CW00540616

#6

0

The Ionian Islands

The Procession of St Spiridion, Corfu

The Ionian Islands

ZAKYNTHOS TO CORFU

Arthur Foss

FABER AND FABER LIMITED

LONDON

First published in 1969
by Faber and Faber Limited
24 Russell Square, London W.C.1
Printed in Great Britain by
W & J Mackay & Co Ltd, Chatham

SBN 571 08944 5

FOR CLARE

Contents

List of maps

CONTENTS

Maps

Illustrations

‿〜∿‿

Acknowledgements for photographs reproduced are gratefully made to the following:- Kokkalis, Corfu, for the colour frontispiece and Nos. 2, 18, 19, 20, 21, 22, 23a, b and c, 24, 25, 27 and 28; Dinos Konomos for 4 and 5; Marinos Sp. Cosmetatos, Argostoli, Cephalonia for 7, 8, 9, 10 and 11; Greek National Tourist Office for 6, 14 and 15; Professor Gerasimos Katopothis for 17, and Clare Foss for 29.

From *Song of the Seven Islands*

KOSTIS PALAMAS

Your waters dazzle like a floor of diamonds
Westward your tides
Grope and caress the shores of Italy.

In a circumference of blue the seven islands
Foam-chiselled, rise, dissolve,
Join hands and dance upon the waves.

Zakynthos drowned in flowers
Cephalonia seamed with toil
Kythera and Paxoi
Corfu the enchantress of the mind and heart
Ithaka a mariner's rhyme in stone
Levkas the watch-tower of the Armatoli.

From the Ionian shore
From the Ionian sea
Since Homer, since Solomos,
The poet's song, the statesman's art
Haunted these islands like sea-birds,

As if here lay the fields of Elysium
And the heroes of myth and of history
The shade of Odysseus, the spirit of Capodistrias
Walked together under a Greek sky.

translated by Ian Scott-Kilvert

Note on Anglicization of Greek names

Because the Greek and English alphabets differ—and because there are unexpected variations in pronunciation as well—the spelling of Greek names and places in anglicized form can create difficulties. Should the Greek or English version of a person or place be used? The island we know as Corfu is called Kerkyra by the Greeks, but to use Kerkyra instead of Corfu in a book written in English would be pedantic. Again, the ends of Greek nouns vary according to sex, whether nominative or accusative and whether singular or plural. A particular case arises here in connection with the names of saints and the places named after saints; the Greek word for 'saint' in its nominative masculine singular form is phonetically 'ayios' (although spelt 'agios' in Greek).

A compromise between the Greek and English versions seems necessary. I have throughout used the English abbreviation 'St' when applied directly to a saint and usually to a place named after a saint as well, unless the English version would sound completely incongruous. An example is the Corfiot village near the Achilleion called in Greek 'Ayii Deka'; to call this village 'the Ten Saints', which is an exact translation of the Greek name, would be incomprehensible to English and Greek alike.

Introduction

Unlike the Aegean Sea, which is the home of many groups of islands, the Ionian Sea nourishes only one group—the Ionian Islands or the Seven Islands (Heptaneesa) as they are known to the Greeks. Formed from the summits of a limestone ridge which runs parallel to the mainland, they are, with one exception, strung out off the west coast of Greece. The most northerly, close to the southern entrance to the Adriatic, is Corfu; the other six islands extending southwards are, in turn, Paxos, Levkas, Ithaka, Cephalonia, Zakynthos and Kythera, together with their dependencies.

The one exception is Kythera, which is not in the Ionian Sea at all but stands out from Laconia in the southernmost Peloponnesos towards Crete. During the carve-up of the Greek Archipelago by the Latins after the Fourth Crusade in 1204, it was successfully claimed by Marco Venier on the grounds that his family—one of the most distinguished in the history of Venice—was, as their name indicated, directly descended from Venus whose birthplace the island was. Kythera—or Cerigo as the Venetians called it—is a fascinating island; but while the other six can be reached via the Gulf of Corinth, the route to Kythera is by boat from the Piraeus down the east coast of the Peloponnesos. There are now no direct communications between it and the islands in the Ionian Sea, so I have not included it in this account.

Each island has its own distinctive personality and beauty and, as a group, they have a much richer history than most Mediterranean islands. From earliest recorded time until they came under Roman domination, they were independent, one from another. After the division of the Roman Empire by Constantine, they remained subject to his successors on the Bosphorus until around the end of the twelfth century when they became separated from Byzantium. Unlike the rest of the Greek Archipelago they never, apart from Levkas, fell under the Turkish yoke for any considerable time. Cephalonia, Ithaka and Zakynthos were under Turkish rule for a few years only at the end of the fifteenth century.

Because the islands came progressively under direct Venetian control from 1387 onwards, they are regarded by some as less purely Greek than, for example, the Aegean Islands which were under Turkish dominion for several hundreds of years, some of them until as recently as 1913 when the Turks were defeated in the first Balkan War. But Venice had a richer civilization to offer than the Porte. Subsequently, between the collapse of the Venetian Republic in 1797 and 1864, there were British, French and, very briefly, Russian influences at work as well.

In 1864, the British, after exercising a protectorate entrusted to them at the end of the Napoleonic wars, ceded the United States of the Ionian Islands to the Kingdom of the Hellenes, an act of perhaps unprecedented generosity by an empire at the height of its power. This however would not have happened if the Ionians themselves had not been proud to be Greek and convinced that union with Greece was desirable. Throughout the centuries of foreign domination, a sense of both individuality and of their historic origins has remained in these islands.

Lying between the ancient Greek city states and Magna Graecia, between Rome and Athens, between Christendom and Islam, between East and West, the Ionian Islands have always acted as a bridge over which both armies and ideas have moved back and forth. A bastion of Christendom, against which the might of the Turk battered twice in vain within less than two hundred years, the Ionian Islands, a centre of the Orthodox Church, resisted the propaganda of the Counter-Reformation from Rome with equal success. Out of all this, the islands have developed their own unique identity, a harmonious amalgamation of the cultures of Byzantium and Venice—admittedly on a very small scale—which can be enjoyed in the various island capitals, villages, churches, monasteries and country houses, when these have been spared by earthquakes and human destructiveness. And if the evidence of the past and the personalities which were involved are considered of insufficient importance or interest, there is always the ever-changing beauty of mountains and sea, the peacefulness of remote harbours, of olive groves and vineyards, the excellence of simple food and good wine, and the companionship of the islanders.

The idea of writing what is an account and an appreciation of the Ionian Islands began, I suspect, as long ago as October, 1944, when I arrived among them after some months' service in the Epirus with the

British Military Mission attached to the resistance forces of the late
General Zervas. Certainly, I then became captivated by them so that
my wife and I—the 'we' of the text—have been back a number of
times. It was however Charles Monteith of Faber & Faber who
brought what was only a dormant idea to life, and I am grateful to
him for this and for his patience and encouragement over the four
years and more which it has taken to complete this task.

I owe an enormous debt to many friends in the Ionian Islands who
have looked after us on our visits, who have most generously spent
much time in answering a stream of questions, who have supplied
written material and many of the photographs. I would like especially to record my gratitude for the help given by Mr and Mrs Alec
Cronopulo, Dr Denis Roma and Mr Charalambos Zois of Zakynthos,
by Mr and Mrs Marinos Cosmetatos of Argostoli, by Professor
Gerasimos Katopothis of Levkas and, not least, by Miss Maria
Aspioti and Mr and Mrs John Collas of Corfu. Anyone who has visited
these islands will know that I could not have had better mentors and
that any mistakes in this book are entirely of my own making. Mr
Constantinos Tsamados, until recently Greek Consul-General in
London, has also generously given much guidance and many useful
introductions. I am also most grateful to Mrs Arnold Gathercole and
Lord Hurcomb for reading the manuscript at various stages and for
much constructive advice and to Mr Ian Scott-Kilvert for his translation of an extract of the poem by Palamas on the Ionian Islands.

Other acknowledgements I should like to make are to Mr Ray
Hutchings and to the Librarian of King's College, London, for permission to use the Burrows Library; to Mr Nigel Nicolson for permission to quote from the late Sir Harold Nicolson's *Byron—The Last
Journey*, first published in 1924; and to Messrs Michael Joseph for
allowing me to reproduce extracts from *The Letters of Private Wheeler
1809–1828* edited by Sir Basil Liddell Hart and first published in
1951. I acknowledge my indebtedness to the late Professor Angelos
Procopiou, whose book *La Peinture religieuse dans les îles ioniennes
pendant le XVIII siècle*, published in Paris in 1939, has been of the
greatest help. I am grateful to Mr W. Y. Carman for much help in
connection with the history of the Greek Light Infantry.

Finally, I would like to thank Clare, my wife, for carrying out so
cheerfully the long and arduous task of transposing my handwriting
into type, sometimes with expressive asides, and for so much help and
companionship throughout the venture. To her this book is dedicated.

Part One

ZAKYNTHOS

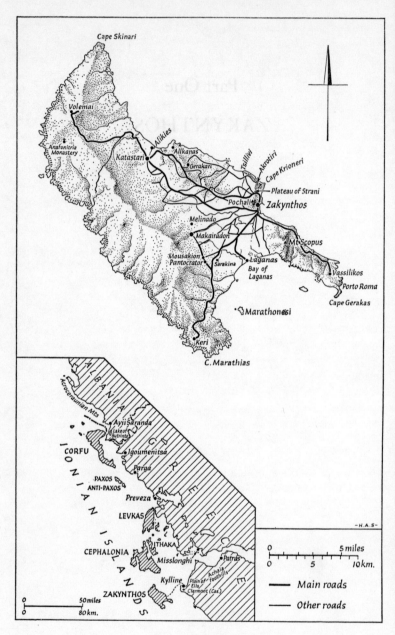

Cape Skinari

Volemai

Anafonitria
Monastery

Katastari

Alikies
Alikanas
Gerakari
Tsillivi
Akrotiri
Cape Krioneri
Plateau of Strani
Pochali
Zakynthos

Melinado

Makairadon
Mt Scopus

Mousakion
Pantocrator
Sarakina
Laganas
Bay of
Laganas
Vassilikos
Porto Roma
Cape Gerakas

Marathonesi

Keri

C. Marathias

ALBANIA

Acroceraunian Mts

Ayii Saranda
Lake of
Butrinto

CORFU

CHEREE

Igoumenitsa

Parga

PAXOS
ANTI-PAXOS

Preveza

LEVKAS

ITHAKA

CEPHALONIA

Misslonghi

Patras

Kylline
Plain of
Elis
Clermont (Cas.)

Achaia
foothills

ZAKYNTHOS

—H.A.S—

0   5 miles
0   5   10 km.

Main roads

Other roads

0   50 miles
0   80 km.

I. Zakynthos

20

I

Arrival in Zakynthos

❧

After pounding south-west and then south along a good road through the coastal foothills of Achaia and the racing plains of Elis, the grey-blue pullman bus slowed down at a crossroads and turned due west. There, straight ahead, high on a brown hill, stood the stark massive walls of the great Frankish castle of Clermont, or Chloumoutsi. It was built between 1220 and 1223 in order to protect the port of Glarentza, the chief port of the Peloponnesos until it was destroyed in 1442. Geoffrey II de Villehardouin, Prince of Achaia, who built it out of confiscated church funds, was one of the most eminent grandees of the Latin Orient; it was his great-uncle, the Marshal of Champagne, who chronicled the Fourth Crusade whose capture of Constantinople in 1204 began the Latin domination. Later it became known as Castel Tornese because Geoffrey's brother William, who succeeded him, established a mint there to produce the coins known as 'tournois', such as had originally been made at Tours.

Clermont is generally described as one of the finest buildings erected in Greece during the Latin supremacy. Its great sandstone mass looked however dourly utilitarian on the day we saw it, and we never got close enough to see if our impression was wrong. Instead, the road swung away to the north-west, affording only an occasional glimpse of the castle walls through the intervening olive trees.

We had left Athens punctually at a quarter past six that early June morning. Now, at one o'clock and fifteen minutes after our first glimpse of Clermont, the bus came to a halt close to the little jetty of Kylline harbour, where the *Ayios Dionysios*, the car-ferry boat named after the patron saint of Zakynthos, was waiting to take us to his island, just under sixteen miles to the south-west. We stepped out into a blustery south wind which was churning the Ionian Sea into milky aquamarine waves fringed with white caps. Although the sun shone fitfully, nothing could be seen of Zakynthos or of Cephalonia to the north-west either, because the south wind always brings rough weather and poor visibility. We huddled for protection under the awning of a little taverna which served delicious souvlakia—little pieces of lamb skewered on a bamboo spit and grilled over charcoal—which we ate with wholewheat bread and washed down with small glasses of ouzo to warm us up.

Half an hour later, the *Ayios Dionysios* pushed its way into the boisterous Ionian Sea. The coast is rugged and dominated by the great hexagonal castle of Clermont, which we could now see to greater advantage. It was last used as a defence point by the insurgent Greeks in the War of Independence against Ibrahim Pasha. He stormed and sacked it with his Egyptians in 1825, smashing the interior into ruins. Of Glarentza, which stood about a mile south of Kylline and below Clermont, all traces seem to have disappeared.

As we moved south-west, the sea mist began to dissolve and Zakynthos slowly to appear. First emerged the upper slopes of Mount Scopus, the most southerly part of the eastern side of the island, rising to nearly sixteen hundred feet above the Ionian Sea; then the ridge appeared above the town of Zakynthos, thickly wooded and surmounted at its southern extremity by the decaying walls of the old castro. The nearer the ferry approached, so more and more detail appeared—the lower slopes of Mount Scopus, the bell tower of the church of St Dionysios at the southern end of the town, then the buildings along the quay and the long mole with the lighthouse at the end, stretching out to greet us.

The harbour had an air of emptiness, almost of melancholy, accentuated by the lengthening golden light of the afternoon sun which was flooding through the great white deserted Solomos Square at the end of the mole. It had been designed for more important craft than the few vessels idling at their moorings. Here the great galleys of Venice had anchored *en route* for Crete; here, in October 1827, had come in turn the fleets of Britain, France and Russia to take in fresh water and vegetables before sailing south to Navarino for their victorious encounter with the Turks. Byron's body had been carried here during April 1824 from Missolonghi and deposited in the lazaretto while its final destination was debated. The arrival of the brig *Florida* with the first instalment of the English loan for the Greek insurgents decided the matter, and Byron's remains departed on board for England some five weeks later.

Private Wheeler, whose letters were edited by Sir Basil Liddell Hart in 1951, passed the brig while he himself was travelling south to Cephalonia by troopship. He seems to have been as moved by the death of the poet as were his Greek friends. He describes in a letter how 'I said to a Greek one day "Byron is dead". He replied, "No, never," then striking his left breast at the same moment his soul was revealed in his eyes, "He will always live here and in the hearts of my countrymen" . . . This generation adores him and future generations will ever respect the name of Byron and class him in the highest ranks of their immortal heroes.' Wheeler has of course been proved right.

One occasion when the mole was packed tight with people was for the arrival of William Ewart Gladstone, the future Liberal Prime Minister, during his visit to the Ionian Islands in December 1858. His purpose was to find a political solution to the mounting unrest of the islanders against the British Protectorate. Lord Morley in his biography describes the scene.

'A concourse of several thousands awaited him; Greek flags were flying on all sides in the strong morning sea-breeze; the town bands played Greek national tunes; the bells were all ringing; the harbour was covered with boats full of gaily dressed people; and the air resounded with loud shouts. . . . Long live Gladstone the Philhellene, hurrah for Union with Greece.' Such was the crush on the mole that he was taken instead to the private landing stage of a house just to the north of the quay, which then belonged to the British Resident; it was destroyed by the 1953 earthquake.

Private Wheeler makes more sinister mention of this mole. Here, in 1827, he watched the execution of a Greek found guilty of murder. On this occasion the hangman, when the steps had been dragged away from under the victim's feet, went back some ten paces, then ran and sprang on the wretch's back, pulled himself on the man's shoulder and clung there until he was dead. Also close by was the quarantine station in which travellers were automatically placed on arrival if it was known that they had been ashore in areas where the plague was active. Edward Dodwell described how, early in the nineteenth century, he was detained in such a building during one of his visits to Greece. Letters intended for people ashore were fixed into a split cane and smoked, sometimes so carelessly that the paper became half-burnt and illegible; money for provisions was put into a bowl of sea-water before it could be handled. Joseph Cartwright, the marine artist from Devon who, in 1815, at the age of twenty-six, became paymaster-general to the British forces in the Ionian Islands, a post which he held for some ten years, depicted such a scene in his view of the harbour at Vathi, Ithaka. It is reproduced in his *Views in the Ionian Islands* which was published in 1821.

The fact that we were the only guests at our hotel, although it was already June, again underlined the emptiness of the town. As the hotel kitchen was not yet functioning for the season, we were introduced to Mr Kardianos, the proprietor of one of the best restaurants in the Ionian Islands.

The Kardianos clan is a large one. In such cases, the various branches of the clan are often nicknamed after the occupation of its family head. Mr Kardianos is generally known in Zakynthos as 'O Bukios', or 'the mouth-stuffer'; we were assured that his father had enjoyed this nickname and that his son would inherit it in due course. 'O Bukios' not only served excellent food but, by the simple fact that he had a telephone which was available to his clients, was the club secretary to the citizens of substance in the community. Sooner or later everyone of note in the town called—for a meal, for a drink and a gossip with a friend, to leave or collect a message and to hear the latest local news. Mr Kardianos specializes in Verdea, the name given to the dry white wine of the island, probably because of its greenish tinge. As early as 1517, its excellence was noted in the account of his pilgrimage to Jerusalem by Sir Richard Torkington, who wrote, 'There is the greatest wines and strongest that ever I drank in my life.' Today, excellent Verdea wines are produced by the Carrer and Comouto estates. The alcoholic content of Verdea is between fourteen and sixteen per cent. A good Verdea, if kept in a cask for a number of years, acquires the bouquet and taste of a good sherry.

The town of Zakynthos, which faces east towards the Peloponnesos, stretches south along the shore, from Cape Krioneri, where the Akrotiri ridge falls to the sea, to the great modern church of St Dionysios in the south. Just beyond the church a little river marks the southern boundary of the town. The streets run largely parallel or at right angles to the sea. Long and narrow, the depth of the town is limited to the gently sloping ground between the sea and the steep wooded ridge which protects it from the west. At the southern end of the ridge at its highest point, stands the old Venetian castro whose weathered walls once encompassed the medieval town, now long abandoned.

The splendours of the town have been noted in the writings of many travellers, from Pliny onwards, and especially by visitors in the first half of the nineteenth century, including Edward Dodwell and Dr (later Sir Henry) Holland, who was to become physician-in-ordinary to Queen Victoria. Dr Davy wrote in 1842, 'Zante [Zakynthos] in any part of Europe would be considered as a handsome town. Subject to earthquakes, from which it so often suffered, unusual care has been taken in the construction of the buildings; they are commonly strongly built, of a light freestone; the streets are well disposed; and the houses generally good and convenient, and well fitted for a warm climate.' This is still true, except that what we see today is virtually a new town.

Davy was describing Venetian Zakynthos which had been built largely between the middle of the seventeenth and eighteenth centuries, when Baroque influences were at their height. There had of course been later additions and modifications, necessitated by the earthquakes which seem always to have blighted the island, but the Venetian character had remained. Then, in 1953, came one of the most devastating earthquakes in modern history and, as a result, Venetian Zakynthos has largely disappeared. Gone are the original arcaded streets, most of the Baroque churches and the Venetian palazzi or palazzini—'the little palaces'—of the nobility. The church of St Dionysios, one of the very few buildings of any importance to survive, only did so because it was built, between the two world wars, of pre-stressed concrete, the material in which the modern town has been reconstructed. Gone too, is much of the population. Instead of some twelve thousand, there is today barely eight thousand. The two main reasons for this have been lack of local opportunities—this is also true of other Greek provincial centres—which has encouraged the departure of the more energetic in search of better prospects and the fear of further serious earthquakes. In many cases, the latter reason was merely the last straw in persuading people to emigrate to Athens or overseas.

The broad outline of Zakynthos today is much as it was before the great earthquake. In the centre of the town, immediately opposite the mole, is the great gleaming white square, named after Dionysios Solomos, the first modern Greek poet of international rank, and dominated by his marble statue dressed in mid-Victorian formality of frock-coat, stiff collar and cravat. Around the square, to the north and west, stand a number of public buildings of unified design. The

Zakynthos Museum stands beyond the statue of Solomos and is separated from it by a road lined with orange trees. Like the other buildings round the square, it is of two stories and its curved windows and balustrades in concrete and stucco give the building a neat appearance, faintly reminiscent of eighteenth-century Venice. The wrought-iron lamps and window grilles are also happy reminders of the past, although a local claim that the Solomos Square is modelled on that of San Marco can only be regarded as fanciful.

To the south of the museum is a good modern commercial hotel. Between it and the quay stand a portentous bank building, the post office and, where the quay joins the mole, the office of the harbour-master and the naval authorities. Arcades run under the first floor of each building to provide shade for pedestrians. From the harbour-master's office, a broad road runs due south along the quay and then, following the curve of the bay, south-eastwards to the great church of St Dionysios beyond.

On the north side of the square are buildings, all of them white like the museum, which house the electricity authority, the public library and public rooms which are intended for lectures, concerts and theatricals. Here, before the earthquake, was the great opera house, somewhat reminiscent of Covent Garden, a moquette of which can be seen in the museum. First built in 1872, it was badly damaged in a severe earthquake some twenty years later. Zakynthos has always been known for its love of music and the opera house was quickly rebuilt in 1893. For many years, until 1939, one or other of the Italian opera companies would start its season here, consequently moving northwards to Argostoli and Corfu, both of which had opera houses before the recent war, and thence back to Italy. English friends have told us of the splendour of these occasions in the 1930s, the men immaculate in evening dress, the women magnificent in tiaras and jewellery.

Also on the north side of the square and closest to the mole itself is the church of St Nicolas of the Mole, the only building here which survives from the Venetian period. When it was first built in 1561, it stood on a small island close to the quay and to a battery point, known as the Castello San Nicolo which also housed the local military commander. Here, occupying part of what is now the Square of Solomos, was a small harbour where ships could shelter from the east wind. The castello was, however, demolished by the Venetians towards the end of the eighteenth century and the modern mole started. This work was continued by the French during their brief occupation between 1797 and 1798 and completed by the British when they took over the southern Ionian Islands in 1809 during their long campaign to eliminate the French from the eastern and central Mediterranean. (This campaign culminated with the occupation of Corfu after the French surrender in 1814.) The church of St Nicolas now serves as the cathedral, until such time as the Metropolis, which was destroyed in 1953, is restored. It has a simple basilica shape and looks, from across the square, as if undamaged by the great earthquake. Walk, however, round the sides and the back on the seaward side and you will see how heavily and well it has been restored.

The distinction of St Nicolas lies in the evenly laid square slabs of sandstone from which it is constucted and the complete absence of any decorative features, unless you include the pale curved tiles of the roof. The contrast of the warm stone of the church with the white concrete of the other buildings grouped around is only partially satisfactory, as it creates a nostalgia for what has gone for ever. Such, incidentally, was the splendour of the Baroque ecclesiastical architecture of Zakynthos that this little church was not considered important enough to be illustrated in the monumental two-volume work in German on the island which was produced in 1901 under the direction of the Archduke Ludwig Salvator, a member of that branch of the Hapsburg family which ruled the Grand Duchy of Tuscany immediately prior to the unification of Italy. Most of his life was spent in Majorca but he travelled widely and, like the Empress Elizabeth of Austria-Hungary who built the Achilleion in Corfu, fell deeply under the spell of the Ionian Islands and especially of Zakynthos. He also published works on Ithaka, Levkas and Parga, a dependency of Venetian Corfu on the Epirot coast.

The road northwards from the mole skirts the east side of St Nicolas, passes the Xenia Hotel and runs along the coast past a straggle of modern bungalows, some of them well built with agreeable surburban gardens. It continues on past the olive oil mill under the cliffs of Akrotiri until it reaches the lighthouse at Cape Krioneri. Then it turns inland and climbs up into the olive groves which cover the low hills beyond Akrotiri until it reaches the unspoilt beaches of Tsillivi. It is a modern road, built largely, for its first two hundred yards beyond the Square Solomos, from the rubble of the old town, deposited there after 1953. Before then it did not exist; instead, the gardens of ancient and lovely houses ran down to their own private jetties. Here were splendid town houses built in the seventeenth and eighteenth centuries; one of them, which belonged to the Mercati family, had more than forty rooms. Other houses belonged to the Anglo-Zakynthiot family of Sargint, to the Carrer family and to the influential Forresti, who owned property in Corfu as well. One of the Forresti, George, was for many years the English consul at the court of Ali Pasha at Yannina where he gained considerable influence, to British advantage, over the tyrant. Only one of those houses, that belonging to the Roma family, has survived the 1953 catastrophe, but without its top floor.

Behind Solomos Square is the little square of St Mark on the north side of which are the ruins of the former Roman Catholic cathedral and on the west the simple white-stuccoed house which is planned as the Solomos Museum. Due south from St Mark's Square, parallel to the quay which is some hundred and fifty yards distant, runs the principal street, the Plateia Rouga or 'broad thoroughfare'. Here, when I first visited Zakynthos in 1945, was the loveliest street in the town, perhaps in the Ionian Islands. It was however a sad time to be there. Although unscathed by bombing or by fighting between Italians and Germans which had taken place both in Cephalonia and Corfu in 1943, the town looked decayed and exhausted through neglect. But in spite of the decay, its charm was still alive. Here along both sides of the Plateia Rouga rose the Venetian pallazzi and palazinni, the living quarters of which were on the first and second floors. The first floors were built above arcades, supported by colonnades, which provided a covered way for pedestrians on both sides of the street. Under the arcades, dark and cool, were offices and shops. Then, before the town could be restored, it had been destroyed by the earth-quake.

The rebuilt Plateia Rouga has arcades for part of its length. No house, however, is now more than two stories high. Each is separated from the next by a narrow gap which is sometimes used for rubbish. As in Solomos Square, a faint Venetian air still lingers. The arcades, how-ever, do not extend far beyond the modern municipal building, which is in the same agreeable style as those in Solomos Square. Beyond the arcades, the road continues south without any character. About two hundred yards past the municipal building, the road forks into two, one branch climbing uphill to Katastari and the north of the island and the other stretching away to Keri in the south-west. Just before leaving the town on the northern route you pass on the left what was once a forge, judging by the lively metal cut-out sign of a prancing Lippizaner horse which is fixed above it. But the days of the carriage and horse finally went with the start of the Second World War and inside a mechanic was stripping down a motor-cycle.

2

Zakynthos until the Fall of Venice

〜∾✕∾〜

Zakynthos is the third largest island in the Ionian group. It is chunky in shape, barely more than twenty-five miles from north to south and about thirteen at its broadest from east to west. Much of the island consists of rugged upland country, especially towards the north, but it has a wide fruitful plain in the south.

The period of prosperity for Zakynthos started with the Venetian occupation in 1483. Prior to that date, knowledge about the island's history is sketchy. Zakynthos, we know, was part of Odysseus' kingdom. The name of the island possibly derives from a legendary king of the same name; equally legendary is the story that Saguntum on the east coast of Spain is an Iberianized version of Zakynthos and was founded by and named after the same king. More likely the name is associated with the word 'kinthos', meaning a hill.

Independent until 455 B.C., when it was forced to accept the supremacy of Athens, the island was later dominated in turn by Sparta, Athens again, and then the Macedonians, until it came under Roman rule in about 191 B.C. The island is said to have escaped the ravages of the civil wars towards the end of the Roman Republic but, like most provinces, suffered from the rapacity of its Roman governors. At one time it was thought that Cicero was buried there but this tale was discounted as long ago as the seventeenth century by Sir George Wheler who, together with his companion, Dr Spon of Lyons, wrote an account of their journey to the Levant in 1675–1676. Of these Roman and pre-Roman years, there are virtually no visible remains. Outside the museum stands a few truncated pillars, probably of Roman origin, while a few Hellenistic and Roman fragments are to be found on the first floor of the museum itself. There is a Roman altar in the village church of Melinado—but for the rest, earthquakes, vandalism and piracy have completely obliterated the past.

After the division of the Roman Empire by Constantine, Zakynthos formed part of the Eastern Roman or Byzantine Empire until
1185, when together with Cephalonia, it was invaded by the Normans
from Sicily. As a result of this and of the conquest by the Latins of
Constantinople in 1204, Zakynthos and Cephalonia became permanently separated from Byzantium. It was a period when the ascendancy of Venice in the Ionian Sea and Eastern Mediterranean was
steadily increasing. As a result of the Fourth Crusade, Venice gained,
at first only nominally, the Ionian Islands as her share of the booty.
Only in 1483 was she in a position to assert her authority over Zakynthos and then only by payment of five hundred gold ducats' tribute
to the Sultan. In the meantime, Zakynthos, together with Cephalonia
and Ithaka, had been ruled first by a branch of the Roman family of
Orsini and subsequently by the Tocchi dynasty, both of which had
looked to the Angevin rulers of Naples, rather than to the Serene
Republic, for support. The Tocchi, who in 1362 became the Dukes of
Lefkadia as well as Counts of Cephalonia, finally collapsed from Turkish
pressure in 1480. Zakynthos in particular suffered from ruthless
brutality during the brief Ottoman occupation which followed, and
most of the churches and houses of the lovely island were destroyed.

The Venetian arrival heralded the beginning of the island's golden
age. From that time onwards, its prosperity grew apace and in the
seventeenth century, the town had a population of thirty thousand.
The Venetians encouraged the cultivation of the olive tree by granting a subsidy for every tree planted, a sum which they more than
recovered when the oil was marketed through Venetian trading
monopolies. In addition—and far more important—there was the
currant trade, first established in the sixteenth century from the
Corinth area. The currant, the name deriving from the 'raisin de
Corinth', grows on a dwarf vine rising little over three feet; it
flourished in the southern Ionian Islands, and especially in Zakynthos
from where a lucrative trade throughout Europe was developed.
Wheler wrote, 'Zant . . . is one of the most fruitful and pleasant
places I ever saw . . . It hath been called by Boterus the Golden
Island: which it well deserves because of the fruitfulness and pleasant-
ness of its soil and abode. But it now more truly merits that name from
the Venetians, who draw so much Gold by the Curran-Trade, from
hence and Cephalonia as beareth the ordinary charge of their Armada
at Sea.'

The English and, to a lesser extent, the Dutch were the principal consumers. The English in particular appeared to have an obsession for this 'liquorish stuff' and were prepared to pay a high price. The Levant Company, first established in 1583, made Zakynthos its principal station in the Venetian provinces and English merchants are reported to have been established there in 1586 for the purpose of organizing the packing and the shipping of the currants to England. Zakynthos had the reputation of being unhealthy and Wheler was shocked to find that these English merchants, who were obviously wealthy, maintained no chaplain . . . 'They have neither church, nor chapel, nor pastor so that it seems to the people of this country that they live without religion and die without hope, which is a great scandal for their neighbours . . .'

Unfortunately, the currant trade was subjected to many difficulties arising from the heavy taxation imposed by the Venetians. As a result, the English transferred much of their business to Patras, the collecting station for the currants of the Peloponnesos then under Ottoman rule. Those of Zakynthos, however, were always recognized as the best and, in spite of the constant bickerings between Venice and England, English traders bought here whenever conditions permitted until, during the last decades of the eighteenth century, the declining Republic priced its products out of the market.

Other exports included silk and cotton fabrics to Smyrna and Constantinople and liquorice and beeswax to England, Germany and Russia. Corn was paid as tithe and enough was sent annually to Venice to pay the yearly tribute to the Turks. There was also the freight trade, although here the Cephalonians were more active. The ships of both islands carried goods throughout the Mediterranean and to the Black Sea. Finally, Zakynthos thrived because it became the Venetian port of call *en route* for the East after the Turks had captured Modon on the mainland. It thus became the richest of the Ionian Islands. It was with good reason that the Venetians talked of 'Zante—il fior di Levante'—the flower of the Levant.

The local aristocracy built fine town mansions as well as those on their country estates, because of the richness of their land. The merchants came to enjoy equally prosperous conditions. Comfortably established in the town, they were members of trading guilds with strict laws of apprenticeship, very like those of the guilds of the City of London. Thus they became a second force in the community as elsewhere in Christendom during this period of expanding frontiers

1. Solomos Square, Zakynthos

2. Bay of Liapades, near Paleocastritsa, Corfu

3. Phaneromene Church, Zakynthos

4. Iconostasis of Pantocrator Church, Zakynthos Museum

and new-found wealth. In 1628, they rose successfully against the Venetian administration and the local aristocracy, who were only able to re-assert themselves after a considerable struggle. The town therefore developed a life which was not merely dependent upon the aristocracy.

Each guild supported a church which they were anxious should be the finest on Zakynthos. For this purpose they commissioned paintings and so became important patrons of the arts. Thus St Nicolas of the Mole was the patron church of the Guild of the Corn Merchants and Seafarers; originally built, as we have seen, on an islet, it had a beacon light on top of the bell-tower as a guide to shipping. The Bakers Guild was established in the lofts of the Church of the Annunciation, the Merchant Tailors Guild worshipped at the Church of St Athanasius and the Bricklayers Guild at the Church of St Basil, and so on. The number of churches on the island was four hundred and ten in 1811, according to records available to Archduke Salvator; half of these were private chapels.

There is a picture in the Zakynthos Museum which gives a delightful introduction to the relationship between the aristocracy, the merchants and the civil, ecclesiastical and military authorities in Zakynthos towards the end of this period. Painted by Ioannis Koraes or Kastrinos, it is of the procession of the relics of St Charalambos and was originally hung in 1759 in the church of that name. The canvas is only about two feet high but some twenty-five feet wide, in concept not unlike the long continuous depictions which were unrolled from a spool and bought for children many years ago at the Lord Mayor's Show in London. The picture now runs the whole length of the far wall in the entrance hall of the museum. It is full of life and gaiety; although the occasion is a solemn one, the painter's sense of amused tolerance is noticeable. The long cortège of dignitaries and their attendants is headed by the presidents of the local guilds, each carrying a distinguishing flag. Behind comes the band consisting of trumpet, flute and drums, the players wearing red or blue frock-coats and black tricorne hats. Next come the relics of the saint in a great silver box carried by deacons, followed by a procession of priests in black caps, but carrying wide, black, brimmed hats, their long black habits covered by gaily coloured flowing gowns. Immediately in front of the bishop or Protopapas marches a group of halberdiers in red frock-coats, red hose and black tricorne hats, carrying their halberds with a certain relaxed ease. The bishop himself is protected from the sun by a canopy carried by what may be representatives of the civic authorities. Behind, bringing up the rear of the official procession, come members of the aristocracy. There are of course no women in the procession. Instead they are to be seen looking out of every window, shutters flung open, of the houses facing on to the long street down which the procession is moving.

But the decline of Venice is by this time visible by the very material on which the picture is painted. A few years previously funds had still been readily available for decorating the Phaneromene church—literally 'the presentation of Christ in the Temple'—with all the richness of carved wood and gold leaf. Now, instead, a picture painted on canvas was used as a frieze on the church wall. It was only a few years before the young Bonaparte gained control of Venice and the Ionian Islands by the Treaty of Campo Fornio, and brought to an end the long history of the ancient Republic.

3

Zakynthos from the Fall of Venice
until Today

∽✕∾

The social centre of Zakynthos is just to the south of the white empty square of Solomos on the road along the quay where there are several cafés. It is a quiet peaceful place. The only sounds are the murmur of conversation from little groups seated outside the shops and at café tables, footsteps and the occasional muted sound of a distant radio. A Venetian atmosphere still lingers faintly; with a great stretch of the imagination, one could be on the Zattere or the further reaches of the Guidecca. The sudden eruption of a near-by juke-box from what otherwise appeared to be a restaurant worth trying, pounding out a record of Bouzouki music or a Beatle song, occasionally shattered this spell when we were there, but these noises were occasional only and the feeling of peacefulness would quickly return.

Peacefulness however is not a word to be associated with the closing days of the Venetian administration or with the years which immediately followed. Certainly at the end of the eighteenth century, life in Zakynthos must have been as riotous and lawless as anywhere in Europe. The Venetian regime had become increasingly impoverished and corrupt during its last declining years. As a result, the rich took the law into their own hands, supported by their own bodyguards of ruffians, imprisoning and assassinating their rivals with impunity. Over two thousand assassinations were said to have taken place in the brief space of three years, without a single criminal being brought to justice. 'For a slight sum,' wrote Christian Müller, 'a wretch was permitted to assassinate whoever he pleased . . . it was considered a common event. Crowds collected around the victim, not to assist, but to behold his agonies, which, to the Zantiots, formed a pleasing sight. The assassin was often among the spectators, nay, he

35

was even daring enough to laugh at the tears and lamentations of the wife and children over the murdered corpse.' Müller, a Saxon Phil-hellene, visited the Ionian Islands in 1821 homeward bound from the Peloponnesos; he and his companions had gone there to join the Greeks at the start of the Greek War of Independence but had been robbed by local Greek bandits and a member of the party killed. By the time he arrived in Zakynthos, the British had imposed the rule of law. He was probably quoting, as do most other writers on this subject, from André Grasset de St Sauveur who was French consul in the Ionian Islands from 1782 to 1799 and who painted a grim picture of social conditions during those years. He reported that the local Provveditore or governor of the island was known to have agreed the amount he was to receive for allowing a criminal to commit a murder.

Because of these lawless conditions which favoured the aristocracy, there was growing support among the populace for the doctrines of the French Revolution. The aristocracy in turn became so worried by the strength of this feeling that certain of them plotted, in the home of the Comouto family, a St Bartholomew's Eve operation against the Jacobins. The massacre never took place but when the French arrived in 1797, skeletons were found chained in the cellars of certain noble houses. Little wonder that the arrival of the French was the signal for the planting of Trees of Liberty and the burning of the 'Libro d'Oro' in which the names of the aristocracy had traditionally been inscribed. There may have been some light-heartedness over the destruction of aristocratic symbols, as the owner of a certain badge of office refused to part with it for immolation in the flames of the new regime without having first received compensation.

The French occupation was short lived. Only a year later, the combined Russo-Turkish expedition, an extraordinary alliance of traditional enemies, brought together only by Bonaparte's invasion of Egypt, and subsequent defeat by Nelson at Aboukir Bay, began to drive the French out of the Ionian Islands. In 1800, they set up, under their joint protection, what was the first modern Greek state. This was the Septinsular Republic consisting of the seven Ionian Islands and their dependencies. After 1802, Russia was the sole protecting power. Corfu was the capital but the first and only president was the head of the Comouto family who was granted the title of prince. This family still owns considerable estates on the island; you pass through their extensive olive groves on the road to Tsillivi.

These were troubled days in the Ionian Islands. The islanders had

shown themselves to be excellent traders since the early days of the
Venetian Republic, alive as well to politics and the arts. They were
however untrained in administering themselves, so that the Septinsular Republic quickly found itself in troubled waters. After the
French defeat in 1799, the Russians, with Turkish approval, drew up
what became known as the Byzantine Constitution. This was found
in practice to favour the aristocracy exclusively and therefore proved
unacceptable to the merchant and peasant classes, the latter of whom
rebelled soon after the withdrawal of Russian troops. Civil war
extended to the other islands; in Cephalonia, Argostoli and Lixouri,
the rival towns, attacked each other and Zakynthos withdrew altogether from the Republic, hoisting instead the British flag. At this
point the British Ambassador in Constantinople expressed George
III's disgust to the Porte at the unauthorized use of the Union Jack.
The Senate in Corfu asked for British protection and, for a while,
British troops kept order from the Old Fort. The goodwill which then
existed in the Islands towards Britain is well illustrated by the gift of a
sword and cane made by the people of Zakynthos to Nelson after his
great victory at Aboukir Bay. When they apologized for not being able
to provide the cane with more than one band of diamonds, Nelson
magnanimously replied that the letter and sentiments accompanying
the gift were 'valuable ten thousand times more than any gold and
diamonds.'

An appeal was made to the Tsar to restore order and as a result
Russian troops were sent back to the Ionian Islands, accompanied by
Count Giorgio Mocenigo as Russian minister to the Septinsular
Republic. For the remainder of the Republic's brief life, Mocenigo
was the real power behind the scenes. A member of an ancient
Zakynthiot family of Venetian origin—an ancestor was one of the
few Venetians who had fought under the last Palaeologue emperor at
Constantinople in 1453—Mocenigo first went as minister plenipo-
tentiary of the Septinsular Republic to St Petersburg, where he found
favour with Tsar Alexander I. He managed to maintain tranquillity of
a sort and introduced reforms which concentrated ever more power
in his own hands. The Senate even voted the Tsar a statue, which he
fortunately refused, seeing that in the following year he threw in his
hand at the Treaty of Tilsit. Napoleon thus regained control over the
Ionian Islands, although French troops were only to remain in Zakynthos, Cephalonia, Kythera and Ithaka for two years.

This turbulent period also saw the development of an intellectual

and artistic ferment, and the emergence of poets of European importance. Ugo Foscolo, one of the great Italian romantic poets of the
early nineteenth century, was born of a Venetian father and a Zakynthiot mother in 1778 and spent his boyhood on the island. Educated,
like so many other Ionians, at the University of Padua, the principal
university of the Venetian Republic, he supported French revolu-
tionary ideals and fought with the Napoleonic army. He eventually
arrived in England after 1815 in voluntary exile, having refused to
accept the Austrians as masters in Northern Italy. He died at Turn-
ham Green in 1827.

Andreas Kalvos, who was born in Zakynthos in 1792, has an
honoured place in modern Greek literature as the author of twenty
patriotic odes, written between 1824 and 1826; he was a classical
scholar, a fact which strongly influenced his style. Like Foscolo, he
spent many years in England where he eventually died in 1869. He
was buried at Keddington, near Louth in Lincolnshire, where Tenny-
son was for a time a schoolboy. His remains were brought back to
Zakynthos in 1960 for internment. Six years his junior, Dionysios
Solomos, the greatest modern Greek poet, was born here in 1798, and
spent the first half of his life here before moving to Corfu where he
died in 1857.

A minor English poet also emerged in these years. The British
consul-general to the Septinsular Republic during its brief duration
was Waller Rodwell Wright who, after the Ionian Islands were surrendered by the Russians to the French in 1807, returned to England
to become the recorder for Bury St Edmunds. He was something of a
scholar and had apparently built up a library which was rifled by the
French when they returned to Zakynthos in 1807; the Dictionary of
National Biography gives the date as 1804 but this cannot be correct.
Two years later he published his *Horae Ionicae*, a collection of poems
about the Ionian Islands which now have a period charm:

> *Ye isles beyond the Adriatic wave*
> *Whose classic shores Ionian waters lave;*
> *Ye plains of Greece! the Muses' ancient pride,*
> *Whose rising beauties crown the western tide. . . .*

Byron was considerably impressed by this work and Wright emerges
with credit from *English Bards and Scotch Reviewers*.

In 1809, British troops from Sicily, under the command of Briga-
dier-General Oswald, chased the French out of Zakynthos and out of

Cephalonia, Ithaka and Kythera at the same time. The local inhabitants were anxious for British protection for their commerce and above all for an end to the chaos which had developed during the Septinsular Republic. Such was the goodwill that existed between the two peoples that General Campbell soon after his arrival in Zakynthos in May 1813 felt justified in writing to London, 'I have introduced myself to the Administrative and other public authorities of the Island from all of whom, as well as from the Heads of the Greek and Latin Ecclesiastical Establishments, I have received the most solemn assurances of the respectful gratitude which they consider this fresh proof of the British Nation and its Government having it in contemplation to unite them more closely to the British Empire and that they desire no blessing so ardently as that they should be conclusively and permanently placed under its protection and I believe in the utterance of these sentiments.' General Campbell worked hard to obtain a proper understanding of the local situation and became extremely popular with the islanders. Eight years were to pass before the start of the Greek War of Independence.

Proof of the excellent relationship between Britons and Greeks was the establishment in 1810 of a regiment known as the Duke of York's Greek Light Infantry, recruited mainly from Epirots who had taken refuge in the Ionian Islands from the oppression of Ali Pasha. Messrs Goddard and Booth, whose work the *Military Costume of Europe* was published in 1812, describe the background of the Greek Light Infantry thus, 'It is composed of continental Greeks, a hardy warlike race, peculiarly well calculated for the service of Light Infantry. In the Russian and French service a prejudice existed that the rude habits of these people unfitted them for anything but the most irregular description of force. The judicious exertions of Major Church, their Inspector, and the other British officers attached to the Corps, have completely done away with this impression and under his able direction they have acquired a competency in military instruction and shown the most subordinate and tractable disposition. . . . The organization of this corps has produced the most beneficial effects on the minds of the Greeks in general who now, alive to the advantage arising from the British service, have shown themselves desirous to enter a career, while it opens to them views of honourable advancement, calls them from a country where their situation is by no means enviable.'

This unit was established along the lines of other local levies which

Britain had raised in the Mediterranean, such as the Corsican Rangers in which Richard Church, later to be commander-in-chief of the Greek army in 1827, had been appointed captain in 1806. Church, like many of his countrymen, was captivated from the first by the Greek temperament and immediately saw the advantages of persuading the exiled mainland chieftains from Suli and elsewhere to join this unit together with their retainers. Those who did so included such worthies as Colokotronis, Metaxas, Nikitas and Petmezas, many of whom became his lifelong friends and comrades-in-arms during the Greek War of Independence.

Although first formed for garrison duties only, the Greek Light Infantry quickly saw active service in the successful attack on the French in Levkas. Later in 1813 a second battalion was raised and we find General Campbell in 1814 anxious to raise two battalions of Ionian Fencible Light Infantry to satisfy the military aspirations of the Ionians. Nothing came of this admirable venture; instead, the second battalion of Greek Light Infantry was disbanded in Cephalonia sometime after taking part in the capture of Paxos in 1814. A similar fate overtook the first battalion in 1816. This took place because the Turks regarded the establishment of Greek troops, composed of rebellious subjects so close to their territory, as an unfriendly act.

In 1815, Britain was formally recognized as the protecting power over the Ionian Islands which were established as a semi-independent state and known as the United States of the Ionian Islands. In these early days of the British Protectorate, the quay and the narrow cobbled streets of the town must have had the appearance of a Levantine Portsmouth Point. 'The Greeks here are strangely mixed,' recorded Müller. 'First a great portion of Moreats, then the Albanese, Epirots, Suliots, Hydriots all wearing their more or less beautiful original dresses.' The Albanians, the Suliots and other natives of Epirus were refugees from Ali Pasha, now nearing the end of his long and treacherous reign. Dark, morose, quick-tempered, feigning indifference or arguing volubly, these exiles from the mainland in their bedraggled finery lounged along the quay or sprawled at tavernas from where they could watch and comment on the coming and going of ocean-going three-masters in the British service or island hopping caiques. In addition, there were British redcoats and the levies of Sicily, Malta and Corsica. Zakynthos also had a Jewish ghetto; it was a small community compared with that of Corfu but until about 1862 its gates were closed every night and woe betide the Jew who ventured abroad after dark. Just before the end of the British Protectorate, its walls were pulled down.

During the Greek War of Independence, Zakynthos was the naval base of Admiral Codrington and his French and Russian allies for containing the movements of the Turkish-Egyptian fleet of Ibrahim Pasha who was trying to subdue the Peloponnesos. Zakynthos was also, ironically enough, an important centre for provisioning the Egyptian forces; this was done with the approval of Capodistrias, elected Greek President in 1827, who considered that the withholding of supplies from the Ionian Islands would only result in greater Egyptian dependence upon local supplies in the Peloponnesos and therefore in further suffering for the Greeks, many of whom were already close to starvation.

Private Wheeler, by then a sergeant, was in barracks up in the castro in 1827. From here he could see the Turkish fleet, lying between the island and the Peloponnesos, harried by the Greek navy under the command of Lord Cochrane. There was no doubt where Wheeler's sympathy lay. He reported with pride a successful action against a corvette flying the Tripoli flag by Lord Cochrane who, as he wrote home, 'does not belong to the family Dolittles, and so has the Musselmen found out to their cost'. Cochrane having commanded the fleets of the newly emerged states of Chile and Brazil, by both of whom he had been shabbily treated, was persuaded to take over the command of the Greek fleet at a vast salary in 1825. The Greek fleet, if all that was planned by the London Committee had materialized, would have been the most modern then in existence. Among other armaments planned were six steam gunboats, but only one was completed in time to take part in operations against the Turks. She was named the *Karteria* and commanded by Captain Abney Hastings, like Cochrane a brilliant but unconventional sailor. He had joined the Greek insurgents as early as 1822 and was extremely popular with them. Wheeler describes a steamship under Cochrane's command during this action, which was one of the few that he was able to carry out against the Turks. This was no doubt the *Karteria*.

Cochrane resigned his Greek command soon after the destruction of the Turkish fleet at the Battle of Navarino on October 20th, 1827, because he was unable to train up a disciplined body of men capable of handling warships in a set engagement. The Greek sailors of the period were essentially privateers, excellent at hit-and-run tactics but with no tradition or liking for disciplined manoeuvring under fire. After the frustrations of his service in Latin America, Cochrane was not prepared to persevere indefinitely. Abney Hastings had more success. With the *Karteria*, equipped with cannon capable of firing red-hot shot, he was able to terrorize the Turkish fleet in the Gulf of Corinth. He was wounded in an attack on Anatoliko near Missolonghi in 1828 and brought back to Zakynthos for medical treatment. He died from tetanus while his ship was in port.

Throughout the period of the British Protectorate—despite increasing political unrest for union with Greece—and subsequently under the Greek state, the Ionian Islands were at peace, if the minor uprisings in Cephalonia in 1848 and 1849 are excepted, until the Italian occupation in 1941. Even this and the brief German occupation which followed in 1943–1944 were uneventful—at least in Zakynthos. Then came 1953.

Most travellers have commented on the frequent earth tremors which shake the island. The earthquake of August 1953 very largely destroyed Zakynthos and the main centres of Cephalonia and Ithaka as well. Starting on Sunday, August 9th, it continued for over a week. The greatest damage was to Zakynthos where the worst tremors hit the town in midmorning when the stoves were alight for cooking the Sunday midday meal. As a result the town was gripped by a fire which spread unchecked as there was no fire-fighting equipment.

Help had been slow to arrive, possibly because the severity of the earthquake was not at first realized. The Greek fleet was at Tinos in the Cyclades for the annual festival of Our Lady of Tinos, nearly a day's steaming away. About the first to bring help were three Israeli destroyers which were on manoeuvres in the vicinity. By mid-week, however, British, United States and Greek services were giving all possible help. Lord Mountbatten, then commanding the Mediterranean fleet, accompanied by Lady Mountbatten, who was head of the British St John's Ambulance Brigade, had visited the stricken islands to assess what further help was required.

The Times on Saturday, August 15th, reported that over one hundred and twenty shocks had been registered during the previous five days and that there were seventy-five thousand homeless. 'British sailors from H.M.S. *Gambia*,' the report continued, 'were today helping Greek troops in fighting widespread fires in the city of Zakynthos, the capital of Zante, where barrels of oil and petrol stored in houses and shops were continually exploding. It was hoped this morning to save some buildings in the south of the town, but tonight there was little left in Zakynthos to burn. Explosions of hand grenades (kept in fishermen's houses for illicit fishing) added to the hazards of fire fighting. Parachutes were being used to drop food to the villages in the north of the island as roads were impassable.'

From then onwards, the tremors became less frequent and less violent. All was over by Wednesday, August 19th, when official estimates gave the number of those killed in the three islands as six hundred, injured as twenty-three hundred, eight hundred of them seriously. That autumn, ironically enough, the grape harvest was the finest for many years.

Despite disasters the traditional life of Zakynthos continues. All Saints' Day is celebrated on the first Sunday in June, heralded by maroons and bells. On occasions such as this Solomos Square really becomes alive. When we were there, St Nicolas of the Mole was already crowded by nine in the morning. Outside, vendors were frying a semolina mixture in oil which when cooked, was cut into long slabs. Perhaps this tradition has some connection with the food for the dead which is still sometimes offered to the local community on the anniversary of a death, the wheat symbolizing the renewal of life.

In the evening, there was a firework display and a concert given by the local high school brass band, dressed in dark blue tunics with yellow facings. We had seen the firework artificer at work in the clear violet light of early evening, weaving long coils of paper, loaded with gunpowder, round bamboo frames, working deftly and speedily in the preparation of various set pieces in different corners of the great square. Throughout, the bells had clanged vigorously, the bell ringers being young schoolboys swinging on the ropes in the three arches of the campanile, each trying to make more noise than his companions.

By nine in the evening, Solomos Square was crowded with family parties admiring the whirling catherine wheels and the exploding rockets. At intervals the band played selections from Italian opera. It was both a family outing and a religious occasion. St Nicolas was a soft blaze of candlelight within; people were continually entering to light a slender taper of wax, to kiss the icons, pause briefly for prayer and then return to the square outside. The stone floor was strewn with branches of laurel, the air pungent with the smell of smouldering wicks.

Then by eleven it was all over and the square itself once more empty. The moon which had now risen was strong enough to touch faintly the distant shore of the Peloponnesos. Only the debris from the fireworks remained; by the next morning this too had been cleared away.

4
The Lost Treasures of Zakynthos

We became very aware of the lost splendour of Zakynthos when visiting the one remaining mansion, only partially destroyed by the earthquake. This belongs to the Roma family. The house, originally built in the seventeenth century, is situated close to the Church of Our Lady of the Angels which stands to the north of St Mark's Square. Originally of three stories, the top one was destroyed in 1953 and has not been replaced. Before 1953 the garden ran down to the sea where there was a boathouse but now there is no longer access because of the new road.

We walked down steps between a fenced-off garden which was alive with flowering trees, into the hall which runs the full length of the house. On its walls and the walls of the staircase to the first floor are portraits of ancestors going back nearly four hundred years, one of the earliest being that of a dark lean man, stern and unbending, who had commanded the Zakynthiot naval contingent at the siege of Candia during the seventeenth century. In the background is depicted his great galley, its long oars striking the sea off the great island of Crete. Close by are his helmet and sword.

At the foot of the staircase, facing into the hall, is the portrait of another Roma in frock-coat, cravat and all the sartorial embellishments of the mid-Victorian era, who was President of the Ionian Senate during the Crimean War. It had, therefore, been his duty, according to treaty obligations with Britain, to sign the declaration of war by the United States of the Ionian Islands against Orthodox Russia, with whom Greek and therefore Ionian sympathy preponderantly lay, especially as the war was in support of the Turks. 'A mosquito attacking an elephant', was the comment of our guide. Count Roma was later appointed Resident of Ithaka, and as such was about the only Ionian to become the direct representative of the Lord

High Commissioner. In this capacity he entertained Mr and Mrs Gladstone in December 1858 during their tour of the Ionian Islands by giving a ball in their honour in Vathi.

Also in the hall is a glass cabinet containing the uniforms, both civil and military, of those members of the family who have held high office in the Ionian and Greek administrations. Conspicuous among them is the red uniform of the present owner's father, who had been a great admirer of Garibaldi and who had emulated his example, even to the colour of his uniform, in raising Greek irregular troops to fight against the Turks both in the ill-fated campaign of 1897 and in the successful First Balkan War of 1912–13.

Running the full length of the first floor directly over the hall is the drawing room, furnished with Regency furniture acquired during the British Protectorate when the old Venetian furniture was given away to the peasants. The other room of particular interest is the ground-floor study, off the entrance hall. In addition to a valuable library, including family archives dating back several centuries, there are some fine icons, together with views and maps of the island. Dominating one wall is a splendid self-portrait by Nicolas Koutouzis, an eighteenth-century painter of some local distinction, who was also a priest, musician, poet and satirist. A dramatic and romantic work. Koutouzis' use of light and shadow is here shown at its best.

The paintings of Koutouzis and of his great admirer, Kandounis, who was also a priest, marked the end of a small but historically interesting and occasionally distinguished school of painting. It had flourished in the Ionian Islands, mainly in Zakynthos and Corfu, in the eighteenth century. The four principal artists of the school were Panayiotis Doxaras; his son, Nicolas; Koutouzis and Kandounis, but little of their work remains. The greatest glory of the school, the interior of the Phaneromene church in Zakynthos, was almost completely destroyed in 1953, although the walls and bell tower were left standing; the church is now being restored. The ceiling of St Spiridion in Corfu, however, which was painted by Panayiotis Doxaras in the first quarter of the eighteenth century, gives some indication—although replaced by inferior copies of the original paintings in the first half of the nineteenth century—of the fine quality of the work of Ionian painters at the summit of the prosperity of these islands and immediately afterwards.

The Ionian School of religious painting marks the final stage in the acceptance of Western ideas and skills by post-Byzantine painters, according to the late Professor Angelos Procopiou, in his authoritative work, *La Peinture religieuse dans les isles ioniennes pendant le XVIII siècle*, published in Paris in 1939. In this work, he traced in some detail the history of Greek painting from the fall of Constantinople in 1453 onwards. It is a fascinating story, much of which is illustrated by the paintings in the Zakynthos Museum. Here are hung paintings not only by native Ionian painters but also good examples of works by many artists who visited or settled in Zakynthos from the sixteenth century onwards.

Byzantine art which derived originally from Imperial Rome, had become formalized during the course of centuries according to rules laid down by the Orthodox Church and accepted by the Imperial court. Although there is every evidence of thriving schools of jewellers, carvers in ivory and textile designers, the greatest artistic works were undoubtedly those commissioned by the Church, such as the wonderful mosaic of Christ Pantocrator in the dome of the church at Daphni, just outside Athens, and the fine mosaics in the monastery church of Hosios Loukas near Delphi.

After 1453, there was an exodus of Greeks—soldiers, merchants, scholars, artists—to the west and particularly to Crete, which had been acquired by Venice soon after the Fourth Crusade. The island was already prosperous because of its geographical position between east and west; the arrival, therefore, of these sophisticated fugitives from Constantinople and Mistra heralded a literary and artistic Renaissance. It was only to end some two hundred years later when, in 1669, Candia, the last great Venetian stronghold in Crete, surrendered to the Turks after a siege which lasted over twenty years.

The great difference between Cretan society and that of the Imperial capital, from the artist's point of view, was the existence of a wealthy commercial class on the island which was anxious to possess paintings. In addition to ecclesiastical work, artists began to paint icons on blocks of wood which were in demand wherever Greek families settled, whether in Egypt, the Aegean or in Venice where a large Greek colony, estimated at fifteen thousand and more in its heyday, had established itself round the Church of San Giorgio dei Greci. In the course of time the work of Cretan artists began more and more to assimilate western ideas and techniques through contact with Venice. There was a further reason, apart from popular demand, why icon-painting flourished and mural-painting declined in the sixteenth and seventeenth centuries. The new style of Baroque architecture did not give the same opportunities for wall-paintings. In no sense however was this acceptance of western ideas deliberate. In Crete, at least, the Venetians were not popular. Through heavy taxation and forced labour to maintain Venetian defences against the Turkish threat and through enmity between the Roman Catholic and Greek Orthodox churches, the Venetians were regarded as oppressors. This however was to change after 1669 when the Venetians realized how much they needed the help of their remaining colonies, above all the Ionian Islands, whither so many Cretans had emigrated. This change of heart by the Serene Republic was rewarded in turn by increasing loyalty and affection on the part of her Greek subjects.

Even before the fall of Crete, painters from the island had travelled widely, both to the remaining monastic centres of the Greek Orthodox Church under Turkish rule in the Sinai Peninsula and on Mount Athos and to the west. The association of the Cretan, Theotokopoulos, better known as El Greco, with Toledo is well known, but there were other artists of note. Michael Damaskinos, whose main work was carried out during the last thirty years of the sixteenth century, and Emmanuel Tzanes, who worked in Zakynthos and Corfu before becoming vicar of San Giorgio dei Greci in Venice in 1659, were two prominent Cretan artists whose works are represented in the Zakynthos Museum. Another influential Cretan painter who settled in Zakynthos during the mid-seventeenth century was Elie Moskos, whose work shows the growing influence of the West on post-Byzantine painting, revealed by a more sentimental approach in feeling and a greater rotundity in the treatment of figures. It should be noted that painting was concerned almost exclusively with religious subjects and that the painters themselves, probably without exception, were members of the Orthodox clergy, the junior ranks of which, as in the case of the parish priests, were allowed to marry.

The reconciliation of Venice and her Ionian Greek subjects after 1669 opened wide the door of post-Byzantine art to western influence. This was the age of the Baroque, the re-affirmation of the splendours of the Catholic Church after the Council of Trent, seen at its finest in the rebuilding of Rome. The Zakynthiot churches built in the prosperous second half of the seventeenth century were in simple classical form without a dome and the paintings commissioned for them both by the aristocracy and the trading guilds were painted increasingly by men who had studied in Italy. Cretans in exile in the Ionian

5. Procession of St Charalambos by Ioannis Koraes in Zakynthos Museum

6
The Ascension, a
post-Byzantine
icon in Zakynthos
Museum

7
Virgin and Child
from Church of St
George, Tzannata,
Cephalonia, by
Andreas
Carantinos
(c. 1660–1740)

Islands and in Venice learned to paint in the Italian style because of economic pressures. According to an article by M. Chatzidakis published in 1953 in *L'Hellenisme Contemporain*, works by Emmanuel Tzanes and by Theodore Poulakis, who settled and died in Corfu, have on occasion been attributed to such contemporary Italian artists as Crivelli and Parmigianini. Cretan artists in Venice on occasion painted on both sides of the block of wood, in Byzantine style on one side and in Italian on the other.

Although no work of his remains in Zakynthos and but a little in Levkas and Corfu, the life of Panayiotis Doxaras (1662–1729), as told by Professor Procopiou, illustrates the Greek-Venetian relationship in the Ionian Islands at its most harmonious. It is also the story of a most interesting man, which deserves to be better known. Born in 1662 in Kalamata in the Peloponnesos, his family emigrated to Zakynthos to be under Venetian protection. At the age of twenty-three, Doxaras was apprenticed to Leo Moskos, a distinguished painter of icons, for four years, after which there was the usual struggle for recognition. Then in 1694, he temporarily gave up his artistic career to raise a troop to fight against the Turks in the Peloponnesos where the Venetians were being hard pressed. It was particularly important at this stage that the Mani, that turbulent and rugged peninsula to the south of Kalamata, should be held for Venice, and that Turkish attempts to establish a base in the Venetian rear should be frustrated. Doxaras, because of his family's influence in this region and because of its well-known loyalty to the Republic, was chosen for the task. The success of his mission played no small part in making possible the Venetian retention of the Peloponnesos for a further generation.

After the successful conclusion of his military and diplomatic mission for which he was knighted by the Republic, Doxaras spent several years studying in Italy, visiting Rome, Venice and other important artistic centres, where he was greatly impressed by the Renaissance painters. On returning to Zakynthos, there is evidence that he was preparing to establish his own school of painting, based on that set up in Bologna by the Carracci brothers, in order to teach Ionian artists the principles and techniques he had learned in Italy. It was basically for this reason that he translated into the Greek of his day a group of three works from the Italian, namely *The Treatment of Painting* by Leonardo da Vinci, three essays on painting and sculpture by Leo Battista Alberti, the late fifteenth-century Florentine architect and sculptor, and finally *Concise Instructions on the Painting of Frescoes* by

Andrea Pozzo, a Jesuit contemporary of Doxaras, whose painting of the ceiling of San Ignazio in Rome, with its illusions of distance and open sky, is one of the finest illustrations of Baroque perspective. Finally he drew up his own guide to painting techniques which he completed in 1726 when he was about to embark on the decoration of the church of St Spiridion in Corfu.

Two copies of these translations exist, one in the Marciana Library in Venice and the other in the National Library of Athens. In both Doxaras has copied scrupulously well the drawings of Nicolas Poussin which illustrated the 1651 edition of Leonardo's *The Treatment of Painting*. This concentration upon the provision of a textbook of religious painting and on the creation of an Ionian Academy explains why only a small number of works can authoritatively be attributed to him; he was too busy writing and teaching. His works, apart from several religious paintings, include a miniature portrait of Field Marshal Count von der Schulenburg, who successfully defended Corfu against the Turks in 1716. He is also known to have done a portrait of Grimani, then the Venetian Provveditore-Generale of the Ionian Islands. Some of his finest religious paintings adorn the altar screen of the church of St Demetrius in Levkas.

The results of Doxaras's efforts were far reaching for Ionian painting. His was the first Ionian Academy of Arts—later to be revived, in 1805 and subsequently by the sculptor, Prosalendis. Secondly he was responsible for overthrowing finally the formalistic principles of Byzantine painting and creating instead in the Ionian Islands what might almost be described as a regional school of Italian painting.

The traditions established by Doxaras were continued by his son Nicolas whose finest work, the ceiling of the Phaneromene church, was destroyed, as we have seen, in the 1953 earthquake. It is impossible to hope that what was undoubtedly the finest example of Baroque architecture in Greece will ever regain an interior like the original. The few examples of Nicolas Doxaras's work in the museum give little evidence of his painting at its best; they look merely unimaginative imitations of G. B. Tiepolo, his Venetian contemporary.

Some idea of the splendour of the Zakynthiot churches built during the island's greatest period of artistic activity can be gained from the two lovely altar screens or iconostasis in the ground floor room to the right of the entrance hall in the museum. One is from the church of Pantocrator and dated 1681, the other from the church of St James of Collas and dated 1690. Their design is similar. At the top of the elabo-

rately-worked gold screen are the portraits of six saints, each supported from below by crowned mermaids in a carved frieze. Below
this are thirteen smaller paintings, each about two and a half feet high,
stretching right across the screen; each depicts a scene from the life of
Christ. Full of action and colour, they are reminiscent of the Giotto
frescoes in the chapel of the Scrovegni in Padua. Finally there are the
great full-length figures flanking the entry to the inner sanctuary,
saintly figures tremendous in their majesty and dazzlingly ornate in
their painted vestments and surrounding gold decoration.

Upstairs in the museum are the frescoes of St Andrew of Volemai,
a church badly battered in the earthquake; these have been re-established completely as if in their original setting. They were painted in
the seventeenth century but their only claim to distinction is that
they are virtually the only frescoes from this period still in existence
on the island. Moreover they have been considerably damaged by
visitors' initials which have been carved into the painted surface,
some, but not all, by Italian occupation troops during the last war.

The one church which was not affected by the 1953 earthquake
was that of the island's patron saint, St Dionysios. Together with the
neighbouring monastery and the separate Venetian-style belfry, its
white reinforced concrete structure with red roof dominates this part
of the town. It was built on the site of an earlier church which was
destroyed by the earthquake of 1893. The mortal remains of the saint
repose in a great silver casket in the south-east corner of the
church. On each August 24th, to commemorate their removal to
Zakynthos from the monastery on the Strophades where his tomb
is situated, the saint's remains are taken in solemn procession round
the town.

St Dionysios of Zakynthos—not to be confused with other saints
of the same name in the Greek Orthodox Church's Calendar of the
Saints—is a latter-day Orthodox saint, born in Zakynthos as recently
as 1547, of parents of Norman origin. He is much concerned with
helping local fishermen, and travels so much in this labour that he is
presented with a new pair of shoes at his annual festival. His story
can be briefly told in the words of a locally produced guide-sheet
(with a somewhat exotic English translation) which accompanies a
good map of the island. 'When going to Jerusalem, he passes by
Athens, he is ordained Archbishop of Aegina . . . Two years later he
abdicates and returns to Zante where he sends for candidature for
the episcopal throne of Cephalonia and Zante. He fails and retires to

the highland convent of Anafonitria (near Volemai on the western ridge of the island). The 17th December 1622 God has taken him. His relics are removed and buried in the Strophades. When the exhumation, the holy body is safe and well. The 1703, by virtue of a Synodical Statement of the Oecumenical Patriarch Gabriel he is classified among the saints. During the war between the Turks and Venetians, a Turkish fleet . . . attacks the convent . . . they pillage it, they take the church utensils and icons and put the monks to death and others to rapture. The holy relics are saved by some hided monks, who embark them on a Venetian corvette . . . and transport them in security to Zante.' A spirited account. The church, however, in spite of the presence of the saint, has an atmosphere which is both worldly and empty of feeling. When we visited it, we were the only laymen there, except for an elderly peasant woman venerating the icons, some of which are by Koutouzis. Two priests were taking it in turn to read the service, each appearing to try and read his part faster than his colleague. Their boredom was obvious. Two elderly monks in dark blue work clothes waved cheerfully to us as we left.

As Italianate techniques and, to a certain extent, feelings supplanted those of Byzantium and Crete in the field of painting, so did the rites of the Roman Catholic Church influence both Greek laity and clergy. The Venetian authorities did everything possible, for political purposes, to create a feeling of reconciliation between the two churches after the fall of Crete. While the principal Roman Catholic representative was held to be senior in rank to the Greek Orthodox bishop or protopapas, the former together with his attendants invariably attended the enthronement of the latter, who was appointed by the Greek Patriarch in Constantinople. Likewise the Greek clergy attended all official ceremonies both of the Venetian administration and of the Roman Catholic Church. The festival of St Arsenius, the first Orthodox metropolitan of Corfu, was celebrated jointly in that city by the combined Catholic and Orthodox clergy, each according to its own ritual. In 1635, a petition was sent from Zakynthos to the Venetian Senate asking that Greek Orthodox clergy be allowed to celebrate Mass in the Roman Catholic Church. In the middle of the eighteenth century, many members of the Orthodox Church, attracted by the ritual and the music, attended Catholic services, which had been developed by the Jesuits after the Council of Trent. There is little evidence however of members of the Greek Orthodox Church being converted to Roman Catholicism. Indeed, an English traveller, A. Drummond, whose *Travels* were published in London in 1754, reported that during his visit to Zakynthos ten years earlier he found Greek priests, among other inhabitants, reading Locke and other philosophers. Drummond was obviously impressed with the cultural standards of the island.

An extreme example of the strength of the Italian influence in both clerical and artistic affairs can be seen in the approach to his ecclesiastical duties and to painting by Koutouzis. Born in 1741 in Zakynthos of a family which sought refuge in the island from the Peloponnesos, he lived through the period of the decline and fall of the Venetian supremacy in the Ionian Islands, a time when the first rumblings of the French Revolution preceded by some years the actual arrival of French troops in 1797. He died in 1811, two years after the start of the British occupation. Apprenticed to Nicolas Doxaras, he quickly roused hostile comment by including self-portraits in his religious paintings. A visit to Italy in his early thirties seems only to have aggravated his anti-establishment feelings. Having become parish priest to St Nicolas of the Mole, he deliberately ran counter to many of the traditions of the Orthodox Church. In the first place he shaved his beard, wore red silk stockings and a short silk cassock. His church was decorated with carpets and pots of flowers. He celebrated Mass with exaggerated fervour, dramatic gestures and feigned weeping. At the same time he wrote bitter satirical verses at the expense of many local worthies.

His religious paintings, more than those of any other Ionian painter of the period, show the influence of the Baroque—the dramatic poses of his figures, the strong interaction of light and shadow, the replacement of walls and ceilings by the limitless reaches of clouds and sky amidst which his heavenly beings were depicted. Procopiou allowed Koutouzis a richer imagination than his teacher, Nicolas Doxaras, and a greater sense of design. He painted, however, with incredible speed and in doing so broke with the tradition of faithfully copying nature which Panayiotis Doxaras had tried to establish. His works and those of his associate, Nicolas Kandounis, who worked even more speedily, show the shortcomings of this approach. Colours are inclined to be muddy, figures incompletely depicted. This way of painting is even more exaggerated in the followers of these two artists; there is nothing more depressing in the Zakynthos Museum than the paintings attributed to the schools of Koutouzis and Kandounis.

5

Akrotiri–Zakynthos

❦

'Over there—that's where the body hung,' said our guide pointing to a wooded promontory at the edge of the hamlet overlooking the town and the Ionian Sea. We were on the way up by taxi to the old Venetian fortress and at that moment approaching Pochali which lies under its massive walls. He was referring to an unhappy event which took place soon after the start of the Greek War of Independence when, among others, a teenage boy was executed, his body dipped in pitch to preserve it and then left to rot in a cage in full view of the town. 'It took fifteen years to disintegrate,' continued our friend, 'they hung the cage here because it was his home; no wonder the poor mother went mad with grief.'

At that time the Ionian Islands, on the instructions of the Lord High Commissioner, Sir Thomas Maitland, were forced to remain strictly neutral during the struggle between the Greeks and the Turks; and the British authorities did everything possible to restrain the Ionians from aiding their brethren on the mainland. In 1821, an Algerian warship, serving with the Turkish fleet in its blockade of Patras where Greek insurgent forces were holding out, got separated from the main body by Greek naval craft. In order to escape capture, the ship ran aground in the Bay of Laganas. A British detachment was sent to take the crew into quarantine but was attacked by local peasants and two soldiers were killed. The officer in command retreated with his troops and the Algerians into a near-by house to await reinforcements, but not before there were further casualties. The authorities at the time not unnaturally decided that forceful action was required, especially as the bodies of the British dead were brutally mutilated. Hence five Greek peasants who were involved in the fracas, including the boy, suffered on the gallows.

The soft grey limestone walls of the fortress, massive but neglected, now enclose nothing but a forest of pine trees which that evening perfumed the cool night air. Underfoot was a carpet of herbs and pine needles, occasionally broken by the stone foundations of now vanished buildings. It was here that the medieval city of Zakynthos with a population of several thousand was situated. A map in Archduke Ludwig Salvator's book shows that in the early Venetian days, the houses of aristocrats and merchants were tightly packed together with the arsenal, the barracks, churches, warehouses and stables. As the Venetian ascendancy became more secure and the island more prosperous, the new town began to grow up alongside the harbour below. As early as 1592, the Venetian governor reported that although the archbishop and government were still situated within its walls, the castro was little more than a ruin. Two views of the town, now in the Zakynthos Museum, painted during the early years of the British Protectorate, show the fortress walls intact and the steep ridge on which it stands devoid of trees. At that time, according to Private Wheeler, the barracks in the castle were occupied by British troops. In both pictures, which are painted in gouache, the flag of the United States of the Ionian Islands is seen flying from the summit at the southern end of the ridge where the radio station now stands. Today apart from the radio station, there are no buildings whatsoever except for a stone building which may have been the arsenal, and the only inhabitants on this occasion were a few goats whose little bells rang plaintively as they moved through the lengthening shadows of the trees.

We climbed on to the parapet which runs along the eastern heights. A thousand feet below lay the greater part of the town, stretching along the quayside in a gentle curve from the mole to beyond St Dionysios. To the south-east stood Mount Scopus with the scar of the gypsum quarry two-thirds of the way up on its eastern flank; there is a road as far as this which can be taken by those climbing to the summit and to the abandoned monastery situated there. In the remote distance the great walls of Clermont on the mainland gleamed faintly in the setting sun. In the violet light of evening the sea was the colour of aquamarine and still, except when little catspaws of breeze suddenly ruffled its surface.

Edgar Allan Poe wrote a charming, mannered sonnet on Zante, the island's Venetian name, the closing lines of which read:

> O hyacinthine isle, O purple Zante
> Isola d'oro, fior de Levante.

Hyacynthine may have been a better description of the sea's colour than aquamarine that evening, but in spite of a local guide-sheet which assumes that he visited the island, Poe never moved further east than Islington in London, where he was taken from the United States for a few years as a small boy.

The western view from the castro revealed the geography of the island. From immediately below the castle hill the great central plain, green from the cultivation of the currant vine, stretches away to the mountainous ridge which runs the whole length of the western limit of the island, at times rising over three thousand feet. On the lower slopes could be seen little white villages, with an occasional plume of wood-smoke lifting above them. The upper slopes, devoid of cultivation, consist of the bare grey-white limestone rock. To the south, the great Bay of Laganas sweeps in a curve from beyond Mount Scopus to the far south-western tip of the island beyond Keri. Nearer the sea, wheat is grown as well as the vine and sunbaked brown was the predominant colour, as the harvest had just been completed there. The plain is crisscrossed by a multitude of white roads, connecting the many smallholdings.

From the northern ramparts you look towards Akrotiri, which lies somewhat lower than the castro, and the hills which border the central plain on its eastern side. Immediately below to the east lies Pochali, the red terracotta and umber roofs of its houses partly hidden by the shining dark green leaves of the orange, lemon and lime trees which flourish in its gardens. Beyond there is a terrace from which there is a fine view of Zakynthos. Close by is the church of St Nicolas, famous for an icon of the Madonna and Child, which is particularly distinguished because the Madonna's hair was proudly donated by a local girl. Known as the Panayia Chrissopi, it is paraded around the village on the first Friday after Easter. The icon, which is said to be dated A.D. 840, is also said to have on the back an excellent painting of its donor in prayer.

The church of St Nicolas is beautifully situated, but unremarkable in itself, as the present structure, built of wood, is temporary only. Its walls are crowded with icons, most of them of indifferent quality. It has, however, historic associations both with the Greek War of Independence and, through indirect association, with the United Grand Masonic Lodge of England. Freemasonry, which was originally introduced into the Ionian Islands by the Venetians, became popular during the second French occupation of Corfu, which lasted from

1807 to 1814. Matthieu Lesseps, whose son Ferdinand built the Suez Canal, was the first Master of the Corfiot Lodge and was succeeded by Count Dionysios Roma of Zakynthos. When masonry fell into disrepute with Napoleon in 1812, Roma founded the Serene Grand Orient of Greece under the Duke of Sussex, who was then Grand Master of the United Grand Lodge of England. In 1814, the Friendly Society (Philike Etairea) was founded by the Greeks to promote the cause of Greek Independence. Roma deliberately used the masonic lodges which he had helped to found throughout Greece to further the cause of the Friendly Society. The executive committee of the Zakynthiot Lodge, the forerunner of the present Star of the East Lodge which is still run according to the English rite, were all members. It was in St Nicolas that they took their oaths of allegiance.

The pro-Hellenic activities of the Zakynthiot Lodge were betrayed in 1821 to Sir Thomas Maitland. Fortunately for Roma, one of the British officers in charge of the British troops rounding up suspects was also a mason and warned him of what was intended; he therefore managed to escape into temporary exile in Venice. Colokotronis, who was also a member, went off to join the insurgents in the Peloponnesos. Roma returned to Zakynthos when Sir Frederick Adam succeeded Maitland as Lord High Commissioner. By then Canning was at the Foreign Office and the cause of Greek Independence was viewed in a more friendly light by the British authorities.

For a time, masonic activities lapsed in Zakynthos but the Star of the East Lodge was established in 1863 on the foundations of the former Zakynthiot Lodge and celebrated its centenary in 1963. It has included Englishmen as well as Greeks. The present Lodge has been much involved with honouring the memory of Dionysios Solomos. It organized the centenary celebrations of the poet's birth in 1898 and was responsible for the erection of his statue in the square named after him. It was made trustee of many important manuscripts and is now active in starting a Solomos museum in a building on the west side of the present square of St Mark to house those papers and other memorials.

The site most associated with the poet Solomos is the little plateau of Strani, named after the family which owned it, which lies between the castro ridge and that of Akrotiri. Here facing north-west, the poet used to meditate and work in the solitude he so loved. From here, surrounded by tall pine trees, rustling slightly in the evening breeze, we had magnificent views over the plain towards the north-western hills. In very clear weather, usually a sign of impending rain, the village of Metaxata and the great mountain of Aenos in Cephalonia are visible to the north. The ridge of Akrotiri cuts off any view of the mainland but did not prevent the sound of gunfire reaching the poet from the siege of Missolonghi during those harrowing few years leading up to the final catastrophe in 1826. His most famous poem, 'The Hymn to Liberty', verses from which now form the Greek national anthem, was written in 1822 when he was only twenty-four and brought him immediate fame, not only because of the timeliness of the theme but also because it was written in contemporary Greek.

The background and upbringing of Dionysios Solomos was typical of that of the Ionian aristocracy of the period. The family itself was originally Venetian and of distinguished ancestry, claiming as a fore-bear Domenico Centranico who was Doge in 1027 and who adopted the name Salomone. Later members of the family were to spell the name variously as Salomos, Saloman and Solomon as well as Solomos. His father, who held the tobacco monopoly for the island, was created count in 1785 by the Venetians. Dionysios and his brother Demetrius were born out of wedlock, his father having taken as mistress a young Greek woman of the island, Angelica Nikli. They were however legitimized by the deathbed marriage of their father, then a widower, to their mother.

Like many other young aristocrats of Ionian and Cretan origin, young Solomos went to Italy for his education. His first attempts at poetry were in Italian, the language of the aristocracy, in which he was educated. It was the publication of some sonnets in this language which attracted the attention of Spiridion Tricupis, who later became distinguished as an historian and a diplomat, but is perhaps best known for the funeral oration he gave over the body of Byron on April 21st, 1824, at Missolonghi. Tricupis was far-sighted enough to appreciate the need for a poet to celebrate in Greek the Greek struggle for independence. He accordingly visited Zakynthos and persuaded the young Solomos that to write in Greek was a worthwhile ambition. The 'Hymn to Liberty' was written shortly afterwards. There is little doubt that the poet was bilingual, as his mother was unlikely to have spoken anything but Greek. Nevertheless it was a remarkable performance and Tricupis was able to write in October 1825 that the poem, then in its third edition, was being read in the original Greek in every civilized country throughout Europe—except in Greece itself!

Dionysios Solomos lived in Zakynthos until he was thirty. A sensitive and, in many respects, tortured man, he grew to dislike the island of his birth intensely. Finally in 1828, because of constant quarrels with his family, he left for Corfu, never to return. In Corfu he was received as a celebrity and became the centre of a literary revival. Although the Ionian Academy which Lord Guilford founded did not develop after his death in the way he had hoped, it nevertheless encouraged in Corfu the growth of an intellectual society. Among Solomos's friends there were such writers as Aristotle Valaoritis, Jakovos Polylas and Lorentzos Mavilis who produced some fine Greek poetry during the British Protectorate and afterwards.

Solomos never married and in his later years took more and more to drink. Nevertheless some of his finest poetry was written while in Corfu. During this time he became reconciled with the English whose politics he had first distrusted. Among his closest friends were Sir Henry Ward, who was British Lord High Commissioner from 1849 to 1855, together with his wife who entertained him frequently at the Palace of St Michael and St George.

His closing years were dogged by ill-health and by drink; his first stroke took place six years before his death, which was in 1857, and he died a few months after his third. During these years, he was a trial both to his friends and to himself. He had however come close again to his brother Demetrius who, always a conservative and in favour of the British connection until the Ionian Islands could join a Greek confederation in equal partnership, had become President of the Senate of the United States of the Ionian Islands; as such he rejoiced in the title of His Highness Count Sir Demetrius Solomos, G.C.M.G.

The aqueduct, which still provides the town with water, and many of the roads of the island were built under British auspices during the Protectorate, much of this under the direction of Lord Charles Fitzroy, a contemporary of Colonel Napier and one of the most successful British Residents of Zakynthos. His success in piping water from Akrotiri to the town encouraged Sir Frederick Adam, when he succeeded Sir Thomas Maitland as second Lord High Commissioner, to embark on a similar but more ambitious scheme for supplying Corfu with water. Fitzroy himself occupied one of the fine mansions on the waterfront. Adam however on one of his rare visits to the island considered that his dignity warranted an official residence of his own. This was a lovely country house on the northern slopes of Akrotiri. It was rented from the Lunzi family, one of the most distinguished and richest of Zakynthiot families. Napier attacked Adam unmercifully for this expense and especially for the cost of a number of improvements. A sketch in Ludwig Salvator's book shows its elegant three-story exterior and terrace, flanked by cypress and olive trees. The great earthquake of 1953, however, brought much of it tumbling down. Its owner was fortunate in being the only islander insured against such an event at Lloyd's; as a result the first two floors have been put back into excellent repair. There is a fine Italianate garden, in which palm trees flourish, surrounded by a balustrade with wonderful views of sea and olive groves beyond. There can be few lovelier sites on the island.

The British Protectorate from the end of the Napoleonic Wars until 1864 marked the revival of the English community which had almost died out during the decline and fall of Venice. The basis was still the currant trade although banking and trading also developed. Nor did this Anglo-Zakynthiot connection die when the Islands were united with Greece. There were Crowes and Sargints on the island until the 1953 earthquake. The last of the Sargints, a family which continued the Anglo-Zakynthiot trading traditions first established by the Levant Company, then left because the family home was destroyed. Miss Isabella Crowe, who entertained most hospitably those members of the British forces who visited Zakynthos after the end of the recent war, stayed on after the earthquake as her own villa on Akrotiri was not damaged, until her death in 1955.

There are now no longer any families in Zakynthos which are of direct English descent on the male side. Disappeared also is a minute facet of civilization, tiny, compact, largely self-contained, provincial perhaps but sophisticated and with a sense of positive enjoyment. The few English families had married among themselves and with the local nobility; there was no feeling of exclusivity on either side. If not rich, they were comfortably off, able to entertain well and travel extensively. Furniture was often imported from England, together with textiles, glass and on occasion nannies for the children. There was a pride in the architecture and art of Zakynthos, in its history and natural beauty. There was a pride both in England and in Greece and in the successful intermingling of the two cultures which created this gracious little society. It was however not strong enough to survive two world wars and sometime between 1919 and 1939 it went into its final decline. The 1953 earthquake buried it. Only a faint memory remains.

The British cemetery, however, is still there. We visited it in suitably elegiac weather—a damp, warm, grey afternoon with a light rain falling gently. It is situated at the rear of St John's Church under the heights of Akrotiri, well away from the shore. We reached it through impressive wrought-iron gates set in high encircling walls, beside which the royal coat of arms of Queen Victoria now lies neglected on the ground. Every square inch is occupied by tombstones of varying size or magnificence, the whole shaded by cypresses, a soaring eucalyptus and a vast magnolia tree. The main part of the cemetery is reserved for officers, traders and members of their families. Up a flight of stone steps is a little sheltered terrace; here are the humbler tombs of the other ranks who died on this remote station.

The earthquake had taken its toll here as elsewhere. The little church of St John is completely gutted. The tombstones are often cracked and the lettering on them has become increasingly illegible through the action of time. It was occasionally possible to decipher a name . . . 'Clementus Harby who was . . . lish consul for the Peloponnesos and Zakynthos . . . who died 1689 . . .', 'James Paul, consul for the Morea, Cerigo, Zante, Cephalonia, Leucadia and Corfu who died in the 39th year of his consulship on 27 August 1728, much lamented by everybody and greatly beloved for his integrity and a benefactor to this island'. It was sad to see the number of young wives who had died in childbirth and of the children who had died at a very early age in the days when malaria and dysentery must have taken a heavy toll. We were surprised to find a Lunzi commemorated here, but later learned that this was because, as daughter of the Danish consul, she was a Lutheran and not a member of the Orthodox Church. The guardian of the cemetery was friendly and patient as we wandered among the tombs. It was rarely visited now, he said, perhaps every other year only when a representative came over from the British Consulate at Patras. No, he knew nothing about the people buried there—it was all so long ago.

A few new trees have taken root since the earthquake; in due course their roots will further push up gravestones. The dripping from the trees in the winter and spring rains will further obliterate the names of forgotten families and regiments.

6

Seaside and Countryside in Zakynthos

(i) ALIKIES

At Alikies on that early June day, the wind blew briskly from the north, so we lay on the sand on the sheltered side of a decaying rowing boat, its ribs staved in by the winter storms. A slight mist overcast the sky but we were conscious of the heat of the midday sun. Inside the crumbling cavern of the boat, cactus had taken root and other plants which seemed to enjoy its cool shade. A large may-bug or scarab beetle competently manoeuvred its great bulk in and out of the exposed ribs. Apart from the beetle we were alone on the sandy beach. To the north the great mountain of Aenos in Cephalonia stood high above the Ionian Sea.

To reach Alikies, we had taken the bus to Katastari, about a mile inland, and then walked. Katastari is a large rambling village at the northern edge of the plain. From here the road climbs north to the Monastery of St John and to the large village of Volemai, where, in 1806, Nicholas Biddle of the distinguished Philadelphian banking family noted in his journal the survival of two ancient customs. One was the placing of a piece of money in the mouth of a dead man at his funeral in order to pay Charon's ferry charge. The other was the measuring of land for purchasing purposes after Dido's fashion, that is 'by the bushel' or by the area likely to be covered by a bushel of seed.

The bus made its way with much puffing and wheezing of air-brakes on a well-made but narrow winding road through the rich countryside. Everywhere the land was cultivated; even the brown sandy soil under the olive trees had been sown with wheat, most of it now harvested. Endlessly across the plain we could see the dwarf vines of the 'raisin de Corinth'. Here and there cottages were being built. The population of the island is now beginning to grow again after the exodus that followed the 1953 earthquake. Everywhere there were flowers—wild flowers along the roadside, and clumps of roses, carnations and geraniums on verandahs and cottage steps—while up the cottage walls and over the verandahs clambered the vine. Cottages and hamlets were protected by trees—pine trees, hibiscus and mulberry trees and vast towering eucalyptus trees with their grey-white bark and festoons of pale green leaves among which swarmed charms of goldfinch.

Most of the passengers were elderly smallholders, the men invariably wearing battered straw hats and the older women headscarves. After dropping a passenger the bus would start off briskly and sigh to a halt a hundred yards further on. The journey of about six miles took over an hour.

We were put down at the entrance to Katastari and a young fellow passenger guided us to Alikies. He had recently returned from Canada where he had worked first in his brother's café near Montreal, known inevitably as 'Nick's Diner', and afterwards in factories. During his two and a half years there, he had learned remarkably little English. Yes, he said, the money had been good but he missed the sun and the open air. In addition, it had been all work. 'They work too much in Canada. Here in Zakynthos, the money is not good, but we rest between the wheat and the grape harvests and also in winter.' So our friend, having gone out steerage, bought himself an air ticket back to Alikies at the beginning of spring. But he was not completely happy; laughing to himself he confessed that he was thinking of returning again to Canada. Perhaps there was some land which he hoped to buy, perhaps it was the question of saving for a dowry so that a sister could be married.

As we came to the crossroads and the two or three cottages which mark the centre of Alikies, only a few yards from the sea, we met another smallholder to whom we were introduced. He had recently returned from Australia for the same reasons as our companion; it was basically a longing for the open air and to be his own master. We learned that there were at least three hundred inhabitants from the Katastari area alone in and around Montreal, and even a greater number scattered in the U.S.A., Australia and Germany. In this way money came back to the village so that there were now few desperately poor people to be found.

Only after a cup of coffee were we allowed to depart. After resting a while by the forlorn rowing boat we strolled northwards along the

sandy beach, on the edge of which were a number of wooden plat-
forms, partly surrounded by bamboo walls. Here in the great heat of
July and August, the local villagers come in search of coolness to
enable them to enjoy a few hours' sleep. There were also a few
summer cottages belonging to the more prosperous inhabitants of
Katastari.

But although Alikies is well known locally for its lovely beach, its
importance lies in its salt pans, which is what the name Alikies means.
These cover some ten acres just inland. They were started as a state
monopoly by the Venetians early in the sixteenth century and have
now been producing salt for well over four hundred years. Channels
are dug through the shallow sand dunes along which sea-water is
passed to the pans themselves. The water evaporates and the thick
deposits of salt are then shovelled into great piles to await collection.
In full summer, the light reflected from the salt pans can be dazzling
and the eyes of the labourers injured unless they wear dark glasses—
which they often omit to do.

The light of late afternoon brought out the full gentleness and
serenity of the landscape. The sky was cloudless as the sun sank
towards the western hills; these were grey and bare except for scrub
and thorn, but everywhere else all was colour and luxuriantly green.
As we waited for the driver to climb into the bus, the conductor
presented us with clove-scented red carnations from a cottage
garden. Quicklime was being unloaded to whitewash the walls of
the village store; a piece fell into a pool of water by the pump
where it hissed and crackled. An old lady came out of another
cottage near by, followed by her granddaughter, with more flowers
for us.

(ii) TSILLIVI

There are two or three bathing places at the town of Zakynthos, to
the north of the Mole. But the nearest country beach is two miles
away at Tsillivi where the upland country, stretching north from
Akrotiri, slopes down to low open fields and the sea. Here there is an
excellent sandy beach which runs north-west below a shallow sandstone escarpment, the only building when we were there being a
recently completed restaurant. Tsillivi is a popular resort because
there is always a breeze even in the hottest weather. To the north-
west is open country stretching away to more olive groves and the

rising ground of the eastern range of hills which ends in the villages of Gerakari and Alikanas above the Gulf of Alikies.

(iii) LAGANAS

The great Bay of Laganas lies between Cape Gerakas, the most south-easterly point of the island beyond Mount Scopus, and Cape Mara-thias, at the far south-west; the straggling village of Laganas lies roughly at its centre. Immediately to the west there is a headland with cliffs and rock-strewn beaches, but eastwards to Mount Scopus there stretches for two or three miles a great wide beach of golden grey sands as fine as any to be found in Europe. Behind the sand dunes there is nothing, apart from the occasional hamlet, until you arrive back at Zakynthos town, some five miles away. Here is the safest bathing on the island with a complete absence of sea-urchins, those black brittle crustaceans whose spikes, if trodden on by the naked foot, can cause so much temporary discomfort.

If you go by taxi, you will be driven through olive groves and past the few whitewashed cottages of the village right on to the beach, where there are several hotels and restaurants. Each of them had its own juke-box or radio. So loudly were they being played that their owners must have thought that the noisiest establishment would attract the most custom, irrespective of the quality of the noise or the cooking. As it was Sunday, three large busloads of schoolchildren had arrived for a picnic; each bus was also equipped with powerful record-players. Finally, there were the elaborate transistor radios brought by individual parties. A quick count revealed fifteen pieces of noise-amplifying equipment along a stretch of a hundred yards. Our choice of restaurant was based on noise (least amount of) rather than on gastronomic considerations and obviously this meant one at the far end of the group, but we should have eaten equally well at any of them. The menus were all virtually the same—freshly caught fish or cray-fish, fresh tomato and cucumber salad, roast lamb, steak and delicious aromatic keftedes together with fried potatoes, as popular now in Greece as in England.

The little headland to the west is wooded and several neat little villas have been built on it. At the beginning of the headland is a little fresh-water stream from where a country lane winds inland. Here is a stone memorial to André Vezal, a Belgian anatomist of the seventeenth century, whose body was washed up here after his ship had been sunk in a storm—a touching reminder of the respect for learning to be found throughout Greece. The lane itself winds upwards through vineyards and olive groves until it disappears from sight beyond a giant eucalyptus tree alive with little fluttering birds.

(iv) PORTO ROMA

An exceptionally attractive beach is that at the Porto Roma which lies beyond Mount Scopus at the south-east tip of the island. The bus goes south out of Zakynthos, past the church of St Dionysios, over the river and south-east along a well-surfaced road parallel to the coast. Originally there must have been a road where the beach has now been covered by the sea as at one point a little stone bridge stands several feet above the water just beyond the mouth of a little stream. Near by is a small eighteenth-century Venetian villa, originally owned by the Domenighini family, which looks in a reasonable state of repair. The good surface ends about a quarter of a mile beyond and the remainder of the eight-mile journey is over a road of hard reddish earth in excellent condition. Here you reach the lower slopes of Mount Scopus which are heavily wooded. The road winds uphill through the trees and there are wonderful views of the sea and the distant coast of the Peloponnesos.

Here on Mount Scopus took place what must have been one of the earliest recorded meetings on Zakynthos between Englishmen and Greeks. In 1599, John Dallam, a distinguished organ-maker, set sail from England for Constantinople on an unusual mission, an account of which he kept in his diary. The purpose of this mission was to take to the then new Sultan of Turkey an organ of great complexity. Ostensibly it was to be the gift of Queen Elizabeth but it was in fact commissioned by the Levant Company who were anxious to develop good relations with Constantinople. The State papers for January 31st, 1599, just before Dallam left on his mission, recorded that 'a great and curious present is going to the Grand Turk, which will scandalise other nations, especially the Germans'. A sad reflection, this, on the changing nature of things. During the Byzantine period, Constantinople had been renowned for the construction of fine musical instruments, including organs. In 757, for example, Pepin, King of the Franks, requested and received an organ from the Byzantine Emperor.

In due course, Dallam's ship anchored off the town of Zakynthos. Mount Scopus so captured his imagination that he vowed that as soon as he set foot ashore he would neither eat nor drink until he had climbed to the top. It was only with difficulty, however, that he persuaded two of his companions to accompany him as they were terrified of falling into the hands of savages; their names were Myghall (Michael) Watson, a joiner, and Edward Hale, a 'cotchman'. Their fears appeared to have been justified when they fell in with a man 'goinge with a greate staffe upon his shoulder, having a clubbed end and on his head a cape which seemed to us to have five horns standinge outrighte, and a greate heard of gootes and shepe folloed him'. It was of course only a shepherd with his flock but one of Dallam's friends refused to go any further and the other was persuaded to stay with Dallam but only with the greatest reluctance. They then fell in with another peasant, completely unarmed, who with typical Greek hospitality led them to his home and filled a silver bowl full 'of a redeishe wyne, which they do cale Rebola', and gave it to Dallam to drink. Dallam offered to pay for his refreshment but this was refused. Instead his host accepted a knife as a gift. After this Dallam was taken to a near-by church where a service was in progress. He was by this time alone as Michael Watson had remained lower down the slopes in terror while Ned Hale, his remaining companion, followed only at a distance. The latter eventually plucked up sufficient courage to enter the church and knelt down at the first empty place, only to find to his consternation and to everyone else's amusement that he was in the part of the church reserved for women.

The service over, they were still not allowed to depart but were conducted to the portico of the church 'wheare we found standinge eyghte verie fayre women and rychly appareled, some in reed satten, som whyte and som in watchell Dameske, there heads verrie finly attiered, cheanes of pearle and juels in there eares, 7 of them verrie yonge women, the eighte was anchante and all in blacke. I thoughte they hade bene nones, but presently I knewe they wear not.' Afterwards Dallam—Ned Hale still hung back—was taken into another house, where he was given eggs 'the shels of them collored lyke a damaske rose'. From this and from his description of the festive garments of the women, Dallam and his companion had obviously come upon an Easter Sunday festival and had been offered the generous hospitality of the Greek countryside.

Beyond Mount Scopus, the country opens out into farmland with extensive views on all sides. Among the upland green fields were patches of gold, where the corn was being harvested. At one point the road runs past thick woods protected by fences, belonging to the French Club Mediterranée but not then as yet developed.

After an hour's journey we reached Vassilikos, a long straggling hamlet of some twenty houses, well-shaded by eucalyptus trees and surrounded by well-worked farmland. The walk down to the Porto Roma through open country takes about twenty minutes. Half-way, you pass a pleasant group of well-shaded farm buildings. The track ends in grass-covered sand dunes on which stands a pleasant little taverna overlooking the deserted beach; close by is a small annexe with beds for visitors. As it was not yet nine in the morning, and too early to bathe, we whiled away the next hour talking to the proprietor over a cup of coffee. He told us that the Porto Roma is so named because it was here that the Roma family used to moor their yacht. He had a great respect for learning. He described with awe the number of languages spoken by a local official. 'French, German, Italian, Russian,'—he ticked them on his fingers—'Why, he even speaks American!'

We were again the only bathers, and the pale sands showed no footprints but our own. High sandstone cliffs encompassed the northern as well as the southern end of the bay. In little pools lived tiny hermit crabs in their delicate fluted shells. Clouds fringed the horizon but over Zakynthos the sun shone from a clear sky.

7

The Central Plain of Zakynthos

We woke up to still June mornings with not a breath of wind. The sea shone while the darker blue, browns and whites of the boats anchored to the quay were exactly reflected in reverse on the water, a painted upside-down extension of hulls, masts and rigging. The heavens were pale blue but sparkled with a rosy glow, which would vanish well before noon when the blinding strength of the midday sun over-powered all colour.

A friend called for us soon after ten and we set out on a tour of the southern part of the island. We took the road for Keri, remote in the rugged heights at the south-western tip of the island. The road runs through open country with olive groves and vines on the southern fringe of the rich central plain. After leaving the road to Laganas on our left, low wooded hills emerged on the same side. A few minutes later we stopped.

'Look', said our friend, pointing due south into the sun, 'do you see the house? That's Sarakina.' This was the country villa of the Lunzi family, one of the most elegant buildings in the Zakynthiot countryside. We could see the graceful lines, the three-storied central block with steps rising from the terrace to the piano nobile on the first floor. On each side was a well-proportioned single story wing. To reach it, a carriage-way, only wide enough for one vehicle, led up to the main entrance from the road, climbing above the terraced vine-yards through which it was built. Beyond the villa were tall trees—cypresses, eucalyptus and pine trees. 'It certainly looks in perfect condition,' we said, knowing this not to be true.

'Then let us go and see what it is really like.' Reversing the car, we proceeded back a few hundred yards, before turning off on to a rough country track which climbed gently upwards through olive groves, standing amid sandy-red soil, to the rear entrance to the villa. As we came to a halt in the courtyard, the air was suddenly pierced with harsh screechings as several peacocks, unexpectedly disturbed in their comfortable dust baths, lumbered angrily off into the protection of the great hangar of trees that stood to the south side of the house, blocking a view of the distant sea. These were fine trees of great beauty; they gave, moreover, an illusion not merely that the villa was over a half-mile from the sea but comfortably inland, perhaps in the Alpine foothills of the Venetia, where the owner's ancestors had originated.

The name of the house, Sarakina, means Saracen, perhaps commemorating an attack by Saracens or kindred Mussulmen. Zakynthos was raided on a number of occasions during the thousand years between the decline of the Roman administration and the brief Venetian naval ascendancy in the Mediterranean. One of the worst recorded cases is that, reported by Procopius, of raiders who invaded the island from North Africa under King Genseric in about A.D. 470, when the bodies of some five thousand Zakynthiots were thrown mangled into the Ionian Sea.

With the fall of Constantinople, the Turks rapidly developed naval forces which they used against the surviving Christian strongholds in the Aegean and elsewhere round the Greek Archipelago. Their aims were furthered by the corsairs who pushed westwards into the Mediterranean in pursuit both of personal and national gain encouraged by the successes of the Algerian raiders against treasure-laden ships returning from the newly discovered Americas. Outstanding among these corsairs were the Barbarossa brothers, Uruj and Kheyr-ed-din, who were said to be natives of Lesbos. Uruj carved out for himself a dependency in Algeria which, after his death in 1515, was expanded by his more famous brother. It was Kheyr-ed-din Barbarossa whose invincible fleets ravaged the Christians from the Aegean to the Balearics and who was eventually commissioned by the Grand Signior to bring Ottoman shipbuilding up to the standards of Genoa and Venice.

After the Battle of Lepanto in 1571, the Turkish navy went over to the defensive and never again enjoyed the same supremacy as under Barbarossa. The Barbary pirates nevertheless became increasingly active, their numbers swollen as a result of the final expulsion of the Moors from Spain in 1609. They operated not only from the North African coast but made full use of Turkish bases in Albania and the Peloponnesos to raid the Ionian Islands for slaves and booty. At the same time, the Venetian navy was proving less and less able to protect their shipping in the Adriatic. A final effort to subdue them was made in 1787, ten years before the Republic capitulated to Bonaparte. An expedition was successfully dispatched against the Algerians and Tunisians under Angelo Emo, who had been equally successful against the Algerians in 1769. He was given for the occasion the resounding title of 'Captain Extraordinary of Ships'.

The air was heavy with the scents of summer and alive with the drowsy hum of insects, but these and the colony of peacocks, whose shrieks had now subsided, were the only inhabitants of this once luxurious villa which, as we could now see, was an empty shell. Originally built in the early eighteenth century, it had been enlarged in the middle of the nineteenth century during the prosperity which flourished under the British Protectorate. Its style showed elegance, simplicity and good taste, with none of the extravagancies which were beginning to develop in Victorian England. The stucco, painted a pinkish terracotta, was in satisfying contrast to the green of the shutters. Under the staircase was a little pillared retreat; here in alcoves were neo-Classical stone portraits of ancient heroes, staring stolidly past us at the courtyard beyond. The steps up to the first floor entrance, however, were crumbling; carob-tree saplings had taken root in the cracks and crannies in the wall. The shell of the building stood only because there had been no fire as in the town.

The western wing had housed the wine and olive presses, now a mass of mangled machinery standing amid cracked vats of stone. On the northern side, facing back towards the road, the great terrace was covered with weed and the front steps leading to the piano nobile were barely negotiable because of the profusion of rambler roses. Only the little chapel at the rear looked reasonably sound; this, containing many tombs of the Lunzi family, was locked. We asked if there was any possibility of restoring it. 'Highly unlikely,' said our companion, 'because of the expense. Of course, a shipowner may eventually turn up.' There followed a discourse on the decline and fall of the Ionian aristocracy, particularly that of Zakynthos.

Originally largely from Italy, especially from Venice, the Ionian aristocracy ruled by means of the feudal system, whereby the peasantry paid over a part of their produce and supplied free labour for their lord's estates in return for protection and sound administration—at least in theory. This system had been first introduced into Cephalonia and Zakynthos by the Orsini at about the time of the

Fourth Crusade. The feudal system, although western European in origin, had by the thirteenth century become widespread throughout Europe and had been introduced into Corfu by the Byzantines.

In Zakynthos, the nobility began to flourish under the more settled conditions of the Venetian ascendancy. There was a considerable community of interests between the nobility and the merchants and the latter were eligible to promotion, should a noble family, the number of which was fixed at ninety-three, become extinct. The peasants, however, remained as serfs and made little headway, in spite of several uprisings, until the establishment of the modern Greek state, when the estates of the great families began to be broken up. 'Look at the situation today,' explained our friend. 'A hundred years ago, the family lands of this house stretched away beyond the road into those foothills of the western mountain range you see beyond. Now they are nearly all converted into smallholdings. Look at all the little cottages scattered among the vineyards.

'The trouble with the aristocracy has been that they never brought themselves up to date. They spent too much time in gambling and litigation. These tendencies seem to have increased as the responsibilities of administration and government which were originally theirs by right of rank were progressively withdrawn, especially when the islands were absorbed into the Greek Kingdom.'

The decline of the great estates was accelerated by two other factors. Before the union of the Ionian Islands with Greece, land was handed down on the male side only; after 1864, it was divided equally between male and female members of the family. Secondly, because the landed aristocracy has never been recognized as a class in the modern Greek state, the exclusiveness of the Ionian aristocracy declined. Territorial family alliances became fewer, and this again hastened the break-up of the large estates. The nobility, our friend continued, should have adapted itself to modern life, should have learnt professions or gone into commerce whereby family fortunes could have been re-established or consolidated. Only since the recent war has this begun to happen. The great names of Zakynthos still exist and their past is remembered, but titles, especially since the Second World War, are now rarely used. Not everyone bearing a distinguished family name in the Ionian Islands is however necessarily a member of that family as peasants have over the years acquired the name of the owners on whose estates they have worked.

The road from Sarakina to Keri rolls up and round the southern foothills of the western range. About three miles before Keri, a very rough road, pleasantly lined with trees, branches off to the south. Within a few minutes we reached the seashore; hills rise steeply to the south-west but there is swampy land to the north-east, where cattle were sleepily browsing. Out to sea stands the little island of Marathonesi, rising to a height of nearly five hundred feet and terraced for wheat and fruit. A few cottages straggled along the shore; there was nothing remarkable in this. More unusual, however, was the rig of a small oil drill standing desolate and rusty by the side of the road. Most remarkable of all was a well in the ground, full of what appeared to be diluted pitch through which bubbles continually forced their way. Here was one of the most renowned features of Zakynthos, the pitch wells, which are still used for caulking local fishing boats against fouling. First mentioned by Herodotus, there is little doubt that the black ships which sailed for Troy under Odysseus' command were treated with the pitch of Zakynthos, as the island together with Cephalonia formed part of the kingdom which he ruled from Ithaka.

These pitch wells have been described by many writers. 'Here,' Müller wrote, in his journal which was subsequently published in several languages, 'the air is noxious and causes protracted fevers; as is evident from the pallid features of the inhabitants'. It is only since the Second World War that malaria has been almost completely eradicated from Greece. Until the introduction of insecticides and spraying from aircraft, malaria was very widespread and was no doubt the cause of the lack of energy of the peasantry, so frequently and prudishly remarked upon by visitors from the West.

Müller mentioned other signs of volcanic activity, notably the deep caverns in the neighbourhood of Cape Skinari to the far north of the island, from which was said to flow 'a white oily substance which coagulates on the surface of the water'. We, however, heard nothing of these manifestations. We also heard nothing of the sport of seal-catching which Müller also mentioned. This used to take place in sea-level caverns at the foot of the great limestone cliffs which stretch north-west from Keri for most of the western coast of the island.

On our arrival towards noon at Keri, a chalky blue heat haze hung over the cliffs and the sea but we could see something of their magnificence. They are at least as high as the chalk cliffs of Dover with endless views to the south and west, where the Mediterranean is at its emptiest. Keri itself appears to be built largely on bare rock. It has many fine houses, which suffered little harm from the earthquake, but there are few trees here and little pattern in the layout of the village. Zakynthos for the most part justifies Homer's description of 'woody' but in Keri and its immediate vicinity vegetation is extremely sparse. Many of the houses appeared to be shut up and a general sense of emptiness and neglect hung over the village.

We returned the way we had come until we reached a point nearly opposite to Sarakina, and then turned on to a good dirt road, sandy-red in colour, which led to the little village of Pantocrator and on to Mousakion and Makairadon. Here we were running along the western rim of the saucer formed by the central plain. There were trees enough by the roadside and in the villages—the usual olives, eucalyptus and cypress trees—but higher up we could see the grey limestone wilderness of the western slopes.

At Makairadon there is one of the finest village churches in the island. It is constructed in simple basilica form with fine wrought-iron grilles over the windows, each of which is supported on both sides by classical pillars in bas-relief and covered by a fine curved canopy. The plain whitewashed exterior contrasts satisfyingly with the curved terracotta tiles of the roof. Rose trees grow against the walls. The church, according to a tablet set in the wall above the north entrance, was rebuilt in 1872, no doubt after an earthquake. The interior looks even more modern, over-decorated and garish; the many icons are in the cloying, sugary style in which so many are now produced. Of considerable interest, however, is the screened-off balcony at the west end of the church for women. Segregation of the sexes during worship has continued far longer in the countryside than in the towns.

Separate from the church itself on the east side of the little stone-paved square is the great campanile. It is crowned with an octagonal turret; high up round the bell chamber is a fine wrought-iron balustrade. A tablet incorporated in the wall says it was built in 1802. Now it has been rebuilt again because of the severe damage received in 1953. Great cracks were to be seen in the masonry and it was feared another severe 'quake could bring it crashing down on to the church and surrounding houses. This fine Venetian style campanile is a symbol of the natural conservatism of the countryside and of the wealth which the soil of the central plain has produced.

We drove on through the village to a little hamlet beyond its northern outskirts. Melinado consists merely of a few peasant cottages and their smallholdings. The little church itself is of historic interest because of Roman remains built into it. The altar of the church, now removed for safety to the basement of the Museum in Zakynthos, was originally in a temple dedicated to Diana. The Latin inscription on its side, which is still clearly legible, reads, in translation, 'Archicleo, son of Aristomenes, and Alcideme, wife of Archicleo, have dedicated their daughter Clenippe to Diana Opitidis'. The church is not now in use as it suffered heavily during the earthquake. In the interior, all was confusion. Much of the ceiling had collapsed; this together with debris of the church furnishings had been piled into the middle of the church and left to rot. Among the litter was a fine brass altar lamp and some fragments of fine woodcarving. We expressed a hope that the church would be rebuilt, but were told that it had proved cheaper to erect a tiny box-like church of pre-stressed concrete a hundred yards away—a sad reflection, either on the poverty or ignorance of the local ecclesiastical authorities.

Outside the church there were more ruins, this time in the shape of four granite pillars with white marble plinths and capitals. These have been mentioned by several travellers in the golden days of Hellenic travel during and just after the Napoleonic wars. A picture in Ludwig Salvator's work shows them supporting a covered entrance to the church. Now they lie haphazardly on the ground. The walls of the church, where the outer stonework or stucco has fallen away, can be seen to have been built largely of material, including broken columns, from the Roman settlement and shrine which once stood here.

These columns and the altar in the church are about the only classical remains on the island outside the few Roman relics in the Zakynthos Museum. The date ascribed to them locally varies from pre-Roman times, which of course cannot be true, to about the first or second century A.D., which is more likely.

75

Part Two

CEPHALONIA

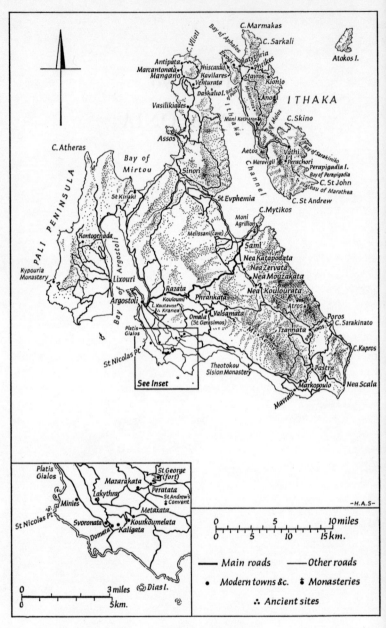

C. Marmakas
C. Sarkali
Atokos I.

Bay of Aphalos
C. Vlioti
Antipata
Marcantonata
Mangano
Phiscardo
Kavilares
Venturata
Daskalio I.
Exoïsi
Platythria
Phrikes
Stavros
Kionio
Vasilikiades
Anogi
ITHAKA
Moni Katharon
C. Skino
Assos
C. Atheras
Bay of Mirtou
PALI PENINSULA
Sinori
St Kiriaki
St Evphemia
Aetos
Merovigli
Vathi
Perachori
Bay of Sarakiniko
Perapigadia I.
Bay of Perapigadia
Plateau of Marathea
C. St John
C. St Andrew
C. Mytikos
Kontogenada
Melissani (cave)
Moni Agrillion
Ithaka Channel
Kypouria Monastery
Lixouri
Bay of Argostoli
Razata
Kouloumi
L. Koutavos
Kranea
Argostoli
Phrankata
Saml
Nea Katapodata
Nea Zervata
Nea Mouzakata
Nea Koulourata
Atros
Valsamata
Omala
(St Gerasimos)
Platis Gialos
St Nicolas Pt
See Inset
Tzannata
Poros
C. Sarakinato
C. Kapros
Theotokou Sision Monastery
Pastra
Markopoulo
Nea Scala
Mavrata

Inset:

Platis Gialos
Mazarakata
St George (fort)
Lakythra
Peratata
St Andrew's Convent
Minies
Metaxata
St Nicolas Pt
Svoronata
Kourkoumelata
Domata
Kaligata
Dias I.

0   3 miles
0   5 km.

−H. A. S−

0   5   10 miles
0   5   10   15 km.

——— Main roads   ——— Other roads
• Modern towns &c.   ⚑ Monasteries
∴ Ancient sites

2. Cephalonia and Ithaka

8

Argostoli

Argostoli, capital of Cephalonia, which is the largest of the Ionian Islands, is a long narrow town built on the eastern slopes of a spit of land which juts northwards from the central land mass into the Gulf of Argostoli. Looking east from our hotel window, we could see the vast slopes of Mount Aenos, with its summit rising to approximately five thousand feet, dominating the whole of the view. At one time, these slopes were covered, from about eight hundred feet upwards, with forests of the cypress dark Cephalonian silver fir. These trees were famous from ancient times for the building of triremes and long ships because, according to Theophrastus, of the lightness and durability of the wood. Odysseus almost certainly built his ships from Cephalonian fir; certainly the Venetians used it for theirs. The first question Napoleon put to a Cephalonian who was presented to him in Paris during the second French occupation was about the forests of Mount Aenos. These, however, have shrunk considerably over the centuries. In addition to being cut down for ship-building and for fuel, fires and the depredation of the voracious goat have both taken their toll so that great stretches of the mountainside are now barren. In recent years, however, there has been some afforestation. The lower slopes are planted with olive, cypress and pine trees.

The town has a sheltered site, at least from the west and east; and the long quay gives as comfortable berth as any in the Ionian Islands to the shipping that comes here to load the grapes, figs and other fruits from the valleys and coastal slopes around Argostoli. In general the inhabitants of Argostoli claim milder weather than Zakynthos; the more southerly island is far more likely to be affected by the winter snows of Aenos, which can cast a chill shadow over it. Still, you do not altogether escape extreme rigours of climate on Cephalonia. In

January and February there is on occasion a plentiful demand for charcoal for indoor braziers.

On this occasion however we were in Argostoli in June, verdant with early summer. The mornings were calm and still cool. In the early afternoon a little breeze sprang up from the north, rustled through the trees in Metaxas Square and was away south-eastwards over pine-encircled Koutavos Lake towards the Venetian capital of St George, its ramparts perched nearly a thousand feet high on an out-spur of Mount Aenos. This is the pattern of summer weather except that it gets hotter and hotter until, from mid-July until mid-August, it is stifling; the whole town is inert then from noon until about six in the evening.

The present town came into being in the seventeenth century as the port to St George. In the same way as in Zakynthos, the port itself rapidly became the main centre. In 1757 it became the official capital and the fortress was abandoned. Colonel Leake when he visited Argostoli in 1806 reported that the houses 'have in general only one story on account of the earthquakes to which the island has the reputation of being more subject than any of the surrounding countries.' The vast majority of houses are still of only one storey but because of the 1953 earthquake are now of reinforced concrete.

Leake also remarked on the prevalence of malaria, as Lake Koutavos was then no doubt a vast breeding ground for the mosquito. The itch he also reported to be widespread but said that the inhabitants refused to have it cured because they believed it to be a preventive of malaria. Fortunately, malaria is now something of the past and Argostoli is as peaceful, agreeable, healthy and welcoming a town as anywhere in Greece.

Leake was writing at a time of turbulence and change when the ill-fated Septinsular Republic was crumbling to its fall. Because of the uncertainty of the political situation, local antagonisms were rife. 'There is little society on account of the family enmities,' he wrote. Certainly the Cephalonians have had a more turbulent record than that of the other Ionian islanders. Writing before the tragic events in Cephalonia of 1848 and 1849, when the only serious troubles during the British Protectorate in the Ionian Islands took place, Davy said, 'Of the larger islands generally considered, the inhabitants of the southern ones, in which the currant vine is cultivated, are held to be the more industrious, active and intelligent than those of the northern, in which the olive is the principal product—which, too, is no more

8. Assos, Cephalonia

9. Beach at Platis Gialos, Cephalonia

10. Napier's Lighthouse near Argostoli, Cephalonia

11. Phiscardo, Cephalonia

than might be expected, taking into account how habits are formed and how the one species of cultivation requires and therefore promotes industry—and how the other, requiring little labour and exertion, has a contrary effect.' Davy goes on to say, 'The inhabitants of Cephalonia and Ithaka have shown a more enterprising spirit than any of the other islanders, leading them to engage in adventure and foreign commerce: and it may be added that the Cephalonians have also shown more freedom of will and love of liberty, prompting them to resist oppression and to break into acts of insubordination.' They have sometimes been compared with the Irish both for their quarrelsomeness and their sense of humour. 'Are you a Cephalonian? Then you are to blame', is a story they tell against themselves.

The enterprising character of the Cephalonians is mentioned by other visitors to the islands. Holland remarked that Cephalonian doctors were to be found in every town in European Turkey. At the time of his visit to Ali Pasha, the physician in attendance was a Doctor Metaxas, a well-known Cephalonian name. Thomas Jefferson, while United States minister in Paris, enjoyed the friendship of Count Carberry, the Royal physician, who was a Cephalonian of the family of Charvouris. A prayer of the 'sages-femmes' of Cephalonia, when a female infant was born, was, wrote Holland, 'may she be happy and have a physician as a husband'. Had he been writing a hundred years later he would certainly have mentioned shipowners. Cephalonia's shipowners—no Greek island has more—are the pride of the community, not only because of their commercial success which is naturally admired, but also because of their generosity to the island of their birth. He would also have mentioned that Cephalonia today provides a greater proportion of Greek university professors than any other part of Greece.

Müller commented with surprise and pleasure on the high standards of social life in Argostoli during his visit in 1821, eleven years after the British had brought peace to the island. In the private houses of wealthy merchants and the nobility 'everything is in European style. The luxuries of the west have entirely supplanted the customs of the Levant, which is not the case in the neighbouring island of Zante. Here we met with looking-glasses, carpets, lustres, elegantly bound libraries of books, with the old French and Italian classics. . . . The amiable accomplishments of the inhabitants of this small town is in perfect unison with this external splendour; and the female sex is not excluded from it . . . I found many young merchants occupied in their leisure hours with astronomy and the study of ancient coins. Almost all the young gentlemen are educated abroad, in Germany, France or Italy; so that none of the Ionians are so well informed as the Cephalonians.' This is borne out by an examination of the private libraries of the period which have survived until today and by the books in the Koryialeneios Library, many of which were donated to it from what was left of private collections after the earthquake. Here, in the well-designed modern building on the upper slopes of the town, is a fine auditorium for lectures and films, together with an exceptionally fine collection, often well bound, of the writings of the most distinguished French, German and Italian writers of the eighteenth and nineteenth centuries in their native languages. There is also an interesting collection of Napier's papers, some of them copies of those in the British Museum.

Müller emphasized the determination of the Cephalonians to succeed at anything they attempted. He also remarked on their hospitality. 'I have met it in the interior, even from the forest; and they offer a draught of water and their coarse bread with the greatest pleasure.' This is still true today as travellers will find when journeying through the island.

It is worth quoting these passages to show that the standards of civilization in the principal Ionian Islands have from the seventeenth century onwards been at the same level as those of the rest of Christian Europe. Although vulnerable to every power which became ascendant, however briefly, in the Ionian Sea, Cephalonia was only under the yoke of the Turks for some twenty years during the last quarter of the fifteenth century. At that time the Ottoman forces were consolidating their grip upon the mainland and islands of Greece after the fall of Constantinople in 1453. Venice, aided by the Kings of Naples and Cyprus and by the Knights of Rhodes, an alliance for which the Papacy was largely responsible, continued to resist the Sultan, but was eventually forced to make peace in 1479. By this agreement, she retained a few of her colonies on the mainland; she also held on to the Ionian islands of Corfu and Paxos to the north and Kythera to the far south. She however deliberately excluded Cephalonia, Ithaka and Zakynthos, because the Tocchi dynasty, which had ruled these islands for nearly one hundred and fifty years with the resounding title of Dukes of Lefkadia and Counts of Cephalonia, had recently made a fresh alliance with the Angevin dynasty in Naples.

The Tocco family, which originated at Benevento near Naples, had originally gained favour both at the Angevin court in Naples, and, through a marriage alliance, with the independent Byzantine Despots of Epirus. Leonardo Tocco I was assigned Levkas and the southern Ionian Islands in 1357 by the King of Naples and thus reunited the island possessions which had previously been ruled by his Orsini cousins. The last of the Tocchi, Leonardo III, who ruled from 1448 until ousted in 1479, had proved himself an able ruler and his islands were a paradise of peace and plenty compared with the chaos on the mainland. Thousands of Greeks had therefore taken refuge in Levkas, Zakynthos and Cephalonia. While the dominant religion was Catholic, Leonardo had granted rights to the Orthodox clergy and recreated the Orthodox bishopric of Cephalonia which included Zakynthos and Ithaka as well.

The Duke of Lefkadia had been in alliance with Venice against the Turks. Venetian ingratitude towards this almost last Christian state in Greece by excluding it from the peace of 1479 because of its Angevin ties, spelt its downfall. The Turks quickly saw in this their opportunity for seizing these islands. Leonardo III fled, first to the hill-top fortress of St George, and then, on the approach of the Turkish fleet, to Italy. The Turks on landing in Cephalonia executed all the Ducal officials, burnt the fortress of St George and carried off to Constantinople most of the peasants; they were then mated with Ethiopians in order to produce a race of grey slaves. Venice finally acquired Cephalonia in 1500 and held it until 1797.

Our first walk in Argostoli took us down the broad avenue into Metaxas Square, the centre of the town; the square is named after the Cephalonian prime minister of Greece who so valiantly defied the Italians in 1940. In the many gardens, the trees and shrubs were at their greenest. The feeling of spaciousness was enhanced by the single-storey houses. The shops are similar in design to those elsewhere in Europe, although the multiple chain is not yet in evidence in Greece. There were a few taxis and lorries about, but it is still possible to stroll down the centre of the street, to pause and speak to friends without fear of being run down.

Argostoli, today a respectable if undistinguished town, had some claim to distinction before the earthquake. During the nineteenth century, as a result of its flourishing economy under the British Protectorate, there had been a considerable amount of building, both public and domestic. Although Cephalonia has never been as rich as

Zakynthos, the Venetians built gracefully and well; houses erected in the first half of the nineteenth century followed the Venetian style. Such houses can only now be found in Corfu. In the Koryialeneios Library in Argostoli is a magnificent set of photographs showing the town at the beginning of this century—rows of great stone houses of two and three stories, embellished with fine wrought-iron balconies and gates. In addition there were the public buildings of the British. The main administrative building stood in the centre of Metaxas Square and was of neo-Classical design. This was unfortunately pulled down early in this century in order to make way for the present great open square, on the western side of which was a delightful small theatre and opera house. This however has gone, as have nearly all the private houses, as a result of the earthquake. Only in isolated cases have the owners rebuilt; instead, most of the wealthier inhabitants have preferred to settle in Athens.

Cephalonia was singularly fortunate in its local administrators during the British Protectorate. General Campbell, in dispatches home in 1813 and 1814, was already discussing the prospect of establishing a Greek school or college in Cephalonia and encouraging Greek teachers to migrate there from the Peloponnesos rather than teach among the Greek communities of Moldavia or Wallachia. Later he seems to have favoured Vathi in Ithaka; it is possible that Frederick North, the future fifth Earl of Guilford, was already exerting his influence in favour of the foundation of an Ionian University which was originally to have been sited in Ithaka but was later established in Corfu.

The first governor of Cephalonia, appointed by General Oswald in 1809 when he occupied the southern Ionian Islands, was Colonel, later Sir Hudson, Lowe, who was afterwards to be Napoleon's gaoler in St Helena. He was succeeded several years later by Colonel C. F. de Bosset, an officer of Swiss origin who served in the British Army for over twenty years. De Bosset was sent in 1817 to hold Parga against Ali Pasha, where he fell foul of Sir Thomas Maitland.

It was de Bosset who in 1813 built the causeway over Lake Koutavos; Mr Gladstone was to cross it on arriving at Argostoli in 1858, surrounded by several hundred demonstrators demanding union with Greece. In the middle of the bridge, which is about half a mile in length, there is a small column on which, according to Private Wheeler, who was stationed in Argostoli from 1824 to 1826, was inscribed, 'To the glory of the British Nation'. This inscription was however defaced by the Italians when they occupied Argostoli in 1941. They apparently planned to convert it into a memorial to Ugo Foscolo, but were ousted before this plan could be carried into effect.

De Bosset started building the excellent network of roads which, in addition to the water supplies, is the principal legacy of the British Protectorate; the main road to Argostoli from Sami was his. He also, according to Holland, tried to introduce the potato into Cephalonia, but was hindered by two local priests who declared that the potato was the very apple with which the Serpent had seduced Adam and Eve in Paradise. Holland adds dryly that bad winters and the need for fresh seed from England were the more serious obstacles. Times have changed; fried potatoes are now as popular on Cephalonia as in England.

The most dynamic British administrator ever to have served in the Ionian Islands was undoubtedly Colonel, later Sir Charles, Napier, the conqueror of Sind, who had announced that event to Whitehall with the single punning word 'peccavi'. He was appointed Resident of Cephalonia by Maitland in 1822 at the age of forty, by which time he had seen considerable service overseas. He immediately fell under the spell of the Greeks and at one stage seriously considered accepting the command of the Greek insurgent army during the War of Independence. He was a tremendous enthusiast; 'the merry Greeks', he wrote home, 'are worth all the other nations put together. I like to see them, to hear them; I like their fun, their good humour, their paddy ways, for they are very like Irishmen. All their bad habits are Venetian; their wit, their eloquence, their good nature are their own.'

His tremendous energy and enthusiasm were given wholeheartedly to Cephalonia. The fine open quay of Argostoli was built on his instructions. In order to make it, he had brought down some of the stones from the Roman walls which formed part of the ancient city of Kranea, traces of which are still visible on the slopes of Aenos immediately above the Koutavos Lake. He also had the waterfront beyond the quay cleaned up and a walk, now expanded into a road, constructed to the grove of trees outside the Xenia Hotel where there had been erected in Private Wheeler's time a bronze statue to Maitland. This statue remained in position until shipped away in 1942 by the Italians for melting down; the boat in which it was being transported was torpedoed in the Ionian Sea and so the image of the great proconsul remains hidden underwater within the realm over which he ruled so ably and where he made himself so unpopular. Instead of

Maitland, there is now a memorial there to those who worked to achieve the union of the Seven Islands with Greece.

Napier authorized a model prison to be built on the site now occupied by the Xenia Hotel. He was also responsible for the Ayios Theodoros lighthouse on the promontory to the west of the sea-mills north of Argostoli; this was destroyed in 1953 but has since been rebuilt in exactly the same way. He also initiated the construction of many other public works. Napier's name is still remembered today, above all for his honesty and incorruptibility, for his reform of the administration of justice, for his work in ameliorating prison conditions and for his protection of the peasants from the tyranny of the local aristocracy. Under him, 'life and property attained to a security hitherto unknown in the island,' according to Lord Kirkwall who wrote an account of the British Protectorate in *Four Years in the Ionian Islands*, published in 1864.

Napier could however be overbearing and was on occasion seized by uncontrollable anger. 'On one occasion,' recorded Kirkwall, 'hearing screams and learning that a titled Ionian was beating his wife, he rushed into the house and inflicted on the spot, with his riding whip, a severe personal chastisement on the astonished husband. To be sure he immediately afterwards sent to offer to the sufferer complete personal satisfaction. But the Ionian, ignorant of western refinements in such matters and unused to the pistol, refused to understand how the being shot at could fully atone for the disgrace of being flogged.'

Napier became a great friend of Byron, when the latter stayed in Argostoli and at Metaxata from August to December 1823. It was Byron who recommended to the London Committee that he be offered the command of the Greek forces against the Turks. Napier actually went to London in 1824 to offer his services, but they were refused. When later the Greeks offered him the command, he regretfully declined as he did not wish to place himself at the mercy of the mismanagement and intrigues which then, in his opinion, marked the running of Greek affairs.

His work in Cephalonia ended under a cloud. On returning temporarily to England in 1830 on account of his wife's health, he was informed that Sir Frederick Adam, the successor to Sir Thomas Maitland as Lord High Commissioner, had seized his papers on a visit to Cephalonia and had then publicly declared that he would not have him back. The most tremendous row exploded with an embarrassed

British Government offering Napier, as a peace gesture, the Residency of Zakynthos, considered senior to that of Cephalonia, which he refused. Instead he wrote a most violent attack on Adam in 1833 called *The Colonies:—Their Value Generally, Of The Ionian Islands in Particular*, which today would most certainly have led to a major action for libel and which gives an interesting and entertaining picture of the period. It was basically a clash of personalities, Adam was something of a martinet while Napier was not of a subordinate nature. The latter grew a beard against army regulations, whereupon Adam instructed him to remove it. This Napier promptly did and sent the whiskers in an envelope to Adam.

The row would never have taken place if Adam had been prepared to allow Napier the same independence as Maitland had. Possibly the seeds of enmity developed from Napier's *Memoir on the Roads of Cefalonia*, which he published in 1825; this he dedicated to Adam without first obtaining his permission and, after praising him for his 'great activity, united with a thorough knowledge of the resources and wants of *all* the islands' . . . added, 'I think Cefalonia may expect full *thirty thousand dollars*, to be annually applied to improvements.' Adam would have been irritated by being thus publicly committed and Napier equally annoyed when the money was not forthcoming. Napier, if autocratic and domineering, knew local conditions thoroughly and resented Adam relying more upon his aristocratic courtiers for information about Cephalonia than on his direct representative, the Resident. Adam, moreover, insisted on keeping to the letter rather than the spirit of the law when dealing with the peasantry; and this too often meant the death sentence, according to Napier who saw himself as their protector against the machinations of the aristocracy.

Napier was never to return to the Ionian Islands, but remained deeply interested in them for the rest of his life. Even during his Indian campaigns we find him writing to his old friend Count Metaxas about Cephalonian affairs, 'I always think of my second country, the (to me) dear island of Cefalonia. I have almost cried with vexation to hear of all that goes on there. I hear that people have been harshly treated in Cephalonia and I know there is no need for that for the people are good and noble.' In this letter of 1851, he went on to denounce the mischief-makers and deplored local attempts to resist Britain. 'Remonstrate, appeal, memorialise the Queen who is good and just. Do all but try the terrible strength of such an Empire as ours.'

He remained convinced that should England give up the Ionian Islands she would quickly be implored to return.

The extent of Napier's love for Cephalonia can be seen from his will. He had christened one of his daughters Emily Cephalonia. He retained to the end two properties in Argostoli, one of which he left to each of his daughters. To Gerasimos Cambitsi he bequeathed a gold ring. He particularly emphasized the value he placed on the antique Ithaka ring given him by Count Demetrius Delladecima of Cephalonia. To his great friend, John Pitt Kennedy, who had been his Director of Public Works and thus responsible for carrying out his development schemes, he left a handsome legacy. Kennedy, on retiring from Cephalonia after Napier's departure, settled in Ireland where he became so absorbed in improving agricultural standards that he refused the Governorship of Australia. He later joined Napier as his military secretary in India.

Napier was for many years commemorated in Argostoli by a statue. This was pulled down by the Italians during the war and thrown on a rubbish dump after it had been defaced. It has since been salvaged by well-wishers who wish to re-erect it when properly restored. A possible site is a small public garden on the upper slopes of the town, near the Koryialeneios Library, known as Napier's Garden. London, in this respect, is more fortunate as there is a fine bronze statue of him standing in Trafalgar Square, his strong hawk-like features dominated by his great broad brow; a replica of this is also in the crypt of St Paul's Cathedral.

Argostoli today has its full complement of public buildings, all of them restored or built since 1953. It is pleasant to find how much of this has been carried out with help from foreign organizations. The General Hospital was donated by the Swedish Red Cross, the children's hospital was the gift of the Swedish Save the Children Fund while the orphanage was given by Britain—to quote but a few examples.

Sunday proved the day to see Argostoli at its liveliest. After the siesta, family parties stroll leisurely round Metaxas Square or along the broad avenue to the monument outside the Xenia and back again. After a while, they settle at one of the cafés on or near the square for a cup of coffee or a soft drink which is made to last endlessly. On occasion in summer there is a Sunday evening concert, with the local band resplendent in white tunics and gleaming helmets. Then, all of the eight thousand inhabitants of the town appear to be present. Modestly well-dressed, the girls demure, the boys cheerful but well-mannered, the men wearing ties and often hats, the skirts of the women comfortably below the knee, conversations quiet and no doubt humdrum, polite bows exchanged as acquaintances pass—it is a Sunday evening scene in summer to be met with all over Greece. Yet in Argostoli at least, the threat of tragedy and disaster can be rarely completely forgotten.

Tragedy and disaster have come not only through natural causes such as fire, which have destroyed vast tracks of forest, and through earthquakes, but in recent years through man-made violence, as in the case of the Germans and Italians in 1943.

The Italians tried during their brief occupation of the islands to revive past memories of Venetian glories by setting up an Ionian administration, but with little success. Although the unwarranted bombardment of the open town of Corfu in 1923 had soured relations between the two countries long before Mussolini's seizure of Albania in 1939, the Italians themselves were not disliked. Until the turn of the century, the older generation of many cultured families still spoke Italian among themselves; for this, or rather the Venetian dialect, had been the everyday language of the aristocracy and the merchants for hundreds of years following Byzantine rule. In any case many Ionian families have, though usually from remote times, a little Italian blood, while others have gained professional qualifications in, for example, the fields of medicine and architecture at Italian universities. The occupying Italian forces, although not welcome, rarely inspired the deep hatred which the Germans were to incur.

Then in September, 1943, Mussolini was renounced and the Badoglio government came to terms with the Allies. The Italian commander in Cephalonia of the Acqui division and supporting units received orders from Badoglio to resist any approach from the Germans. Unfortunately the Italian command in Athens, dominated by the Germans, at the same time ordered him to place himself under German orders. The general hesitated. While he was quite capable of resisting the few units of crack German troops which began to arrive on the island soon after the Italian armistice was announced, he knew that without air power—and he had none—he would ultimately be at the mercy of the German Air Force, especially of its dive-bombers. Accordingly he played for time, hoping perhaps for the arrival of the Allies who were already advancing, although only temporarily, in the Aegean. But no help came. Meanwhile the tempers of the Germans and Italians rose until the Germans, supported by Stukas, launched an all-out attack upon the Italians whose morale was already low. The Stukas rapidly finished off what artillery the Italians had at their disposal and made the roads unusable for wheeled transport. The Italians, with no real leadership, were forced to surrender piecemeal, although here and there they put up considerable resistance.

Then came the final tragedy. The Germans, probably because their troops, however excellent, were so few and because the problems of imprisoning and provisioning a whole division were so great, decided in cold blood to massacre their former allies. Killer squads of Germans encircled the Italians, herded unarmed into camps, and cut them down with automatic weapons. The bodies were then heaped together and burnt; the fires were seen at Kardakata, at Kourouklata and Trojanata and at many other places on the slopes of Aenos. The headquarters staff was mown down at the northern tip of the Argostoli peninsula near the sea-mills. Altogether 341 Italian officers and about 4750 other ranks were massacred in this way. Occasionally in Italy today, you will come across references to 'the martyrs of Cephalonia'.

Visitors to Cephalonia have remarked on the feeling of melancholy which occasionally surrounds the island. The dark forests of Cephalonian firs which still cover considerable stretches of the remoter slopes of Aenos, the long shadows cast by the clouds that often stand above the mountain, the stillness in the air and the humidity which casts a haze over the view—all contribute in some indefinable measure towards creating this impression. There must have been a particularly strong feeling of melancholy about the island in the autumn of 1943.

9

Lixouri

❧✦❧

Lixouri is the second largest town and port of Cephalonia with a population of some four thousand; before 1953 there were half as many again. In fact when Napier was Resident, it had a larger population than Argostoli. Capital of the administrative district of Pali, the most western part of the island, it faces due east across the Bay of Argostoli to the central massif of Aenos. The surrounding area is about the most fertile part of the island.

Lixouri is connected with Argostoli by a frequent car-ferry service which takes barely thirty minutes. Its berth in Argostoli is on the quay just to the north of the Navy administrative building. Before sailing out into the great open Bay of Argostoli, you pass the promontory, famous for its sea-mills, one of which still functions. In the early days of the British Protectorate, a certain Mr Stevens, an English resident, decided to harness the power of the sea at one of the two points where it rushed inland to disappear down potholes to emerge no one then knew where. He accordingly had a water-wheel erected to work a mill for grinding corn. A Greek neighbour followed this example by harnessing the other sea race in the same way. These two sea-mills quickly became famous and no visit to Argostoli was considered complete without a visit to them. They were destroyed in 1953 but one has been repaired, although it no longer functions as a mill. From the boat you get an excellent view of it.

Close by the water-mill is a small bathing beach and beyond, at the western tip of the promontory, is Napier's rebuilt gleaming white lighthouse in the shape of a rotunda with classical pillars. From here the coastline of the Argostoli peninsula stretches south to St Nicolas Point. The western slopes of the peninsula are pleasantly wooded, leading down at Platis Gialos to the favourite beach of Argostoli with its gleaming sands.

Lixouri is a completely modern town, as pleasant and as undistinguished as other rebuilt towns in the islands. On its waterfront, Napier had erected the administrative building for the town, perhaps his most impressive public building judging by contemporary prints, but this of course has been destroyed. There is as usual a spacious public square, around which eucalyptus and acacia trees have been planted. There are one or two formal flower beds at the eastern end, in the midst of which stand two bronze busts to members of the Typaldos family of shipowners, who have contributed much to the island both before and since the earthquake. The effect of the white concrete paving, the whitewashed walls of the surrounding houses and the whitewashed curbs to the sidewalks is almost blinding in the sun at noon; even the trunks of the trees are whitewashed. The roads leading off the square are also tree-lined but here the washes of the house walls and the colour of doors and window frames are in soft pastel shades so that there is some relief for the eye.

The only house of distinction not to have suffered complete destruction is the impressive Venetian villa which originally belonged to the Jakovatos family. The quality of its restoration is regarded locally as exceptionally good. In addition, it houses one of the finest libraries in the Ionian Islands. Asking our way to the house which is situated on an elevation on the outskirts of the town, a Lixouriot insisted on guiding us there. On arrival, a Sunday morning, we found it had shut at eleven; now it was half past eleven. But because we were visitors from abroad, he said he would take us to the house of the custodian. On arrival, we found he had gone to Patras, and that his stand-in lived out at Lascaratos Hill, some three kilometres to the north of Lixouri.

Our friend without further ado commandeered a taxi, insisted on our getting in, rushed off to collect his two small children and off we set. On the outskirts of the little town, the road suddenly degenerates into a barely passable earth road. The taxi lurched at a walking pace between verges of prickly pear and shallow bone-dry ditches. Just before reaching our destination we passed the site of the ancient castro which had been fortified by the Venetians at the beginning of their occupation. As in the case of Argostoli and Zakynthos, the old fort was abandoned when the modern town developed. Now only a few feet of Venetian wall remain.

Eventually we came to a halt under the shade of eucalyptus and umbrella pine trees near a flat roofed whitewashed house, only to find that the young custodian had disappeared down the slopes and into the sea. Instead we visited the house which contained a few relics of Andreas Lascaratos after whom the hill is named. He was a nineteenth-century savant who brought upon himself for a time the hatred of the Ionian Islanders—and especially of the clergy, who excommunicated him—because of his savage and satirical attack upon Ionian morals in a book entitled *The Mysteries of Cephalonia*, published in 1856. He was eventually to regain the respect of the community because of his outstanding honesty and his fine intelligence, in spite of the fact that he favoured the continuation of the British Protectorate. His attacks on the hypocrisy of priest and politician were recognized in due course as being valid and he is sometimes referred to as the 'Voltaire of Greece'. Today, although nobody may read his works, there are large notices both at the ferry landing stage in Argostoli and in Lixouri advertising Lascaratos Hill as a tourist attraction.

Lascaratos was educated in a school or college at Fort St George, one of several institutions founded in the Ionian Islands by Lord Guilford between 1815 and his death in 1827. The first headmaster was one Thistlethwaite, a mathematician, and at the start there were twelve pupils. Neofitus Vamvas, an orthodox priest and a distinguished scholar who taught Napier Greek, was also a master. Originally from Chios, he settled for a few years in Cephalonia until the school was disbanded after the death of its founder, Lord Guilford. Later, he was appointed professor of philosophy at Athens University. Vamvas is perhaps best remembered for having translated the Old Testament into modern Greek for the British and Foreign Bible Society, using the Hebrew text instead of the official Septuagint version. This aroused a storm of criticism from the Orthodox Church, which distrusted in those days the Protestant missions which began to arrive in Greece after independence.

Like Kalvos and Foscolo, Lascaratos spent some time in England; this was because a writ for libel was issued against him after the publication of the offending volume. (In any case he spoke English extremely well, having been brought up by an English stepmother.) On returning to Cephalonia, he gave himself up to undergo a four months' sentence in Napier's model prison. But because of the brutality of the prison governor, he was released by the British authorities after only two months.

While Lascaratos lived most of his life in Argostoli where he died in 1901, the family estate was on and below the hill; his main income was from the sale of the currants produced there. The original house had stood next to the little stream which we could see making its way across the gentle slope below the hill; all that was salvaged in 1953 was a battered old desk, oil paintings of his mother and brother, and a sepia photograph of himself, showing an earnest, bearded, hollow-cheeked man in early middle age.

The father of the missing custodian of our quest produced Turkish Delight and excellent water—not from his own well but from a spring half-way up the hillside which was rated much better. It is common to discuss the differing qualities of well and spring water in the remoter regions of Greece. On returning to Lixouri, we offered to pay for the cab, but our friend would have none of it; nor were we allowed even to provide ices or chocolate for the children.

About six miles to the west of Lixouri high up on the cliffs above the sea is the Kypouria Monastery, built on three sides of a square. The monastery is now in a poor state of repair, both on account of the earthquake and through neglect. The views are magnificent, but the road to it is bad. A far better idea of post-Byzantine monastic architecture can be seen above the Bay of Paleocastritsa on the west of Corfu.

10

The District of Kranea

❧

South-east of Argostoli is a serene upland countryside which rolls gently down to the southern shores of the island. Here and there, neat little villages nestle in the hollows or under protecting slopes with fine views of the blue Ionian Sea and of rugged Zakynthos beyond, high on the southern horizon. Behind from north-west to south-east stands the great dominating ridge of Aenos at its steepest and most impressive. It is a warm, sunburnt land with olive groves, orchards, vineyards and open heath where flocks of goats and sheep browse. Above all here is an air of peacefulness. Many successful Cephalonians retire here.

We hired a taxi for the afternoon. The hotel general factotum arranged a price with the owner of the newest American limousine taxi, who agreed to take us to the Mycenean remains, to Metaxata, where Byron lived for some months and to St George, the former Venetian capital of the island.

We drove down the tree-shaded road out of Argostoli to the south, passing the Old People's Home and the Agricultural College. We could not see Koutavos which was to our left because of the thickness of the intervening pine woods, which stretched on well after the lake was left behind. For the energetic, there is an interesting walk along a rough road, now being much improved, which branches off to the left and encircles Koutavos, meeting the main Argostoli–Sami road at the eastern end of the causeway across the bay.

Leaving the woods behind, we drove higher into the rolling country which is dominated by the hill-top fortress of St George, its encircling walls intact. At Peratata, the fortress rising almost sheer above, we turned southwards into a region of many villages, which are connected one with another by a network of country roads. We passed one or two fine modern houses, which we were told belonged to prominent shipowners.

Just beyond the village of Mazarakata are a number of Mycenean graves, cut deep into the limestone and dating from about 1400 to 1100 B.C. During this period the Achaeans were expanding throughout Western Greece and may well have helped colonize the Ionian Islands of Ithaka and Zakynthos as well as Cephalonia. Odysseus, the most famous Ionian of them all, was almost certainly of Achaean stock. Other tombs have been discovered at near-by Lakythra, about two miles west of Mazarakata, at Mavrata, towards the south-east tip of the island, and at Kontogenada, north-west of Lixouri on the Pali peninsula. Many skulls showing signs of wounds, thus indicating a warrior race, have been found in these tombs. We could not help noticing how small they were, little over five feet long.

We asked if we could next visit the Cyclopean walls, mentioned by Leake and other visitors to Cephalonia. Our taxi guide had never actually visited them. 'You are the first people who have ever asked me to take them there. I've heard that they are at the far end of the Lake of Koutavos somewhere up on the mountain slopes. If I take you to Koutavos, I can't tell you which way to go. They may be two, three, four kilometres away from where the road ends—who knows in what direction. You'll need a guide and that has to be arranged in advance.' 'But they are at Kranea,' we insisted. 'Kranea? Why the whole area is called Kranea.' It is in fact one of the three administrative districts of the island, the other two being Sami and Pali.

Instead we drove on to Metaxata with a wonderful view of the channel between Cephalonia and the great scarred cliffs and wooded heights of Zakynthos; far away to the south-east we could see the distant faint coastline of the Peloponnesos. It was in these calm dark-blue waters that an incident once took place which was to lead to one of the sternest contested sieges of all time. In 1564, a great Ottoman merchant galleon sailing south-east from Venice through the Zakyn-thos channel *en route* for Constantinople and laden with valuable merchandise, was captured by a squadron of three galleys, manned by the Knights of St John, and was then conducted to Malta. The Knights who had previously been driven from Rhodes by Suleyman the Magnificent in 1522 and had re-established themselves in that hard and barren island, were as resolute as ever in their determination to attack the Infidel whenever possible, especially if there was booty obtainable. Here in the central Mediterranean they proved as powerful as ever. The great merchantman belonged to Kustir-Aga, the Chief Eunuch of the Sultan's seraglio, and several ladies of the harem were

12. View of Vathi, Ithaka, by Joseph Cartwright

13. Distant view of Levkas Town with mainland Greece beyond, by Edward Lear

14. Valaoritis Villa on Madura island off Levkas

15. Levkas Town and the lagoon

participating in this venture. For some time the Sultan had contemplated evicting the Knights of St John from their new home and freeing the seas from these piratical enemies. The capture of this merchantman was the ultimate provocation. In the following year a fleet of over one hundred and eighty warships set out from the Golden Horn for Malta. The defeat of this Armada after four months of the bitterly fought siege of Valetta was the greatest humiliation that Suleyman the Magnificent suffered.

Here in Metaxata stood the house which Lord Byron rented from Count Metaxas from early September 1823 until the end of December of that year when he crossed to Missolonghi. It was a period of waiting in the hope that the various Greek factions could be persuaded to end what almost amounted to civil war and to unite against the common enemy. 'The emissaries of the various Greek parties,' wrote Sir Harold Nicolson, 'flocked to Metaxata, attracted like vultures by the savour of Byron's fabled wealth. There were emissaries from Colokotronis, who would represent how their enlightened patron had by now firmly established his humane government throughout the Morea, and how Mavrogordato, that dishonest and incompetent phanariot, had been forced by popular clamour to fly the country. There were emissaries from Mavrogordato who would explain how the Klepht leader Colokotronis, with his big nose and brigand mercenaries, had destroyed the legal government of Greece. . . . There were emissaries from Odysseus who would point out . . . that it was only by allying himself with the Captain of Eastern Greece that Byron could secure the unity and liberation of the country.' The emissaries came from all corners of Greece, even from Mount Athos. 'Byron would receive these conflicting missions impartially . . . And at times, when they arrived together, he would confront them the one with the other; and Count Delladecima would act as interpreter, summarising, in his prolific way, the voluble insults which they would hurtle at each other across the little room; forgetting at moments to interpret, and launching out, upon his own, into a torrent of argument and invective.' Count Delladecima was the uncle of Andreas Lascaratos, who described to Kirkwall many years later how, when a boy, he had seen Lord Byron during his stay in Cephalonia. Byron had called upon Delladecima; because he was wearing muddy boots, the English poet would not enter the sitting-room but instead passed the time while his uncle was dressing by chatting affably with the boy.

Apart from waiting for greater unity on the mainland, this stay in

97

Metaxata was also a period, according to Nicolson, when Byron was steeling himself to take an active part in the campaign against the Turk, hoping that his presence as well as his money would serve as a rallying point. There were of course lighter moments. Other visitors included young officers from the garrison who would come out from Argostoli to drink gin with Byron; moreover there was his kinsman, Lord Sidney Osborne, who had joined the British Ionian Service to escape his creditors in England, and James Kennedy, a Scottish doctor who had strong religious convictions and who felt that the British community in Argostoli and especially the noble author of *Childe Harold* and *Don Juan* needed constant reminders about the fundamental doctrines of Christianity. To all, Byron remained patient and friendly while he waited for a sign from the mainland that circumstances were propitious for him to commit himself. He was eventually persuaded to move to Missolonghi by Prince Mavrogordato that December.

The Metaxata house which I had visited in 1945 I remembered as a simple white-painted single-storey building made of wood, very much the sort of house to which a mariner would retire; from it he could watch the sea from the shade of his balcony, that same balcony on which Byron used to sit wrapped in his Stewart tartan cloak. Now there was no chance of testing the accuracy of my memory. Like all other buildings in the vicinity, the house had disappeared. But not Byron's memory. Here, on a whitewashed wall next to a wrought-iron gate through which there were views of a pleasant garden and bungalow, was a little marble slab with the simple inscription 'Lord Byron's Ivy'. The ivy itself, a vigorous plant, was being encouraged to climb freely about the wall, as it had when the poet had lived there.

Metaxata is an extremely well-kept and agreeable village. An even more delightful village is Kourkoumelata a little lower down the same slope. It has been rebuilt completely since 1953 by the well-known Cephalonian shipowning family of Vergotis. The present village has a fine model hospital, an equally fine school, a church and a playing field. It is a village of trim lawns, beautifully tended flower beds and flowering shrubs. We might almost have been in California but for the quietness, the absence of automobiles, and the old peasant riding his donkey up the opposite hillside.

We then went to the convent of St Andrew (Ayios Andreou), which we reached down a narrow lane close to Peratata. The convent is recommended as a tourist attraction, especially as it contains the saint's velvet-shod left foot. We were, however, unlucky. The long, low stone church, obviously largely rebuilt since 1953, was shut and the only nun in sight, a heavily-built peasant woman in a long grey garment, was unwilling to find the key. We tried to see something of the interior by peering through the one window at eye level on the north side, but we could only see a clutter of junk like an overcrowded storeroom. The site is a pleasant one with a fine view of the fortress of St George. Towards the end of his Residency, Napier brought out a young clergyman called Dixon and his wife to start a girls' school in the convent for the young ladies of Cephalonia, the first establishment of its sort to be set up in the island. I was unable to discover how successful this venture was, but in the nineteen thirties, there were two frail old maiden ladies called Dixon still living in Argostoli.

It was to St George that we next went. At the crossroads at Peratata, we bumped off the main road on to a very rough steep track which zigzagged upwards. Then suddenly the road became smooth and new as a modern trunk road before it is tarred. Perhaps the island authorities had allocated a sum to make it easier to reach what undoubtedly should be a tourist attraction and then found it insufficient. We were told it would be finished in due course—but when? Perhaps later in the year, perhaps in the following year.

Before reaching the entrance to the fortress, we visited the adjoining village, pretty but decaying, although no doubt a bustling settlement when the fortress was occupied. The villas looked as if they were first built by Venetians and subsequently renovated. The walls of the houses were green with the vine and the little gardens filled with a colourful and untidy profusion of flowers. Half-way down the village which sloped gently eastwards away from the fortress was a small church of simple basilica shape, dedicated appropriately to St George. As we so often discovered, the church was locked and there was nobody we could find to let us in. The main attraction of the church, which we did not see, is the group of five icons in the post-Byzantine style by Andreas Carantinos (c. 1660–1740), almost certainly Cephalonia's most distinguished artist of this period, whose family came to Cephalonia after the fall of Byzantium in 1453; we were however able to admire in Argostoli the lovely icon of the Virgin and Child which he painted in 1705 for the Cambitsi family church of St George at Tzannata. In front of the church is an arch, which may at one time have served as a belfry, on which are carved in bas-relief several curiously squat figures.

We walked up to the top of the village towards the entrance to the fortress. Here several girls displayed locally made lace but of rather dull design, although there are some excellent examples displayed in the Tourist Office in Argostoli. Here also we met the custodian who conducted us round the fortifications, massive stonework with tunnels sunk deep into the rocks for use as arsenals. The fortress has not been used since the end of the British Protectorate and now, as in Zakynthos, great pine trees stand tightly packed on the site. Here was the capital of the Tocco family in Cephalonia and probably of the Orsini before them. The Turks occupied it during their brief ascendancy over the island until 1500 when their garrison of three hundred was overcome by the Venetians, aided by a Spanish contingent under Gonzalo de Cordoba. The fortress was subsequently brought back into full repair by the Serene Republic until abandoned soon after 1756, when Argostoli became the capital. It was used for the last time when British troops arrived in 1809. Private Wheeler mentions in a letter home in 1824 that a strong British army detachment was stationed there.

The views from these ramparts, nearly a thousand feet high, were magnificent. A cool pine-scented breeze sighed through the trees. Here it is always cool even on the hottest of days. Far below just off the coast, we could see the tiny island of Dias, now completely deserted, but once the site of a temple to Zeus. In ancient days there was another temple to Zeus high up near the summit of Mount Aenos far above; when sacrifice was being offered on Dias, the incense, curling up into the air, was a signal to the priests officiating at the summit to sacrifice in their turn to the Father of the Gods.

At the western end of the fortress, the outer wall falls several hundred feet to where a rough track winds into the foot-hills of Aenos. There is also a secondary road to the Shrine of St Gerasimos, the island's patron saint, some six miles inland. Four miles away, we could see the pine woods around Koutavos glowing in the lengthening light of late afternoon. Beyond was Argostoli, the great inland bay and, further still, the peninsula of Palé.

We asked the custodian about the history of the fortress. 'There was a war', he began, 'many years ago. After this the Italians left and the British came. The governor lived in a house over there,' he continued pointing back in the direction of the village. Here the story ended.

Cephalonia as well as Zakynthos was richly endowed with fine churches. A great many were destroyed partly or completely in 1953.

Where repair has proved impossible, a new church has been provided
as in the case of the cathedral in Argostoli, an imposing reinforced
concrete building with a simple whitewashed exterior and with lavish
interior decoration in a style which might be described as mellow-
modern. The church of St Spiridion, however, in the main street of
Argostoli has been restored with most of the original icons on the
iconostasis intact; the usual separate bell-tower, this time in ferro-
concrete, has also been rebuilt. At last the Ionians feel that they are
building for ever and not merely until the next severe earthquake. It
is only sad that the age of craftsmanship has largely departed.

Fortunately there are some fine old churches which were only
slightly damaged or have been successfully restored in the villages on
the slopes immediately below Metaxata and Mazarakata. Take the
road out of Argostoli through Lassi, on the western flank of the ridge
on which the town is built, and follow it south towards the village of
Minies. In Lassi, there is a school where non-Greek-speaking children
are educated in Greek. There are several groups of Greek nationals
whose first language is not Greek; in Greek Macedonia, for example,
the villagers speak a distinct Slav dialect, in the Pindus mountains the
Vlach clans speak a language akin to Roumanian, while there are large
Turkish groups in Eastern Thrace. On the right you see the well-kept
bathing beach of Platis Gialos with its umbrellas, its restaurant, its
facilities for changing and, above all, its clean white sands. A little
further along you pass the little point of St Nicolas. From here onwards, the land by the coast is almost completely flat for some two
miles and is the most likely site for an aerodrome, should one ever be
built. At the moment Corfu is the only Ionian Island with an airport.
The ease with which tourists from the north wanting a two weeks'
package deal in the sun can reach Corfu, compared with the time
needed to reach Cephalonia and Zakynthos, is reflected in the vastly
higher prices of land, especially by the sea, in Corfu. The Cephalonian
Tourist Board has done very much more than most regional com-
mittees to develop the island's attractions but funds, until far more
tourists come, are naturally limited.

Beyond Minies the road winds inland through olive groves and
scattered smallholdings. At Svoronata just off the main road, is the
restored church of St Nicolas whose shining cream-white walls
dominate the village. The funds for this work came, as often, from
members of the village who had emigrated to the United States.

The driver went off to find the key to the church. Near by were the walls of what once must have been a fine small Venetian villa, judging by the attention given to minor decorative details such as the curve of a stone balustrade. The house was not occupied. Instead, for safety's sake, the family had moved into a little corrugated iron hut near by; vines growing up the wall and over the doorway made it look a little less rough. It was the same everywhere—fine deserted stone villas standing neglected amid crumbling walls and overgrown gardens where the occasional flourishing almond or fig tree alone proclaimed that all this had once been cultivated and cared for.

The church door was in due course opened. Pleasantly tiled and clearly painted in light pastel colours, the glory of this church was as usual its great iconostasis. It covered the east wall like a great golden hedge of acanthus whose branches and leaves twisted and entwined upwards, guarding the entrance to the Holy of Holies and supporting the icon of the patron saint, in this case St Nicolas, together with those of St John the Baptist and the Mother of God. The icons alone are well worth a visit. St Nicolas, who is considered by some to have inherited the powers of Poseidon, is shown enduring his various ship-wrecks; the icon is dated 1780. There is also a fine, somewhat damaged icon of St John the Baptist, painted in the Cretan tradition. That of the Virgin and Child shows them in the centre of a family tree which springs from the bosom of a turbaned gentleman, no doubt Abraham, who is reclining at the base of the picture, which is dated 1790.

In the centre of the church is a great wooden ship suspended from the ceiling as a thanks-offering for mercies received at sea. Svoronata, like many other of these villages, is inhabited by seamen although it is a mile or two inland. Most of the men are away; only the women are at home to cultivate the family smallholding and to look after the aged and the young.

Some two miles further is Domata, another village nestling on fertile slopes. Here the church is set well back above the road. To reach it we climbed up a narrow lane, past a perfect little classical gateway with columns in bas-relief on each side supporting the archi-trave; the gate itself is of finely wrought-iron. Several stones of the architrave were missing and the next severe tremor could bring the whole structure tumbling to the ground. The church itself was being rebuilt from government funds; we found it hedged in with scaffold-ing and the iconostasis covered with great dust sheets. Over the entrance, set into the wall, is a white marble slab on which is depicted a great sailing ship. A vessel belonging to the village, it was sailing through the Bosphorus when the captain saw a coffin floating on the waters. On being salvaged, it was found to contain the mortal remains of the Patriarch Gregorius who had been martyred by the Turks at the start of the Greek rising in 1821. The coffin itself is still the revered possession of the church, but the body is elsewhere. The elderly decorator, who told the story, said that rumour had it that the Russians, who were once known for their love of relics, had acquired it. There are some fine wrought-iron grilles in the windows on the south side of the church; we could not see the north side because the hillside had collapsed against it.

Another church which should be visited is that of Kaligata, the village immediately below Kourkoumelata. The key was readily available as the church is popular with tourists, perhaps because of the richly embossed silver throne in the centre of the church, an unusual feature. The iconostasis, which contained quite respectable icons, but not as interesting as those at Svoronata, is particularly grandiose, even oppressive. Unlike the two other churches, it has no grilled section at the west end for women. More interesting perhaps than the church is the bell-tower from which the dome is missing. It stands on the south side of the church and is surrounded by trees. Over the door to the staircase leading to the belfry is the dove of peace while in the centre of the wall facing east there is a stone carving of the two-headed Byzantine eagle. Above the eagle is a lion whose head is missing, while below, is a perfect carving of a crocodile although it might be more exact to describe it as a salamander.

The road continued to Kourkoumelata but then, instead of driving on to the main road into Argostoli, we took that leading to Lakythra and so along the top of the ridge of the Argostoli peninsula. Lakythra, rebuilt by the French after the earthquake, is unexceptional but just beyond is a finely situated restaurant, the Kallithea (Belvedere or Bellevue), looking south towards Zakynthos, with Cape St Nicolas immediately below. Continuing along the road, we had a splendid view of the inland slopes above Koutavos but looked in vain for signs of the Cyclopean walls of ancient Kranea.

II

Pronnos—Poros and Scala

❧

To see Argostoli at its most animated, go to the quays between seven and nine in the morning, when the buses set forth for Athens via the Sami–Patras car-ferry and for various parts of the island. There are of course other bus services at different times of the day, such as the hourly departure to the local bathing beach of Platis Gialos, but the real bustle and uproar is early in the morning. Streams of people going to buy their tickets get involved with those coming out of the ticket office in search of the right bus. The buses move portentously into position. Suitcases and the inevitable round wicker baskets are flung on to the roofs or heaved into baggage boots. Passengers, clutching paper parcels, shopping bags and the occasional cluster of hens hanging upside down by their legs like great brown feather dusters, clamber determinedly into buses and then remembering last-minute messages to be given to friends and relations who have come to see them off, push back off the bus to deliver them. In and out of the road move vendors of Turkish Delight and of koulouria—delicious hoops of brown bread covered with crisp nuts. Here, in addition, is a vegetable market which straggles along the roadside by the buses with displays of water melons, marrows, and potatoes, onions and tomatoes. Tied up to the near-by quay are caiques, loaded with great water melons ponderous as cannon balls.

We were bound for Poros twenty-five miles away, a little port on the east coast in what was once the district of Pronnos, in Roman times one of the four city-states of the island; now it is merged into the districts of Sami and Kranea. As the bus started up, the springing to life of the engine coincided with an upsurge of conversation, and, a moment later, with an attempt to start the radio, which fortunately did not work. We were off.

The road is the same one which passes the St George fort, which

104

we could see some way ahead, peering at us from over the top of its hill. Slowly the road climbs up the side of Aenos to a height of between eight hundred to a thousand feet, as the great mountain edges nearer to the sea. We realized this when we saw several clumps of the elegant tall Cephalonian fir tree standing just above the road. Here and there between the road and the sparkling sea were scattered hamlets surrounded by cornfields, fruit trees and the occasional market garden. Near the Theotokou Sision Monastery, two bearded monks were harvesting wheat. On the skyline, three thousand feet above us, serried ranks of Cephalonian fir trees stood guard around the lofty summit of Aenos.

The further east we went, so the shape of distant Zakynthos changed. As we passed Peratata, the island appeared compact, but as we proceeded further, more and more of the eastern coastline came into view so that by the time we reached Markopoulo not only the low hills of Akrotiri could be seen but also Mount Scopus; somewhere between the two, we knew, lay the enchanting town of Zakynthos itself.

At Markopoulo which local humorists have claimed as the birth-place of Marco Polo, the narrow road begins to turn north-eastwards round the flank of Aenos. From here to the sea falls an open and lovely valley, down which tumbles a stream, its force in the rainy season strong enough to turn the several water-mills standing along its course. According to Napier, writing about his plans for road construction in 1825, it was to these mills that corn was sent for grinding from most parts of the island. Wheat is grown in the valley while on the slopes near the little scattered hamlets are a large variety of conifers and fruit trees plus the occasional plane tree, a sure sign of ample water. Here also are beehives, painted a pastel shade of blue, a colour used throughout the island for this purpose.

Beyond Pastra there is a twisting mountainous road going over the little pass to the pleasant district of Pronnos, well watered and protected on all sides by hills. The bus gently eased itself round the hairpin bends into the valley. Two streams, one flowing north and the other coming from the north-west meet just below Tzannata: the force of the water is such that it has cut a small gorge through the limestone rock into the little coastal plain where stands the fishing port of Poros. Just to the east of the Pastra–Tzannata road on a little hill above the village of St George are signs of a pre-Christian settlement. There is similar evidence on the steep hill called Atros, which rises to some two thousand six hundred feet immediately to the north of the port. Here have been found a number of steles or gravestones. One was being used as a stone for washing clothes and is now in the museum in Argostoli, others had been made into steps of a staircase of a house: these are also to go to the museum. There must still be an immense amount of valuable material to be discovered in these islands. In the fine modern museum in Argostoli are pots, figurines and coins, well displayed and annotated, going back to the earliest known civilization in the Eastern Mediterranean. Of much more recent origin is a fine bronze head of the Roman period, found in a well in Sami, obviously of a man of action, who may have been a local military governor. The delightful gravestone of a little boy holding up a ball which his dog is leaping up to seize is of approximately the same period.

The main valley of Pronnos, in the centre of which is Tzannata, was perhaps the district of Cephalonia that Colonel Napier loved best of all—for its beauty, its fertility and for the friends he made there, above all Gerasimos Cambitsi and his family. It was here that he conceived the imaginative idea of setting up a model farm to teach the Cephalonians the basic principles of good husbandry. In addition to this, he saw the opportunity of making the island self-supporting with wheat instead of buying from overseas. We find him writing to Sir Frederick Adam before the great quarrel, 'Just consider, my dear Sir Frederick, this island "*en masse*". Its aspect is rocky, mountainous, arid; but in the midst of this sterility we find one large district, rich in the abundance of the finest water, and a deep soil of the finest description; and adding to these advantages that of an *excellent port* (Poros) opposed to the Continent and *nearer* to it than any other: I ask you and any man of clear understanding whether such a district does not *hugely* demand all the attention and aid that the Government can give?' The enthusiasm and boundless energy of the man shines through.

Napier accordingly appointed a Scot, one Edward Curling, to run the model farm which became known as the Colony, because a group of Maltese were brought over on account of their industry to work it and set a good example. The farm, however, needed funds for rather longer than originally planned and the whole scheme fell foul of Sir Frederick Adam after he had dismissed Napier. According to Lord Kirkwall, 'the jealousy of the Greeks, and the discontent of the Maltese themselves, together with the great expense of carrying out the plan all combined to render the enterprise abortive.' We find

Curling writing in July 1832 from Suffolk in defence of the Colony when its whole future was being weighed in the balance, 'Government brought over a multitude of Maltese, undoubtedly under the idea that they understood farming, whereas, as has since been proved, they received a set of men collected from the streets and hospitals of Malta and with scarcely an exception, wholly incapacitated for the purpose intended. Is it surprising then that with such men a number of expenses should have been incurred?' There is nevertheless evidence to show that with a little more patience the scheme could have been a success, even under these circumstances. Poor Curling, 'I like my situation very well as I am in England,' he replied in September 1832 to Napier, who had written to tell him of the collapse of the Colony, 'but . . . I would rather live one year in the Colony near old Cambici with my dogs, gun . . . than twenty years here, where everyone that has a shilling looks down with contempt on him that has only sixpence, and where one sees nothing *new* from one year's end to another.'

In 1845, soon after his conquest of Sind, we find Napier still hankering after Cephalonia. In a letter to Demitrios Cambitsi, he wrote, 'you give me great pleasure in telling me that the Colony at Poros is to be revived. I am sure it will become again a great town and port . . . I would give *all Sinde* for Poros. Here in Sinde I am a king, it is true, but they say *first* love is the truest, and Cephalonia is mine.'

Poros faces due east towards the bare rocky Echinades Islands which can be seen in the distance through the mist of summer heat like slumbering dinosaurs. Due north, beyond Atros, the bare flanks of Ithaka rise sharply out of the sea. Poros today is a little community of modern pre-fabricated bungalows standing huddled together under the towering hill which rises southwards up to Petrovouni, on whose lower slopes was the original settlement. Trees and flowering bushes have already done much to soften the little concrete dwelling cubes, built since the earthquake to accommodate the inhabitants of three near-by hill villages which were destroyed. In addition to the modern community, there is also an older fishing village two hundred yards or so to the south under Cape Sarakinato. Both settlements have quays against which a few caiques were berthed and from which there is excellent bathing, but the tourist beach adjoins the newer port. Here are ideal sands for children, grey rather than golden but soft underfoot and with no sign of the sea-urchin.

The local community seems particularly enterprising. Between the old fishing village and the new township is a little promontory on the top of which has recently been built a small well-run hotel. This belongs to the community and the local president is chairman of the board. The rooms are marketed on a package-tour basis through an Athens agency whose contemporary approach to business is indicated by the posting on the notice-board of menus for the forthcoming week, typed on stationery headed 'Technical Data Sheet'.

Another recent achievement is the building of a rough road along the coast from Poros to Nea Scala at the south-eastern point of the island. The scenery is quite magnificent. As far as Cape Kapros there are ever finer views, as one moves south, of Atros and Ithaka beyond. The grey limestone, the brown earth, the olive trees, the little terraced fields, the occasional inaccessible sandy beach and the deep blue sea beyond, would make it one of the loveliest roads in the world if it were asphalted. But the potholes remain and so does the beauty of the scenery, unspoilt by villas and hotels.

After Cape Kapros, Ithaka in the north fades from sight and Zakynthos on the southern horizon takes over—and so does talk of the Odyssey. For in this area, according to local opinion, was the site of Odysseus' capital. There are two mosaics in Nea Scala, quite obviously Roman, which are carefully protected against the weather by walls and a roof; one is of a man being killed at the stake by leopards and tigers, the other of a sacrificial altar, guarded on each side by a Roman soldier, with a bull and two other animals which cannot however be identified as the mosaic has been worn away. We were told, however, that these fine mosaics are Mycenean or earlier and could well have been part of Odysseus' palace; that if these views have not been accepted it is merely because there are vested interests in Ithaka hogging the whole story.

Of course, the identification of Homeric sites invites endless speculation. If you accept that the mosaics mark the site of Odysseus' palace, then the vast old olive tree, certainly with the largest girth I've ever seen anywhere, on the road to Scala from Poros, must certainly be the tree under which the wanderer slept the night he was brought back to his island by the Phaeacians. The fact that there are caves near by in the limestone cliff, one of which must equally certainly have been the cave of the nymphs, would strengthen the case. The tree is near the crumbling Venetian chapel of St George and just to the south of the site of a temple to Apollo. The chapel has remains of three pillars which once formed a portico, as at Melinado in Zakynthos; but digging on the temple site has had to be postponed through lack of funds. In the same way, Dulichium was, so they say, a tiny port a few miles to the west of Nea Scala, which has now sunk below sea-level because of earthquakes. Here, local opinion —acute, as all things Cephalonian—may have a real card up its sleeve, namely the effect of the earthquakes on land levels. This factor scholars may not have taken completely into account. In any case, if Dörpfeldt favoured land-encompassed Nyddri on Levkas as the home of Odysseus, and Samuel Butler looked for it to the west coast of Sicily, then why not search for fresh angles within the Kingdom of Odysseus itself?

The modern village of Nea Scala, laid out in a neat series of streets, is up a gentle incline from the Roman mosaics. The name Scala is apparently of Byzantine origin, indicating a landing place for merchandise, and was regularly used for such descriptions in Italian documents from the eleventh century onwards. It is a pleasant place; trees and bushes have grown rapidly to provide both colour and shade.

We bumped back over the same road up the coast by the clear blue sea, the sky aglow with the golden light of late afternoon. Zakynthos disappeared behind us and Ithaka came back into view. The eastern slopes of the mountains were already darkening in preparation for night. We passed no vehicle of any description either going or returning. Where the road descended to run along by the seashore, an elderly woman in black was gathering herbs while a white pig, standing ankle-deep in the water, watched us pass without moving. A lone turtle dove flew off a rock up the scrub-covered hillside and out of sight. A crescent moon came up from behind the mountains at the next turn of the track.

The little port of Sami, facing Ithaka, gives its name to the district. There is no bus direct from Poros to Sami, the gateway to Cephalonia, but only via Argostoli which would have meant spending the night there. Instead we preferred to travel the eighteen miles direct to Sami by local taxi over a rough secondary road out of Tzannata.

Tzannata itself flourishes amidst a variety of trees, flowers and bushes. In the centre is a fountain surrounded by a stone pavement and sheltered by enormous plane trees. Once out of the village, the road winds along the side of dried-up spring torrents and up into the mountains which rise steeply on all sides. Wherever the soil is at all fruitful, it is terraced and divided, one tiny field from another, by stone walls. Here and there are those little towers of stones, piled one on top of another, to indicate that the grazing is private.

Soon after leaving Tzannata, a rough track branches off up the hillside to the right, leading to the monastery of Atros. It is situated high up on the mountainside overlooking the sea. Here is a tower locally known as the Norman tower; land records show that in 1269 this area was granted to a group of Normans, possibly from Sicily.

Now in the middle of the afternoon, the light was beginning to lengthen and we were constantly moving in and out of shade as the car bumped round the hairpin bends. Abundant rain falls on the limestone mountains during winter and spring and here and there we came across springs gushing into troughs built by the local authorities. Ruins of villages stood scattered about the mountain slopes; the names of Nea Koulourata, Nea Mouzakata, Nea Zervata, Nea Katapodata along the road proclaim the resurgence of old villages on new sites. Wherever possible the inhabitants of two or three destroyed villages have been concentrated in one new area. The old ruins, however, remain. Many of the houses look habitable from a distance; it is only when you come close that the great cracks across the walls, an inch or more wide, can be seen.

There was a feeling of incompleteness, almost of chaos about this mountain landscape. Houses seemed unfinished either because the building materials had not yet mellowed or the trees surrounding them were not yet fully grown. The hillsides, where building material had been blasted away, looked rusty and raw. Then, as we came over the top of a rise and into the long fertile valley at the end of which Sami is situated, we were conscious of a subtle change. At least one corner of the horizon had depth and simplicity—the dark blue haze of the distant sea.

12

Argostoli to Phiscardo

ↄ⋙⋘ↄ

The bus for Phiscardo, in the far north of Cephalonia, leaves Argostoli at about two in the afternoon and takes about four hours to complete the thirty-mile journey. The route is up the east side of the Bay
of Argostoli, across the neck of land separating it from the Bay of
Mirtou and thence up the west coast of the northern pan-handle. From
the bathing beach near the Xenia Hotel, the road can be seen winding
due north up the mountainside, climbing ever higher until it disappears over the head of the pass.

We had bought our tickets in the morning, but on arriving fifteen
minutes before the bus was due to leave, found that all seats were
occupied. Cephalonians are insistent upon their rights but they are
also courteous to foreigners. Yes, we could be squeezed into the
Phiscardo bus by sitting upon camp stools in the gangway but there
was a more comfortable way. Another bus was due to leave at once for
the northern pan-handle and would arrive at the village of Vasilikiades,
some four miles north of Assos, at about the same time as the Phiscardo bus which by that time would have plenty of room. No, there
would be no question of not waiting for us—we were not to worry. We
were later very grateful for this promise.

The second bus into which we climbed was an ancient pre-war
Mercedes-Benz with an exceptionally high chassis and seats for no
more than eighteen. The seven other passengers were already deep
in conversation with the driver, a young man with an air of confidence
and a mind of his own. It was not given to all, we understood him to
be explaining, to go to Athens University; some had to stay at home
to ensure that things were properly organized. Moreover there was
much to be said for getting to know one's own island thoroughly
before going abroad to the mainland. Cephalonia had in any case much
to offer—at which there were solemn nods and grunts of approval. It

was a discussion which would no doubt have continued longer if the superintendent had not indicated that we were already late in starting.

We trundled over the causeway across the lake but then, to our disappointment, turned inland towards Aenos instead of on to the road running due north overlooking Argostoli Bay. We now realized that our route was via Sami and up to St Evphemia, opposite Ithaka, and then north-west to link up with the coastal road to Assos and beyond.

The drive to Sami took, as usual, about three-quarters of an hour. Just before reaching Razata, under its umbrella pines, the first village *en route*, about two miles out of Argostoli, we saw a large notice pointing southwards off the road to the Cyclopean ruins of Kranea; at least the tourist authorities knew where they were even if nobody ever visited them. A heat mist lay over the Bay of Argostoli so that it was impossible to see Lixouri and the surrounding countryside. Afterwards the road climbed steadily with frequent hairpin bends to the first watershed of Kouloumi where a road branches off to Phrankata, Omala and Valsamata. All three villages were rebuilt, as was Sami, by funds raised in Britain. At Omala is the monastery of St Gerasimos, the patron saint of the island. On his two feast days—August 16th and October 20th—the shrine is visited by many thousands, as St Gerasimos is famous for his healing gifts, especially the casting out of devils. His remains are contained in a great silver casket. The monastery was founded in 1554 by Gerasimos Notaras, a monk and hermit from the mainland. He lived a simple life of faith and good works, very like that of Dionysios, his neighbour in Zakynthos.

From Kouloumi onwards we were out of sight of the sea until well over the central backbone of the island. Here, the peculiar melancholy of this part of Cephalonia asserted itself, arising from the dominating silver-grey of the olive trees and the limestone rock which in the midday sun swamps the sandy colour of the earth (although if you travel the same road on a sunny evening you will find the landscape warm and glowing).

Sami is an expanding but raw little town, compact against the west ridge of the mountain where it comes down to the sea ending with Cape Mytikos. Its two-story buildings are made of reinforced concrete, and the walls are painted in white and various pastel shades. There is good bathing in the vicinity but few travellers stop here. Sami gives its name to one of the three administrative districts of the island, Sami; it was also the name given to the island by Homer. High up to the north of the town is the site, spread over two hilltops, of the original township of Sami. It was only here that the Romans met with resistance when they landed in 189 B.C. to pacify the island, long a thorn in their side, because of piracy against their communications in the Ionian Sea. The war against Carthage had at long last been brought to a successful conclusion and the Aetolian League subdued. Now it was to be the turn of Cephalonia. The consul, Marcus Fulvius, quickly received the surrender of the island's four cities— namely Sami, Kranea, Pali and Pronnos—taking four hostages from each of them. 'The radiance of unexpected peace had shone upon Cephalonia when suddenly one city, the Sameans, it is uncertain for what reason, revolted,' says Livy. This may have been because of their fear of being sent away from their homes, as their city was in a strategic position. In spite of all entreaties nothing would make them change their minds. Fulvius accordingly brought over his siege artillery from the mainland and settled down to four months of grim siege warfare. The outcome was inevitable; the city was at last captured and plundered, and the remaining inhabitants sold as slaves.

A little further north towards Cape Mytikos is the Moni Agrillion where Byron and Trelawney together with friends and servants spent the night on their return from an expedition to Ithaka, soon after Byron's arrival in Cephalonia. According to Trelawney, who made much of what happened there in his *Records of Shelley, Byron and the Author*, the monastery was situated in Ithaka, but Sir Harold Nicolson in *Byron: The Last Journey* makes it clear that the monastery was in Cephalonia. 'On coming up to the walls,' wrote Trelawney, 'we saw the monks in their grey gowns, ranged along the terrace; they chanted a hymn of glorification and welcome to the great lord, saying "Christ has risen to elevate the Cross and trample on the crescent in our beloved Greece" ' . . . After further ceremonial greetings, the Abbot 'took from the folds of his ample garments a roll of paper, and commenced intoning through his nasal organ a turgid and interminable eulogium on my "Lordo Inglese" in a polygot of divers tongues.' And then 'suddenly Byron burst into a paroxysm of rage and vented his ire in a torrent of Italian execrations on the holy Abbot and all his brotherhood . . . Seizing a lamp, he left the room.

'The consternation of the monks at this explosion of wrath may be imagined. The amazed Abbot remained for sometime motionless, his eyes and mouth wide open . . . At last he thought he had solved the mystery, and in a low tremulous voice said, significantly putting his finger to his forehead:

' "Eccolo, è matto poveretto!" '

Nicolson added that circumstances indicated 'that Byron was then assailed by one of those sudden convulsive fits which had previously attacked him and which were to be renewed in force on his arrival in Missolonghi. . . . On the following morning Byron was all dejection and penitence.' We do not, however, know whether the Abbot and his brethren ever revised the opinion they formed that evening of the Englishman admired above all others by succeeding Greek generations.

We stopped at the petrol pump on the edge of the town. As the garageman failed to respond to persistent hoots on the horn, our driver stepped down and helped himself. The petrol tank was situated in front of the bus under the driver's seat; after the tank had been filled, the cap was fitted back into place with Sellotape, a roll of which was kept handy in a near-by locker. It was while the tank was being filled that the original conversation about the ennobling virtues of first knowing one's homeland was revived, stimulated by several passengers who had joined *en route*. The cause for its revival was the proximity of the recently discovered cave of Melissani. The upshot was that the driver decided that all in the bus, and especially the foreigners, namely ourselves, would benefit by visiting it and promptly turned off the main road in order to do so.

Such natural phenomena as caves, with their accompanying stalactites and stalagmites, are highly prized by the Greeks and are sometimes publicized to a greater extent than historic sites. When therefore the great cave of Melissani with its underground river was discovered some four years ago, funds were immediately made available for exploiting its tourist attractions. Steps have been cut down into the hillside to the level of the river where a boat is available for exploring the further recesses. At the entrance to the steps is a café and a ticket office.

The beauty of the Melissani cave lies in the intense blue of the lake which it contains, mirroring the blue of the sky which is visible through a great cavity directly above. We floated in the little boat as if on air, as the light above and below the water-line seemed fused into one crystal element. Far beneath us, we could see eels unhurriedly threading their way, their shadows clearly visible on the sandy bottom. The river flows round the edge of this great still bowl of water, emerging from its underground channel at one end and disappearing into further caves on the seaward side into which our boat was only able to penetrate a short distance. Ferns and lichen flourish on the deep walls of the cave but the hurrying river keeps the channel clear of weeds.

In the museum at Argostoli are two terracotta plaques, which were found by workmen engaged in opening up the cave; they date from the third or second century B.C. One of them shows three women in flowing robes moving gracefully one behind another, each of them carrying a torch. The other, round in shape, depicts women dancing round the central figure of Pan. From this it is surmised that the cave of Melissani was a sanctuary to this rustic deity. It is possible that the cave at that time was roofed in, otherwise torches would not have been necessary unless the god's celebrations were always nocturnal.

A curious but fully authenticated story links this underground river with the sea-mills just to the north of Argostoli. Until recently no one had ever known exactly what happened to the waters which rush into the potholes, although various attempts to find out had been made. Two visiting Austrian professors decided a few years ago to make yet another effort to find out and, for this purpose, poured a very strong dye into the water. For a number of days nothing emerged but at the end of three weeks, very real traces of the dye were found pouring into the Melissani cave. No signs of it were found in Argostoli Bay between the town and the main body of the island, so it is assumed that the water of the sea-mills flows underneath the sea bed and then under the central land mass of the island, eventually emerging into the cave within a hundred yards of the Bay of Sami. Full details of their findings have been published in a French spelaeological magazine which I was shown. Previous attempts failed because the search for traces of the dye were given up too quickly.

Our expedition lasted at least half an hour and we were beginning to wonder whether the other bus would in fact wait for us. From Melissani onwards the road deteriorated and was little better than an earth track until well past St Evphemia, an uninteresting scattered modern village. St Evphemia, and not Sami, was the port used by Byron and his friends on going to and returning from Ithaka. Here was the local quarantine station and the headquarters of the British collector for this part of the island.

In spite of the bad road, however, the journey up the long Pilaros valley beyond St Evphemia was worth making. On both sides the mountains rise to about three thousand feet. In the valley itself the little cornfields had just been harvested; on the hillside stood the homes of the farmers, old, crumbling, sun-soaked buildings of wood, plaster and stucco, wreathed with vines. The sun was now beginning to sink westwards into late afternoon and the colour to flow back into the landscape.

At Sinori at the head of the valley, our road joined the road which runs up directly from Argostoli, the route taken by the Phiscardo bus. Partly asphalted, partly cobbled and partly earth, where much of the surface had been worn away, it began to climb steeply up the mountainside. To our left the great sweeping Bay of Mirtou came into view. Above it were steep cliffs and to the south fine sandy beaches round the distant village of St Kiriaki. Westwards stretched the limitless expanses of the Mediterranean. Looking ahead, however, the prospect was even more awe-inspiring. The road, now no wider than a cart-track, seemed to get ever narrower and the drop to the sea, at least a thousand feet below, ever steeper; there was no protecting balustrade, not even an occasional stone to give an illusion of safety. Sitting high over the back wheels, our sense of impending doom became very real when the driver edged over to the rim of the road to avoid a particularly deep hole. We tried to banish from our minds conjectures of what might happen if a vehicle from the opposite direction suddenly swung round one of the hairpin bends. Fortunately none did, but we were glad to note that most of the other passengers fell silent. Perhaps after all it was better to allow the driver to concentrate on the task immediately before him—or were they really listening to the bouzouki music on gramophone records which continued to blare out for most of the journey?

The road wound on, hugging the precipitous mountainside for about two miles. Ahead the little peninsula of Assos stood out to sea. The village itself, about forty scattered houses on the slopes leading down to the little neck of land which joins the peninsula to the mainland, has been largely rebuilt. It is, however, an old settlement with a little harbour. The Venetians built in 1593 an extensive castle on the peninsula beyond, the walls of which still look in excellent condition. Leake mentioned that a stretch of Hellenic wall was incorporated into that built by the Venetians as evidence that this was a fortified site long before their arrival.

During the first French occupation it was at Assos that the French troops attempted to concentrate on the approach of the much stronger Russo-Turkish expedition in 1799 under Admiral Ousakov. The islanders however do not take kindly to invaders, especially when they do not pay their debts, and many of the French were trapped and taken prisoner along the road. It was on this road again that fifteen hundred Italian troops, who had become prisoners of the Germans in September 1943, were marched to their death. They had been garrisoning the north of the island, many of them stationed at Phiscardo. Their German captors marched them south until they reached one of the most precipitous stretches south of Assos. Here they were told to right turn and keep going—and the whole detachment hurtled to their death on the rocks and in the sea a thousand feet below.

Beyond Assos, the road began climbing again but this time inland towards the top of the mountainous backbone of the peninsula. From here, the sea, which remained always in sight high on the horizon, looked even more serene and enchanting. The countryside also underwent a transformation. We were now entering an upland country of terraced fields, whose golden crop was already harvested, and of fruit trees, figs, apples, cherries and mulberries. Everywhere there was a profusion of wild flowers, in the cornfields, under the trees and amid the low hedges which here and there bordered the rough cart-track into which the road had now deteriorated. The bus lumbered slowly through potholes caused by the spring rains, its sides brushing against the leafy branches of overhanging trees. Here and there it paused at a hamlet to set down passengers, who were greeted by groups of elders which invariably included the village priest. On the terraces of the cottages, geraniums, carnations and roses were flowering in pots and in whitewashed petrol cans, while shade was given by vines, now in full leaf. Here was a vision of Arcadia.

Vasilikiades is a large scattered village and there in the centre stood the Phiscardo bus, its passengers peering angrily out of the windows in our direction. 'Oh, dear,' said our driver, by no means disturbed, 'they do look annoyed. But we can't be more than forty minutes late.' As we were the only passengers transferring to the Phiscardo bus, we appeared to be momentarily in disgrace. According to one garrulous old farmer, there had been general pressure on the driver to push on after they had waited about fifteen minutes. Fortunately for us, the driver, conscious of having given his word that he would wait, had insisted on doing so. He was a quiet, polite man who worked a long day. We later discovered that he left Phiscardo at about six each morning for the four- to five-hour drive to Argostoli, arriving back the same evening between six and seven.

The road deteriorated still further and our speed was reduced to a walking pace. The beauty of the countryside with its background of sea and distant mountains seemed to increase even more. Soon after leaving the large village of Mangano, Cape Ducato at the south-western extremity of Levkas came into view across nearly ten miles of sea, its white cliffs capped by its lighthouse. It was from these cliffs that Sappho leapt to her death. Beyond rose the rugged mountains of Levkas, at times reaching over three thousand seven hundred feet, whose peaks were capped with darkening clouds.

A little further on we saw a signpost pointing down a lane to the hamlet of Marcantonato. Whether its name derives from Mark Antony, we did not discover. It is possible that he visited the island, perhaps to see his uncle, the ex-consul Caius Antonius Nepos, who was exiled here from Rome and who is said to have ruled Cephalonia as if it were his own property.

Finally the road turned eastwards, and we bumped downhill towards the sea. Turning a bend we saw in front of us a group of houses and beyond a great inlet of water. The bus came to a halt by the quayside, against which a few caiques were moored, and the engine was turned off. The air was cool and still and there was a quietness in the evening sunshine. Here at last was Phiscardo.

13

Phiscardo

❦

We lay sunbathing on the beach under a creamy sky—a faint radiant haze sufficient to protect us from the full strength of the summer sun. The beach faced north to the savage magnificence of Levkas with Cape Ducato at its south-western extremity. To the north-east, beyond the Ithaka Channel stood Cape Marmakas, the most northerly point of Ithaka. Immediately at the western end of our shallow sandy bay was Cape Vlioti, the northernmost point of Cephalonia, a low scrub-covered promontory of limestone out of which the sea had carved rock-pools and hollows, the homes of lobster and octopus.

Suddenly from over the eastern wing of the bay glided a raven. Half-way across the bay it ponderously beat the air to gain height before again putting its bulky black shape into a glide, now revealed as a most graceful movement. As it passed over Cape Vlioti, it uttered several harsh cries, and then disappeared from sight—but only for a few moments. Almost at once it was back again, this time accompanied by a second and then a third raven. As they flew over the headland, warmer air rising from the sun-baked land lifted them higher into the air. There was obviously a small colony somewhere in the maquis behind us; at one time we saw up to five of these great black birds sailing round the sky above us. Ravens are said to scorn human company. They settle as far away as possible from human habitation, preferring rough uncultivated country.

Here on this remote Cephalonian beach, to which we had been brought by caique, we were indeed in raven country. From nine in the morning until five in the afternoon, we were alone apart from the ravens and two cormorants which we watched flying low towards Ithaka. It was a day of reading and swimming, sunbathing, sleeping and swimming again until we heard the familiar clug-clug-clug of the caique engine, several minutes before it emerged round the eastern end of the bay to take us back to Phiscardo.

We sailed back into the Ithaka Channel, nearly two miles wide, which separates bare steep-backed Ithaka from the bay-indented eastern coastline of northern Cephalonia, which also rises, more gently, to the high ridge of hills which we had traversed on our journey hither. On the top of the Kavilares ridge of Ithaka were two derelict windmills; these in former days probably performed the dual purpose of grinding what little locally grown corn there was for the large village of Exogi on the eastern slopes of the hill and of acting as look-out towers for the community. These waters were notorious for piracy during the Middle Ages.

The entrance to the little port of Phiscardo is marked on the north side by a lighthouse, a tall functional concrete structure. Below it, nearer the water's edge, is a smaller, more elegant, lighthouse, although it is no longer used as such, with a small house attached. This second lighthouse has round windows in circular frames of white stone, while the walls are painted a parchment yellow. The buildings appeared to be deserted. We visited them on foot during our stay on a day when a strong wind was blowing up the Ithaka Channel from the south, churning the chrome-blue sea into chalky white caps. It was too rough for local boats to be out and no living thing was to be seen except an occasional seagull tumbling down the wind. I was unable to discover whether this one was one of several lighthouses constructed while Napier was Resident.

Many of the villages in this area have the typical Cephalonian ending of 'ata'—Antipata, Tselentata, Venturata. Phiscardo as a name, however, stands alone. It in fact commemorates the name of Robert de Hauteville, nicknamed Guiscard, the 'Wise' or the 'Cunning', who died here in 1085. Robert was born in 1016 in the little village of Hauteville-la-Guichard, close to the windswept peninsula of Cherbourg in Normandy, the sixth son of a minor baron of Viking descent. It was not until he was thirty that he joined his older half-brothers who were already successfully carving out territories and titles from the decaying Byzantine provinces of Apulia and Calabria. Here in Southern Italy, the Normans proved themselves skilful intriguers, offering their swords to the highest bidder and emerging triumphant on the winning side. Above all, they were splendid fighters and few armies were able to withstand the disciplined charge of the armoured Norman knights.

In due course, Robert Guiscard proved himself to be not only the greatest warrior of them all but also a highly successful negotiator. Within eleven years of his arrival in Southern Italy, he had been so successful in playing off Lombard against Greek and in holding his own against all-comers that in 1059 he was invested by the Pope with the duchies not only of Apulia and Calabria which he already held, but also of Sicily, then still under Saracen rule. During his later years, Robert Guiscard, most of whose fighting had been against the Greeks, conceived the idea of usurping Byzantium for himself. The Greeks, although no match for the mounted Norman knights, had proved stubborn and determined fighters. They had constantly risen against their Norman conquerors in Apulia and Calabria whenever sufficiently encouraged, which was not infrequently. Constantinople, however, torn by internal dissentions, was then facing increasing pressure from her enemies, especially from the Seljuk Turks. Here, it appeared, was a plum ripe for picking. Lord Norwich has pointed out that it is not unusual for peoples in close proximity to Greek culture to develop a marked inferiority complex; for the Normans, who had fought against the Greeks almost continuously for many years and who had at the same time adopted many of their customs, there was only one answer, which was to conquer.

After much preparation, which included the construction of a great Norman naval fleet, Guiscard lay siege to Durazzo, now in Albania, on the eastern side of the Adriatic. It was a lengthy siege and before he eventually overcame the defenders, early in 1082, he had to defeat in pitched battle the Byzantine army led by the Emperor Alexius 1st Comnenus, who is generally described as outstanding both as a general and as a politician. With the collapse of the Byzantine forces, however, Guiscard's advance into the interior was swift. A few weeks after the fall of the city, he had already pushed on as far as Kastoria in Greek Macedonia before being recalled by events in Italy.

In 1084, however, he was back again, this time in Corfu which his son Bohemund had seized in the previous year; this was his first stepping-stone in his resumed advance on Byzantium. Here his army wintered and at the same time met what proved to be a mightier foe than Byzantine military power—the plague. Robert Guiscard himself escaped the disease but later in 1085, when setting forth with his main forces to join his vanguard which was already established on Cephalonia, he fell victim to it. His boat put in at the first safe anchorage—Phiscardo—and here within five weeks he was to die.

Anna Comnena, daughter of Alexius 1st Comnenus, reports in her Alexiad, one of the most fascinating products of Byzantine literature, that a local personage told Guiscard that on Ithaka was a ruined town once called Jerusalem. Guiscard is then said to have remembered the words prophesied to him long previously, 'As far as Ather you shall bring all countries under your sway, but from there you shall depart for Jerusalem and pay your debt to nature.' Cape Ather was the name given by Anna Comnena to the most northerly point of the island. Today Cape Atheras is the name of the northern tip of the district of Pali, west of the Bay of Mirtou.

The body of the great warrior was borne back to Apulia for burial in the family tombs of the Hautevilles at Venosa. It is possible that some Normans remained on. A hundred yards or so to the north of the lighthouse, we were pointed out the ruin of what is said to be a Norman building, probably a church. What is left of the walls is constructed of grey-white limestone, hewn out of the rocky foreshore where only a few yards away the sea rustles and sighs. Whether it was ever completed I do not know, but its construction must have taken several months, perhaps a year or even longer. As it was never intended that Robert Guiscard should be buried anywhere except in the family vaults, there must have been some idea of creating a small settlement here, no doubt because of the excellent harbour. The idea was obviously abandoned. Perhaps it was not Norman after all but Byzantine. Leake does not mention it but instead refers to some Roman ruins near the shore.

Phiscardo is worth a visit for other reasons than its medieval Norman associations. It is about the only village in Cephalonia which was not completely destroyed in 1953. On the west and south sides of the little bay stand a number of solid two- and three-story houses which date back not only to the British Protectorate but to earlier Venetian days. They are finely proportioned with whitewashed walls, russet-red tiled roofs and green painted shutters, simple in design and very satisfactory to look at. In front of them is a broad quay along which orange trees stand at intervals like sentinels under the command of a giant eucalyptus; the evergreen leaves of the former are as refreshing to the eye as the sound of the sea breeze, never long absent, rustling through the long feathery leaves of the latter. The edge of the quay is of well-cut stone; one or two local boats were tied up to iron rings sunk into its side. To mark the inner or south-western corner of the harbour, there is a fine old street lamp, faintly reminiscent of

Venice in design but probably a Victorian importation of the 1850s from Birmingham. It is here that the two cafés of the village are situated and what little local life is concentrated.

We took a room in a tall solid stone house which looked down on to a little open space where fishing nets were laid out to dry and to be mended. Here we found modest comfort and complete cleanliness for only a few shillings each. Conditions for the traveller have changed considerably in the last hundred years. Murray, in the 1854 edition of his *Guide to Greece and the Ionian Islands*, wrote thus about the only accommodation often then available in remoter places, 'The keepers of the coffee-houses and billiard-rooms (which are very general) will always lodge a traveller, but he must expect no privacy here. He must live all day in public and be content at night to have his mattress spread, with some twenty others belonging to the family and other guests, either on the floor or on a wooden divan which surrounds the room. Where particular honour is to be shown the guest, his bed is laid upon the billiard table; he should never decline this distinction, as he will thereby have a better chance of escape from the vermin.' Murray was probably thinking of the mainland. We never found vermin throughout the Ionian Islands, nor a billiard table either.

I asked our host about the inhabitants of Phiscardo. 'Oh, you'll find very interesting people living here—engineers, mechanics, seagoing people, people who have travelled everywhere. We're not just ordinary country bumpkins, you know. Indeed not.' Certainly the houses round the quay would have made admirable houses for retired sea-captains and other men of enterprise. Many of them were empty as their owners were away in Athens and overseas; a few returned for a brief visit every year, others far less frequently. These houses are rarely for sale. Greeks, however well established they become in foreign countries, usually like to feel that they have a home in their native village to which they can return, even if only occasionally.

We remarked on the number of half-finished houses on the edge of the village, little houses without doors and windows, without interior decoration and exterior stucco work. After 1953 the Greek government was able to make available to those who had lost their houses sufficient money to build the simplest type of small house. If members of the same family had been prepared to share a home, the funds should have proved adequate. But if Greeks are the most independent people in the world, then the Cephalonians are probably the most independent of the Greeks, and there would be no question of sharing.

In any case many lost interest. Although the Greek government was prepared within limits, to pay one drachma for every further drachma laid out by the individual, the latter were often unable or unwilling to incur further expense and so the houses were never completed. Now it is unlikely that they ever will be as the owners have moved to Athens or elsewhere. They are sad, unattractive little houses, many of them doomed to moulder away into rubble.

It is not only the funds of individuals that run out but also those of the public authorities. We climbed up broad steps to the village church, which we found locked, and on the other side of the ridge, which here faced towards the sea, we found standing deserted a great yellow half-finished single-storey structure. This was the tourist pavilion on which work had stopped over a year previously through lack of funds. The difficulties of building must not be underestimated. While good materials for foundations and walls are readily to hand in most areas, the expense of transporting them to the site can be heavy, and may involve the building of roads or even the use of a boat. There is also the cost of bringing in such accessories as sanitary equipment, some of which may come from as far away as Stoke-on-Trent. All loading and unloading is by hand and timetables can be completely dislocated if for some reason local labour suddenly dries up. We were told of one lovely villa on a remote headland which took three times longer to complete than originally planned. This was because the young men from the only village in the vicinity who were employed in lifting material from lorry into caique, and from caique on to the beach and up to the villa, decided to seek better paid work in Germany, when the villa was only half finished. The only remaining labour available were the women of the village. As funds started to arrive back from Germany, they too found less inclination to work.

We took our meals at the café run by the wife of Kristo, the caique-master, whose three boats rode easily in the harbour close by. In looks she and her two daughters seemed French rather than Greek—and Norman-French at that with their fair chestnut hair, blue eyes and pink and white cheeks covered with a pale golden bloom from sun and wind. While we do not know whether any Normans actually settled in Phiscardo, we do know that they never hesitated to attach themselves to the local girls. More likely our hostess's forebears may have included traders who settled in the island from one or other of the North Italian city-states—Venice, Genoa or Pisa, whose merchantmen competed with each other for the trade of the Levant well

before the Latin conquest of Byzantium. The great kindness of Kristo
and his wife was typical of Cephalonia.

The café was the meeting-place for the community. In the dark,
cool room with cooking stove in one corner and barrels of local wine
in another there were usually one or two groups quietly discussing
the political situation, local events or merely contemplating a cup of
coffee. Kristo would occasionally depart, taking a merchant back home
to Ithaka or Sami; the caique was a much more comfortable way of
travelling there than by bus or taxi. Our hostess was always busy,
preparing coffee or peeling potatoes and cleaning fish. All garbage
was flung into the harbour. In due course it was consumed by the fish
which fattened healthily on it and we in due course consumed the
fish, grilled or fried, sprinkled with lemon juice and accompanied by
bread, salad and a glass of pale golden robola.

Part Three

ITHAKA

14

Ithaka South

⟨ ❧ ⟩

There are various ways of reaching Ithaka. One memorable journey was in 1945 with a friend; a small caique, fitted out with a single kitchen chair in the rear for extra comfort, took us from Sami, Cephalonia, to the little landing beach of Piso Aetos (behind Aetos) on the west coast of Ithaka, Aetos being the name of the great conical hill overlooking the narrow waist between the north and south parts of the island. A generous offering of robola, the distinctive light dry wine of Cephalonia, at luncheon averted any competitiveness as to which of us should occupy the seat of honour; instead we had preferred to sleep in what shade was available during the forty minutes' crossing. When eventually after an hour's walk we reached the island capital of Vathi, we found, as we were the first British army personnel to visit Ithaka since the departure of the Germans, that the whole town had assembled to greet us. There followed five enchanting days as the guest of Mr Anastasios Kallinikos, with Cardiff trading connections, who has presented the Molfetto Centre, which contains a valuable library, to Vathi in memory of his brother and who has given so much in other ways to his native island.

Another memorable crossing, one that my wife and I made, was by caique from Phiscardo to Polis, the little harbour below Stavros which is the largest village in northern Ithaka. Polis, as the name implies, was a city in ancient days and a possible site for the Palace of Odysseus. It was a cold evening in June with a strong south-east wind coming up the Channel. White caps broke over the bow of the caique as we plunged towards the headland which hid Polis from us. A long line of shearwater fluttered away ahead of us, flying low over the waves. The island of Daskalio, flat, low-lying and surmounted by a little chapel, lay to our right. This could be Asteris of the Odyssey; Pallas Athene warned Telemachus that Penelope's suitors would be lying in ambush 'in the straits between Ithaka and the rugged coast of Samos', intent on murdering him before he could get home from seeking news of his absent father in the Peloponnesos. This would have been a poor place to have hidden; Telemachus returning from Pylos in the south, would have seen the suitors' ships from a considerable distance, unless the island stood higher out of the sea three thousand years ago. A much better area in which to have laid an ambush would have been somewhere near the southern approaches to Ithaka.

Having rounded the headland, our caique master unearthed a great conch shell, the end of which had been sawn off; then raising it to his lips, he blew sonorous calls in the direction of Stavros, whose houses could just be seen above us, to call the attention of the local taxi driver to our approach. As no taxi appeared, three fishermen, who had just berthed their boat at the little mole, carried our luggage up on their motor scooters.

The normal approach to Ithaka is by the comfortable car-ferry which leaves Patras in the early afternoon for Vathi via Sami. As the boat approaches the entrance to the Ithaka Channel, at the southern end of which Sami is situated, mountains rise steeply on three sides, the higher ones of Cephalonia to the left and straight ahead, the steep but lower slopes of Ithaka to the right. Behind, the sea is more distantly encircled by the Echinades, that scattering of mostly uninhabited islets close to which was fought the Battle of Lepanto in 1571. Here the final attempt of the Ottomans to control the central Mediterranean was overthrown by the Christian alliance under Don John of Austria in which many Ionian sailors, especially those from Corfu, distinguished themselves. The Turkish fleet was almost annihilated; one hundred and thirty galleys were taken by the allies and others sunk or burnt. Moreover some thirty thousand Muslims, three times the Christian losses, perished. Only Ochiali, a famous corsair admiral, distinguished himself among the Turks, overrunning the flagship of the Knights of Malta and making off with the Standard of 'the Religion' in haste to Levkas to the north-west when he found himself in his turn outnumbered. Don John's fleet had anchored in the Bay of Sami before the battle.

On leaving Sami the boat moves north-east close under Ithaka whose bare slopes rise steeply from the sea. Here and there is an occasional inlet but of no practical value to man or boat—except for the bay of St Andrew. This has a little sandy beach at the far end, up which a small boat could be drawn and from which the slopes up into the hills are not too steep. 'Land in Ithaka at the first point you reach,' said Pallas Athene when briefing Telemachus on his return from the south. It is probably here that Telemachus landed secretly in order to climb up to the plateau of Marathea to find out, from Eumaeus the swineherd, the latest news about the suitors and there unexpectedly to meet his father.

As the boat progresses up to Cape St John and passes the island of Perapigadia which lies close in to the rugged coast beyond, the great rocky cliff, generally accepted as Korax, the rock of the ravens, can be clearly seen above the plateau of Marathea. The suitors would have been far better advised to wait behind the island of Perapigadia, posting a look-out high above Cape St John, than to have lurked at Daskalio. Supported by the prevailing north winds of summer—and it is unlikely that Telemachus would have undertaken the journey in winter—they would have had a flying start in swooping down on any boat beating up towards Ithaka from the south.

The coast becomes gentler beyond the Bay of Perapigadia. As the boat approaches Cape Skino, the great central mountain of Neritos, nearly two thousand five hundred feet high, increasingly dominates the scene. Just to the south of the highest point stands the Bell Tower of the Moni Katharon. Below is the great Gulf of Molos which nearly divides the island in half, reaching to the foot of Aetos; the island extends some twelve miles to the north and five southwards from here while nowhere is it more than four miles from east to west. The boat swings left into the Gulf of Molos and left again into the Bay of Phorkys at the end of which is Vathi. From the open sea, the little town, of some two and a half thousand inhabitants, is completely invisible. Only when the boat has passed through the narrows and enters the great inner bay does the town come into view. Its centre is in the far south-west corner with its square, two banks and the marine administrative buildings. The boat however comes to rest on the west quay, a little distance away, having first passed a little island, covered with young trees on which stands a chapel. This was originally the lazaretto, the Venetian prison, the ruins of which still existed in 1945. Byron rowed out to it each morning for a swim, during his stay in Vathi in 1823. Now there is excellent bathing in the north-east corner of the bay; fishermen will take you across in their boats for a nominal sum from the square. Here also was the quarantine station during the British Protectorate.

The arrival of the boat in the evening is invariably a social occasion and its hoot as it approaches Vathi from the Gulf of Molos is the signal for the whole town to stroll with the greatest deliberation towards the landing stage to ensure that the berthing of the vessel coincides with their arrival at the barrier. Accommodation, incidentally, is of the simplest, but comfortable beds can be found; reasonable, if unexceptional, cooking is available in the town's two restaurants.

Vathi came into existence during the latter half of the Venetian regime; Leake, however, remarked on the number of wrought stones of Hellenistic origin in the houses he visited, which seemed to indicate the existence of a Graeco-Roman settlement in the area. Previously the main settlement in this part of the island was above at Perachori, the large scattered village high up on the eastern slopes of Merovigli, whose great limestone ridge rises to some two thousand feet to the south-west of Vathi. From here on a clear day it is said that you can see Parnassos and even Taygetus in the southern Peloponnesos. In summer, however, there is usually a heat haze and visibility is limited to Atokos to the north-east, bare and uninhabited, rising like a sugar loaf from the sea.

The road to Perachori is rough, climbs steeply and winds considerably. The lower slopes are covered with vines and fruit trees and there are a number of now disused windmills at various vantage points —as there are indeed on all the hills around Vathi. Higher up, it is mainly rock. The houses are scattered up the road and over a fairly wide area, many of them showing signs of fortification from an earlier period and most of them badly damaged in the earthquake. The road eventually ends at a house with a threshing floor at its side and a sheer drop beyond. Below is the rugged eastern coast of the island with the Bay of Sarakiniko at the foot of a steep decline but where bathing is possible. Note again the name—the Bay of the Saracen. No wonder it was necessary to build on these exposed, windy heights if a community was to survive.

Just to the north of Perachori on Merovigli is a tall Greek-style bell tower next to a little grey chapel, which was used as a watch tower. The very name of the mountain itself indicates its importance as a look-out—'meros' is Greek for place and 'vigli' derived from the Latin word 'vigilare'—to look out, to watch; the hybrid word is of Byzantine origin.

The Ionian communities prospered during the first three hundred years of Venetian rule and each island built up its own armed trading fleet which became increasingly a match for North African corsairs. Eventually only the isolated communities suffered from slave raids. Not that the Venetian navy was able to rule the seas—far from it. Venetian foreign policy was to remain neutral in the continuing clashes between Islam and Christendom and later between Protestant and Catholic Europe, when English and Dutch vessels from about 1580 onwards penetrated far into the Mediterranean to harry Spanish and Neapolitan shipping. Venetian traders were fair game for all, as the Venetian navy during the seventeenth and eighteenth centuries found it increasingly difficult without allies to give protection to their own merchantmen. Increasingly, therefore, Ionian produce—currants and olive oil—was traded direct with the armed merchantmen of other nations, in the case of currants, especially with English importers. According to Wheler, English trade flourished in the second half of the seventeenth century with Ithaka as well as with Zakynthos and Cephalonia. Thus, while the Venetian merchant navy might lose the carrying trade to those of other countries, the islands continued to prosper until the increased taxation, poverty, corruption and the ossification of the Venetian administration began directly to affect the islands themselves towards the end of the eighteenth century.

Vathi, in spite of the earthquake, looks little changed from what it was before. Neat houses, with their reddish-terracotta roofs and their walls in pastel shades stand round three sides of the harbour, the west side being the most favoured because the harbour outlook gets the most shade. These are mainly the houses of retired seamen from ship's captains downwards, men who have travelled by sea to the ends of the world.

One of them, Captain Gerasimos Kolaitis, courteous and weather-beaten, was firmly of the opinion that Odysseus' journey to the distant gates of hell was not merely to the Pillars of Hercules but far beyond. He presented us with a copy of his lecture, 'The Circumnavigation of Ulysses', given to the Cultural Centre of Ithaka in 1958. In it, he gives his opinion that Odysseus sailed not merely to the Straits of Gibraltar but, taking advantage of the north-east trade winds well known to sailors, sailed to the West Indies. His return journey to Europe would have been by the Gulf Stream. If the Phoenicians had been able to navigate to not only Cornwall for tin but as far as the Baltic for amber, is it completely out of the question that Odysseus sailed across the Atlantic during his ten years' absence from home? The Captain makes several interesting points. Ancient Atlantis could well have been America.

Because the Romans were not a seafaring people, the knowledge of
Atlantis and how to reach it faded and was lost; the sea-routes to the
Baltic and to Cornwall fell into disuse during the Roman supremacy
because it was easier to bring amber and tin overland. This is all hypo-
thesis, as the author admits, but he still feels confident that Odysseus,
together with a crew from Ithaka, was the first to sail the Atlantic and
the forerunner of Christopher Columbus. In Ithaka at least these
opinions enjoy much support. It is certainly fitting that there is a fine
cadet training school in Vathi for the Greek merchant navy.

Vathi is conscious of its Homeric traditions, but carries them
lightly. Immediately on leaving the town to the west you will see on
the crest of a little hill a large notice, pointing up a secondary road
which leads towards Merovigli. On it is neatly painted 'Nimfis Cave'.
The grotto is a good half-hour's brisk walk uphill; don't forget to
take a torch with you. There is a second notice, labelled 'Bay of
Phorkys' further on to the north. The direction in which this notice
points could be taken to indicate the little Bay of Dexia where it is
sited, instead of the bay on which Vathi stands.

Vathi's interests in the island's legendary past is perhaps summed
up in the words of one of its boatmen who claimed to be Ithaka's
official guide. We asked him if his duties kept him very busy.

'No,' he replied, 'Why should they? We all know that this is the
home of Odysseus. The authorities have confirmed it. There is therefore no reason to go scrambling over bad roads in the burning heat of
summer to look at a trickle of water or the remains of an old well.
Does a gloomy cave in the hillside look any more interesting by calling
it the Cave of Nymphs? Does a little trickle of water become a spring
by being called Arethusa's? Of course not. Still,' he added somewhat
grudgingly, 'I am always at your disposal.'

The history of Ithaka during the Roman and Byzantine domination is very obscure but was no doubt closely linked with that of
Cephalonia and Zakynthos. If this was so, then it was severed from
the Byzantine Empire in 1185 by invaders from Sicily. Benedict of
Peterborough, writing in 1191, reported that the island was infamous
for piracy. It was also then generally known as Val de Comparé, not
as Ithaka. This name is said to derive from an Italian sea-captain who
was driven to anchor close to the island by a storm; seeing a light
shining from the hillside he went to investigate. On arrival at the hut,
he found that a child had just been born, and was accordingly invited
to be godfather (phonetically 'koombaros' or 'koobaros' in Greek of

which 'comparé' is an Italian corruption). Ithaka was ruled success-
ively by the Orsini and Tocchi dynasties and suffered the same fate as
Cephalonia and Zakynthos during the Ottoman eviction of the
Tocchi in 1479 when the population of the three islands was deci-
mated if not completely wiped out. In 1504, Venice took steps to
repopulate the island with families from the mainland.

Vathi, although its population is so small, is the seat of a bishop.
Partly because of this and partly because it is the largest town on the
island it is often referred to as 'the town'. The metropolis, dedicated
to the Panayia or Mother of Christ, is situated in the south-east
corner of Vathi, which was the least damaged part in 1953; in size it
is no larger than most churches or chapels in the Ionian Islands. There
is an Italianate belfry separate from the main church and a very fine
rather elaborate gold iconostasis, restored towards the end of the
nineteenth century. There is a little pulpit high up under the roof of
the north wall. Steps fixed to the wall above the side stalls lead to the
entrance of the pulpit; to get to the steps a ladder has to be placed
against the wall—a perilous journey should the bishop be old and
frail. I was assured it was not used more than once or twice a year.

It is not always easy to get exact information about local features
of interest. Churches, for example, are usually locked and the key left
with a family close by. Someone, often a girl, will come very obligingly
with the key and answer what questions she can. Even priests and
vergers often know little about the history of their church and in-
quiries as to detail usually elicits a response such as 'I am not exactly
certain' or 'it happened a long time ago.'

Vathi was at one time scheduled to be the site of a university or
academy for the Ionian Islands. These plans were conceived by Frederick North, later fifth Earl of Guilford. Born in 1786, he won a
classical scholarship to Christ Church, Oxford; such were his accomplishments that he was awarded a studentship when little over sixteen.
Because of ill-health, he then spent a number of years in southern
Europe. The years 1788–1791 were spent in Greece; the first in Corfu
and in Levkas, the second in Ithaka and the third in travelling via
Athens to Constantinople and back. By this time, his philhellenism,
which had first taken root at Oxford was fully grown. Little is known
about this period of his life, but the late Z. D. Ferriman in his study of
Lord Guilford quoted from Papadopoulos Vretos who in 1846 published his *Memoirs of the Earl of Guilford* in Athens.

Vretos who was later to become University Librarian to the Ionian

Academy, was himself born in Ithaka but not until 1800, so that what he reported about Frederick North's stay in the Ionian Islands some ten years earlier is largely hearsay. Nevertheless there is no doubt that North was completely enchanted by the inhabitants and by Ithaka itself. From this time onwards he became a devotee of contemporary as well as of ancient Greece. He became fluent in modern Greek, adopted local costume and completely associated himself with the life of the island. In Corfu, on his return from Constantinople he was baptized into the Greek Orthodox Church.

Throughout his life, Frederick North, who enjoyed in his earlier years an active career in parliament and as a colonial administrator, devoted his energies and resources to the spread of education. When in 1817 he succeeded to the family title, he started in earnest on the creation of an Ionian Academy. Although Sir Thomas Maitland was not enthusiastic, Guilford's close connections with Whitehall won the day; Lord Bathurst, a cousin, was Secretary of State for the Colonies. Maitland therefore announced in March 1820 at the opening of the Session of the Legislative Assembly of the United States of the Ionian Islands, that he had been commanded to propose Lord Guilford as 'President of the University which is to be established in these States'. At the same time the Prince Regent bestowed on him the Grand Cross of the Order of St Michael and St George.

Guilford at once proposed Ithaka as the site and this was also advocated by Ugo Foscolo. Local enthusiasm was enormous; the land was given free and gifts both of money and of building material were contributed from all sides, including nine thousand, five hundred tiles by the ladies of Ithaka. Maitland, however, decided against Ithaka and eventually persuaded the Legislative Assembly to agree that the site be transferred to Corfu.

This decision caused considerable controversy. Napier, writing at a later date, said, 'I could see no advantage in establishing a college at Corfu; a town fraught with all the vice and abominations of Venice and shut up within walls. Lord Guilford was very averse to it and wanted to have the college at Ithaca, an island remarkable for being healthy, where no large town or temptation to vice existed and where the students would not have been diverted from their studies; in short, Ithaca was exactly the place for a Greek school, being classical ground, retired, healthy and central to the islands generally.'

'Central to the islands generally'—that is certainly a strong argument in favour of Ithaka. But there is something to be said for the official point of view, argued by Jervis in his *The Ionian Islands during the Present Century* published in 1863. 'What would it have been if Lord Guilford had succeeded in carrying out his object of establishing the University at Ithaka! Visionary ideas of academical groves and of the birthplace of Ulysses, do not form young men to be useful citizens; and for the one student who would have been sent from there, a hundred men would have been turned out upon the world with their ideas confirmed to a barren rock and a few goats.' Alas, poor Ithaka.

15

Ithaka North

❧

The most fertile part of Ithaka is in the far north. Here, in a triangle between Stavros, Platythria and the little port of Phrikes on the east coast, the land is intensively cultivated, growing not only olives, but fruit trees, vines and some wheat. This area is remote from Vathi by local standards; it is about twelve miles from Stavros to Vathi, going along the west flank of the great central mountain of Neritos. The taxis which leave the northern villages early each morning for their daily run to Vathi follow this road; the views over the Ithaka Channel to Cephalonia help to distract one from its narrowness and bumpiness. There is another road, longer and in indifferent condition, which twists round the east side of Neritos to the village of Anogi, the highest village on the island, and on past the monastery of Moni Katharon. Here the goat reigns supreme except for the immediate vicinity of the village and the monastery; in those places there are still a few trees and some patches of cultivation.

The name 'Moni Panayia Kathariotissa', to give it in full, is held to mean 'the Monastery of the Virgin of Purity'. In the old dialect of Ithaka, however, the word 'kathara'—whose usual meaning is 'clean' or 'pure'—used to denote the weeds which were removed from a vineyard. It was among a heap of such weeds that an icon of the Virgin was discovered in the seventeenth century and a monastery built on the site. The original building, destroyed in 1953, provided accommodation for some twenty monks and no doubt in its early life was fully occupied. Even the rebuilt monastery—and very well it has been done; its little church has great dignity and good taste—can house about ten monks. I can remember the abbot Kallinikos being in residence alone during my visits in 1945 and 1946. He was a kindly, affectionate, simple man with no pretensions to scholarship—who insisted that his visitors spend the night after he had wined and dined them at his table. He was still there in 1967, in his eighties and still as generous as ever; he took much pleasure in conducting me round his rebuilt monastery. Since it was a Friday, the main dish was boiled fish and skordalia, a compounded mixture in equal weight of potatoes and garlic—nourishing although startling at first taste.

There is little sign today of any monastic revival. In spite of great difficulties, there has been a certain quickening of the Greek economy in recent years. Unskilled labourers can now earn at least thirty shillings a day and skilled men at least two pounds ten. Material standards are generally improving, as the number of electrical equipment shops opening in quite small towns illustrates. And the Greeks, as one Greek friend pointed out, are people of logic rather than mystics. When extreme poverty was widespread and opportunities for the very poor non-existent, a life of idleness in a monastery, living on the offerings of the devout, held certain attractions among the villagers. But under present conditions, such a life no longer appeals.

An abbot, however, is not an illiterate monk drawn from the villages, but a senior official of the Orthodox Church. He receives special training and is responsible for the administration of church funds and property. Far more important, he is a living symbol of the continuity of the Orthodox Church, in which St Peter was not supreme and apart, but only the first among equals; where Rome was not the sole source of authority but only the most senior of the great patriarchates which included Constantinople, Alexandria, Antioch and Jerusalem as well. Here on this island, which has been severed from Byzantium for nearly a thousand years, the abbot is a symbol of the survival of the unquenchable Greek spirit from its most ancient manifestations. As the Roman Empire absorbed the territory and culture of the ancient Greeks, so the Byzantine Empire was the direct continuation of the Roman Empire. When in 1453 the last Palaeologue emperor was killed in a vain attempt to save Constantinople from the Turks and the Byzantine Empire finally disappeared, the Orthodox Church was the inheritor of what could be salvaged. In his office and in his person, the abbot represents an immense and awesome tradition. It therefore followed that when the monastery was partially destroyed in 1953, funds from islanders both in Greece and overseas quickly became available for its reconstruction, even though it was inhabited only by the abbot. The tradition had to be continued. As for Kallinikos himself, he is well-beloved throughout the island. The words 'a good man', invariably follow any mention of his name.

Having made my way up Neritos alone in 1967, I was received on arrival in the official guest-room—a large sparsely furnished room, decorated with faded photographs of bishops and a highly-coloured print of Lauterbrunnen in the Bernese Oberland. On the chimney-piece was a plaster cast of what appeared to be some fabulous beast from Revelations, a large four-footed monster, charging upon some sinner. Closer inspection revealed it to be a wolf or alsatian from which the upper jaw had disappeared, broken off perhaps in the earthquake; on its base the name of Rin-Tin-Tin was just decipherable. The room faced inwards to the courtyard, sheltered by sweet-smelling pine trees. The little walls, which bordered the different garden levels, were whitewashed and geraniums and fuchsia grew in pots. A cool, pleasant, restful place. Off this main room were two bedrooms, one of which I was invited to use for an afternoon siesta; clean sheets and pillow slips were provided.

The only way back to Vathi, which could be seen far below in its sheltered bay, was on foot. The view from Moni Katharon is more magnificent even than that from Perachori on the south of the island. For from here, the whole of southern Ithaka falls into perspective and there is a fine view of Cephalonia as well. The walk back to Vathi, nearly all of it downhill took two and a half hours, a distance by road of nearly eight miles. The road is rough and there appeared to be no short cuts. I'd asked about a footpath—a 'monopati'—which might cut off many bends of mountain roads. But I was warned that it was not well-trodden and should I miss my way, the going could become impossible. Best keep to the road, they said.

But nevertheless the walk down was both magnificent and repre-sentative of the island's landscape. Here it was very steep, and the vegetation typically Ionian. The slopes, both above and below the road, were covered with great limestone boulders in between which grew profusely thick bushes of laurel and privet, thorn bush, nettles and scented thyme, sage and rosemary.

From just below the monastery there is a good view down on to the summit of Aetos, where it stands dominating the narrow strip of land which joins the two parts of the island. The remains of the walls of an ancient settlement can be seen running east a little way down from the top. Although Leake dismissed them as third century B.C., Schliemann described them as Cyclopean of the Mycenean period.

Here is an obvious site for an ancient settlement—strong, defensible and with commanding views of the Ithaka Channel and the sea to the east as well; could this perhaps have been Odysseus' capital?

Another possible site is Polis, which lies below Stavros. Although there is a little beach here up which boats could be pulled, it is a poor site for a harbour. For it is exposed to the south, the direction from which the sirocco blows, bringing rough water and rain. On the other hand, shipping here would have been safe from marauders; for an enemy to have entered the Ithaka Channel with both Cephalonia and Ithaka under the same ruler would have been to have sailed straight into a trap.

In caves in the Polis area, early Helladic potsherds dating back to about 2600 B.C. have been discovered, so it is a very ancient settlement. These remains, together with others from the Middle Helladic period, 1900–1600 B.C., and from the Mycenean period, are displayed in the little museum at the hamlet of Pelikata, a little to the north of Stavros. The key of the museum is kept on behalf of the community by the local schoolmaster. The village president kindly sent a girl to collect it and personally conducted us round on a particularly hot morning in July. The exhibits have been very efficiently catalogued and labelled both in Greek and English by Miss Sylvia Benton, who has also been responsible for cataloguing the exhibits in the museum in Vathi.

For an island so famous, the remains of its glorious past seem disappointingly few. Perhaps there was never much of interest. Both the Romans and the French in the Napoleonic Wars were great collectors of booty. Whether the latter found anything of value during their occupation of Ithaka between 1797 and 1798 is not known. During the early years of the British Protectorate, troops were not respectful of antiquity. H. W. Williams in his *Travels in Italy and Greece* published in 1820, wrote, 'We were informed that a helmet and various ornaments in silver and gold have been dug up. . . . These were melted down and formed into a coffee pot and many duplicates of the silver coins made into skewers. A late capo (not an Englishman) was the person guilty.' Müller, the Saxon, and Holland record the same story. Holland wrote querulously, 'the sole excavator is the Corsican commandant of the isle, who appears in this instance to have exercised a monopoly, to which it is very doubtful how far he is entitled.' Ithaka at this particular period was garrisoned by a unit of the British-raised Corsican Rangers. But there is no mention to what period these objects belonged.

Just beyond the Pelikata Museum, which stands cheek by jowl with several undistinguished villas, is another possible site for Odysseus' palace, perhaps the most likely of all. The ground here slopes gently uphill to a little ridge, from where the land falls sharply to the north. From here you can see the Bay of Aphalos straight ahead, and those of Phrikes to the east, Kionio to the south-east and Polis to the south-west. Ernle Bradford in his *Companion Guide to the Greek Islands* points out the advantages of such a position as it would have been easy for the mariners to move their wooden longboats from one bay to another in order to take full advantage of prevailing winds. The finest position on the ridge is occupied by a square concrete villa. We refreshed ourselves with plums as we reviewed the possibilities. Could the ancient stronghold have been here, was this the sort of place from which a king ruling over Cephalonia, Ithaka and Zakynthos would have chosen to control his kingdom? Near by was a little white-washed chapel which is said to stand on the site of an ancient building, sometimes called Homer's School. Byron, Trelawney and company visited this site, travelling by boat from Vathi and refreshing themselves on the way with gin and water from two stone jars.

Alexis Sanderson, a classical scholar of Balliol, who was staying in Vathi during our visit, was especially interested in the geopolitical aspects of the Odysseus story. He thought that if we could decide on the economic basis of his power, we might find a clue to the site of his capital. This we proceeded to discuss over luncheon.

First we agreed that Odysseus ruled his group of islands through control of the sea-routes between them and the mainland. He must therefore have had good harbour facilities for his fleet; we also assumed that his palace or headquarters would most likely have been close by. The basic structure of all the Ionian Islands consists of high inhospitable cliffs on the west with a gentler coastline on the east, where the port is almost invariably situated. Greek shipping, according to all traditions, hugged the coastline so that shelter could easily be reached if required. It is highly unlikely that there would have been any shipping moving to the west of the islands. Even today the route of the regular Brindisi–Patras ferry, once south of Levkas, moves to the east of Ithaka; while other services take the Ithaka Channel, they never travel to the west of Cephalonia. It can therefore be assumed that Odysseus' capital faced the inland seas which means it must have been situated on the east and not the west side of his realm.

But on the eastern side of which island were his headquarters likely to have been? This would no doubt have been dictated by the direction from which danger was most likely to have come. The people over whom he ruled are thought to have been Achaeans who had probably emigrated to the Ionian Islands from the Peloponnesos where we know Odysseus had friends and allies. Penelope, his wife, came from Sparta. It was to consult Menelaus in Sparta and Nestor in Pylos, that Telemachus went in search of news of his father. There was therefore little to fear from the mainland to the south-east and few boats to raid, as most would have belonged to friends. This rules out Zakynthos and probably Cephalonia as well as possible sites for Odysseus' capital.

What about to the north? Here circumstances were very different. Levkas itself was probably friendly and may also have been ruled by Odysseus. Dörpfeldt, the German archaeologist, considered this island, and not Ithaka, to have been the true site of Odysseus' kingdom. But what of the inhabitants of the wild mountainous mainland of Aetolia and Acarnania and of the Epirus beyond? There is no indication of any alliance between Odysseus and these people. The islands to the north-west of Levkas are the Paxi islands and Corfu. These, as we know, were ruled by the Phaeacians who were very friendly towards Odysseus when he was shipwrecked there. But we know little else about them. Beyond Corfu lie the Adriatic and the Balkans, always a pressure area for conflicting ethnic groups. From this direction the danger to Odysseus could have been considerable. If these assumptions are acceptable, then Ithaka becomes a highly practicable headquarters.

Another factor to be taken into account is the basis of Odysseus' wealth, such as it was. He could not have been a farmer because his home, according to Telemachus, was not farming country: 'there is no room for horses to exercise in Ithaka, nor are there any meadows. It is a pasture land for goats and more pleasant than those lands where horses roam.' This is still an apt description of the island. So skilful a sailor as Odysseus did not gain his experience of the sea as a goatherd among the rocks and evergreen bushes of Mount Neritos. It is not unfair to assume that the royal coffers owed much to Odysseus' success as a pirate, a favourite occupation of Ionian sailors until recent years. Odysseus' first action, on leaving Troy, was to sack the city of Ismarus in Thrace because he felt his troops had received insufficient booty. Piracy presumably meant that the ships of any nation or city with whom Odysseus was not in alliance could be considered fair game if caught when passing through what he regarded as his own territorial waters. As ships to the south-east were more likely than not to be friendly, his attention would primarily have been given to the waters north and north-east of his kingdom. Odysseus' main base is therefore most likely to have been in northern Ithaka.

Finally there is the question of seasons and winds. Sanderson had particularly noticed that in the Gulf of Molos a strong west wind arises, owing to the physical structure of the island, when the north and north-west winds blow. These are the prevailing winds of summer; after a calm and windless morning they start up soon after noon and continue until sundown. Summer was probably the time when there would have been most activity at sea; trading or raiding expeditions are unlikely to have been undertaken during the winter storms. The west wind blowing strongly out of the Gulf of Molos would have been a wonderful way of catapulting intercepting craft against ships sailing down the east coast of Ithaka with a following north wind. Without this west wind, interception would have been very much more difficult.

Carrying this argument a stage further, similar conditions operate in the much smaller Bay of Phrikes to the north. At about three in the afternoon the west wind roars through the gap in the mountains on which the little port of Phrikes is situated. Owing to the indented coastline, shipping keeping close to Ithaka would have been far more likely taken by surprise here than in the Gulf of Molos. This wind together with a system of look-outs and signals deployed from a central point above at Pelikata would have had much to offer as intelligent a commander and as experienced a seaman as Odysseus.

We spent one night in the Stavros Hotel but there was not much sleep to be had. It was an extremely hot night and the frequenters of the café below did not leave until after midnight. After the shouted good nights, the noise seemed to become worse. The dogs, also light sleepers, were aroused by the sound of their returning masters and started barking. The barking was taken up by the dogs in Exogi, Platythria and Phrikes; soon the whole island seemed to echo with their frenzy. H. W. Williams mentioned a gigantic and savage species of dog with a loud bark which he claimed might be descended from that of Eumaeus. The dogs in Ithaka today also have a deep and penetrating bark. In due course, about 2 a.m., they awoke the mules and donkeys whose brays and neighs added to the cacophony. Finally the cocks started crowing at about 3 a.m. and silence and sleep only arrived with the dawn at about 4 a.m.

The direct road down to Phrikes from Stavros is a little over a mile but the taxis prefer to go the longer way round via Platythria, where there is a collection of fine stone houses scattered among the olive groves and orchards. Damage in 1953 was less here and at Phrikes than elsewhere. The surrounding coastal hills do not quite meet at Phrikes and in the intervening hundred odd yards of shore lies the tiny port, protected by a little jetty, broad enough for lorries to drive on and off the car-ferry, since the produce of northern Ithaka is exported from here. On each side of the port there is a watchtower, with loopholes for firearms, clinging to the precipitous hillside. Fire from these two stone towers would have made the landing of raiding parties an unattractive proposition.

There is a broad open space, well shaded, in front of the dozen or so houses which face the little harbour. At the north end, cottages huddle close to a whitewashed stone path, fringed on the seaward side by clumps of young shrubs of the vitex family with long thrusting spikes of blue flowers; this is know as the Chaste Tree and grows freely in the Ionian Islands. According to Messrs Polunin and Huxley, this plant has been celebrated since the time of the ancient Greeks for possessing the power of subduing the 'inclination natural' between the sexes, hence its name. They were therefore thought to be especially useful to those leading the monastic life and have been called 'monks pepper'. On the other hand, the fresh seeds have been considered by others to have aphrodisiac properties. Perhaps on the whole a plant to be left well alone.

The Ionian Islands produce, on the whole, excellent wines and it is rare to be offered a bad one. Ithaka wine itself is considered first class; at its very best, the finest of all wines in the Ionian Sea. Many travellers have commented on its excellence. Leake, in 1806, was offered a delicate old Malmsey, made from the currant. Great quantities of a strong dry red wine, he noted, were exported. Though the soil of the island was useless for corn it was not ill adapted to vines, 'the stones being of service to the plant by keeping the earth moist in summer'. H. W. Williams, who visited the island some fifteen years later, said that the island produced perhaps the finest wine in Greece, especially red. Properly kept, it had, said Williams, a Hermitage flavour and a good sound body. The quantities produced today do not appear to be more than sufficient for the island's requirements and the wine has the reputation for not travelling. Yet another good reason for going to Ithaka.

Part Four

LEVKAS

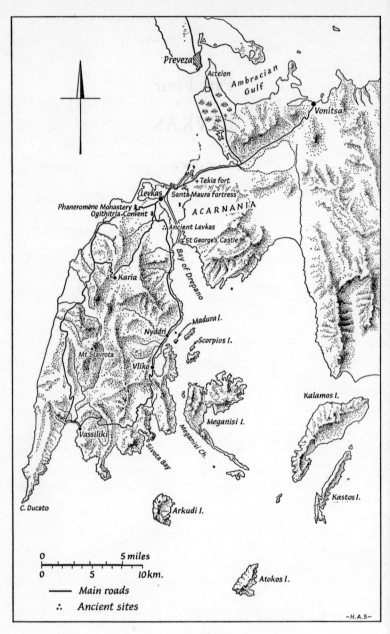

3. Levkas

16

Levkas—the Island

Once a week in summer, the *Ayios Gerasimos*, that most elegant of car-ferries, pulls out from Sami harbour in Cephalonia before eight in the morning and gathering speed, moves through the dark blue Ionian Sea to Ithaka. After pausing briefly at Vathi, it sails north again through the Gulf of Molos and along the east coast of Ithaka. The stony slopes of Neritos are too rugged and steep for cultivation or building, but on every little point jutting out to sea there is a warning light that works automatically at night, and close by a little red-roofed whitewashed chapel as if each headland had its own deity.

At about nine o'clock, the *Ayios Gerasimos*, announcing its approach on its siren, comes to a halt at the little stone jetty at Phrikes. There it is moored briefly, so that lorries—if any—and passengers can get on or off, and then continues its journey.

It rounds Cape Sarkali and the whole southern aspect of Levkas comes suddenly into view, ranging from the thin white promontory of Cape Ducato on the far west, crowned with its lighthouse, to where the steep eastern slopes intermingle with the islands of Meganisi and Arkudi; from this distance at least it is impossible to separate one from another. Further east still are the islands of Kalamos and Kastos with the high rugged mainland wilderness of Acarnania beyond. Due east, behind the sugar loaf of uninhabited Atokos, lie the Dragonera Islands, which were regularly visited on manoeuvres by the British Mediterranean Fleet up to 1939.

Fourth in size of the islands in the Ionian Sea—about twenty miles from north to south and about ten at its widest from east to west—Levkas consists very largely of high plateaus and of mountains rising above them, the highest, Mount Stavrota, reaching to just on three thousand seven hundred and fifty feet. Only on the southern and eastern sides and at the northern extremity are there valleys and

149

plains among the spurs and foothills of the mountains. The great central ridge, seen from whatever direction, looks dramatic and unapproachable.

Strabo thought that the island was named after Leucatas, the ancient name for Cape Ducato, because of the white colour of the rocky promontory (*leukas* is the ancient Greek word for white). 'It contains,' according to the Loeb translation, 'the temple which was believed to put an end to the longings of love.' Strabo then quotes Menander as saying, 'Sappho is said to have been the first when through frantic longing she was chasing the haughty Phaon to fling herself with a leap from the far-seen rock, calling upon thee in prayer, O Lord and master' . . . 'It was an annual custom,' continues Strabo, 'among the Leucadians every year at the sacrifice performed in honour of Apollo for some criminal to be flung from this rocky look-out for the sake of averting evil; wings and birds of all kinds being fastened to him, since by their fluttering they could lighten the leap, and also for a number of men, stationed all around below the rock in small fishing boats, to take the victim in and, when he had been taken on board, to do all in their power to get him safely outside their territories.' The leap itself must have been on the sheer western side of the promontory, for the eastern ridge slopes down a considerable way and there is no place where one could be made. Although at least three hundred feet high, Cape Ducato looks dwarfed against the rugged grandeur of the central ridge. The temple referred to by Strabo was dedicated to Apollo but nothing noteworthy remains.

During both the Venetian occupation of the island, from 1684 until 1799, and the British Protectorate, Levkas was more usually known as Santa Mavra, or the Black Saint. There was a very early virgin martyr of whom little is known except that she was held in great veneration, so much so that Julian the Apostate, in order to overcome this cult, gave it out that the martyr was in fact Aphrodite in disguise. At a later stage, this legend may have become involved with that of the virgin saint called Anne or Susanna, who is recorded in Butler's *Lives of the Saints*. Born in Constantinople about A.D. 840, she was both rich and beautiful but nevertheless refused several offers of marriage. Having turned down one suitor who had the Emperor's support, she fled to Levkas where the rest of her fifty years' life was passed in complete solitude. Her tomb was the scene of marvellous cures, especially of those possessed of evil spirits. It was therefore decided to open it, when her body was discovered to be quite undecayed and giving off a sweet smell, a splendid first step towards sanctification. Henceforward, St Anne was held in great veneration. Today, however, her memory is largely forgotten.

There is a remote and primitive air which hangs over this least developed of the Ionian Islands. The little port of Vassiliki, the only inhabited place on the south coast, supports this impression. Nestling under high bare coastal hills which partly protect it from the east and south-east, it is a pleasant place of some five hundred inhabitants. The houses themselves are grouped around a plain, well-proportioned modern church standing on a slight eminence. Along the sea front are fine plane and eucalyptus trees, a few fishing boats drawn up on the beach and nets hanging up to dry. Like the church, much of the town looks new, for it must have suffered some damage in its last great earthquake. The island is on the same earthquake belt as Ithaka, Cephalonia and Zakynthos, but was miraculously spared damage in 1953. Instead Levkas was the focus for a severe earthquake in 1948, which received little publicity.

There is no harbour at Vassiliki, and would-be passengers have to be rowed out to the steamer. A wood and stone jetty protects its southern approach. The fertile plain, stretching away to the steep slopes of Stavrota, bears a flourishing crop of citrus fruit; vast wicker baskets of oranges or lemons are manhandled into the wide shallow rowing-boats and up the narrow gangway of the ship. Here the countrywomen, both old and young, still wear traditional costume. Usually in either russet-brown or a fine dark green, the dresses reach down to their ankles, like the costumes of the Epirus.

After the *Ayios Gerasimos* leaves Vassiliki, it moves close under the round bare slopes that thrust southwards into the sea, and then follows the north-easterly trend of the coast at a respectable distance. Where the ground is sufficiently level to hold earth, olive trees intermingle with the maquis, but there are no houses. Sivota Bay half-way from Vassiliki to Meganisi is occasionally visited by yachts because of excellent anchorage and protection from storms but the nearest village is about a mile and a half away; it cannot be seen from the car-ferry. Gradually the boat edges round to the north and before long is sailing through a long green channel with the bare hills of Levkas to the west and the lower, tree-covered flank of Meganisi to the east. Vathi, the capital of the smaller island, is tucked away in a sheltered northwards-facing bay towards the eastern end of Meganisi and is the steamer's port of call after Nyddri, the only stopping-place in Levkas besides Vassiliki. From Vathi the boat proceeds south to Kalamos and on past Kastos to reach Patras eventually at about five in the afternoon.

Kalamos and Kastos are associated with the distinguished Cephalonian family of Delladecima. Colonel Floriano served under Morosini in the campaign of 1684 which resulted in the capture of Levkas and the neighbouring islands from the Turks. As a result, he was ennobled by the Venetians and granted the tithes of Kalamos and Kastos. Floriano took the title of Count Delladecima (of the tenth part) or Count of the Tithes.

Nyddri itself—to return to Levkas—lies on the edge of a large fertile plain and is encircled, except on the east, by mountains. Protection is also given by several other islands between which the boat weaves its way before reaching the wooden pier. The largest of these islands is Scorpio, acquired in 1962 and being developed by Mr Aristotle Onassis, the Greek shipowner; it is here that he married Mrs Jacqueline Kennedy, the widow of President Kennedy of the United States, in October 1968. A fine road now runs round the island and groups of buildings have recently been erected for storage, generating electricity and for housing employees—but these materialistic luxuries do not entirely tame the wildness and grandeur of the scene.

Between Scorpios and Nyddri lies the much smaller island of Madura or Moodra, its rocky roots shining through the clear brown water. Facing westwards and completely surrounded by pine trees on all other sides is a small, simple but enchanting villa in the Venetian style. The island and the house belong to the Valaoritis family. Its most distinguished member was Aristotle Valaoritis (1824–1879), a romantic poet who followed the tradition of Solomos by writing in demotic or popular Greek. His work reflected the Greek struggle against the Turk and the Ionian struggle for independence from Britain. When the British authorities, on ceding the islands to Greece, were forced by the Austrians to demilitarize most of the fortifications, they soured Ionian pleasure in what was otherwise accepted as a most generous gesture; at this time, Valaoritis was one of only three dissidents against a Resolution by the Ionian Assembly asking for modification of the British terms. 'Without the sympathy of the British nation', he declared, 'it would be impossible for us to realize speedily our national hopes.' A cousin of Aristotle Valaoritis, Sir Stephen Valaoritis, was an Ionian senator who favoured, as a minority did, the continuation of the British Protectorate.

Nyddri is at the entrance of a large inland bay on which is situated the little port of Vliko, which offers a safe berth for yachts. This bay is protected on the east side by a rocky ridge which tapers down to a pine-covered headland which ends about four hundred yards across the water due east of Nyddri. Here stands the villa built by the archaeologist, Dörpfeldt, who insisted that Levkas was the home of Odysseus, as we were often to be reminded while on the island. But surely not. Although Mycenean remains of the right period were found by Dörpfeldt in the hills above Vassiliki, it is impossible to associate a pirate-king ruling a group of islands from this remote and confined area. No canal then separated Levkas from the mainland as it now does a few miles to the north of Nyddri; it remained for the Corinthians to do this some six hundred years or so after the siege of Troy. It is possible to imagine Vassiliki in the south as a serviceable base for Odysseus' fleet, allowing for a complicated system of signals from look-out posts above the western cliffs, but it would have offered few of the advantages that Odysseus would have enjoyed on the northern heights of Ithaka. The Nyddri area, however, seems out of the question. Because access to the open sea in those days was only to the south, Odysseus' fleet could have been bottled up by a deter-mined enemy gaining control of the Meganisi channel. From here it would have been impossible, in any case, to prey on shipping, as the main sea highways were to the west of the island. Finally, as Ernle Bradford has emphasized, it is impossible to associate Levkas with Telemachus' description of his home. From Dörpfeldt's villa, you can look due west to the fertile fields which encompass Nyddri; these are ideal for horses!

We were rowed across from Nyddri to the headland and climbed up under the pine trees to the villa in the hope of visiting the little neighbouring museum which houses a number of the archaeologist's finds; as usual the key was not available. The villa itself, which is built of wood, looks due north. Facing it is the rugged fist of moun-tains which lie between this inland sea and the Gulf of Ambracia, whose exit to the sea is at Preveza. There was a serene beauty about the view—but a feeling of the sea was absent. Nyddri, with a popula-tion of some three hundred people, acts as a market for the cultivated plain beyond and I suspect only really comes to life twice a week when the car-ferry calls. It consists of one long well-shaded street along whose gutters wells a continuously running spring, proclaiming the fertility of the island. When we were there, a group of peasant women, both old and young, in traditional costume sat under a vast plane tree, several of them twisting sheep and goats' hair on spindles into yarn, while their husbands sat across the road drinking coffee. Through them stalked a young sailor carrying a vast basket of cray-fish for Mr Onassis and his friends. A small speed-boat whisked him away to Scorpio.

A bus meets the car-ferry but on this occasion we shared a taxi to travel the ten miles into Levkas, the island's capital. The road is an easy one, running parallel to the empty, sandy shore. A ridge of mountain, over two thousand feet at its highest, looms over the road as it approaches the Levkas canal. At the same time, the mainland coastline of Acarnania—rugged and uninhabited—leaps towards the island from the north-east, before it turns north-west to the canal entrance, thus forming the east side of the Bay of Drepano. Here we passed the occasional café among the orange groves, much frequented by townspeople in the summer. The mountains on the left quickly lose height; on their last remaining foothills, and parallel to the canal entrance, are what little remains of the ancient city of Levkas or Leucate. Here, amid the olive groves, are traces of ancient structures—an acropolis, a theatre, a little Cyclopean masonry—but nothing of any size remains standing. As at Kranea in Cephalonia, there were probably several settlements raised hereabouts in ancient times, but the islanders were able to tell us nothing about them.

Below the ancient site of Leucate are the salt pans which have been producing salt of excellent quality since the Venetian occupation. To the north of these, there was a causeway and a bridge over the canal which, according to Strabo, existed in the reign of Augustus. To the south of the salt pans was the ancient harbour of Drepano at the head of the bay. Today, close by, there is a pleasant country tavern with splendid views over the canal to distant Acarnania, and to the grim fortress of St George on the mainland which stands prominently over the entrance to the canal.

The great sandstone coloured fortress was occupied and strength-ended in 1810 by Ali Pasha, the tyrant of Yannina, whose territorial ambitions included the possession of the island. He had in fact attacked it in 1807 during the reign of the Septinsular Republic but his troops had been repulsed by the defendants, commanded by Count John Capodistrias. During the Napoleonic Wars, Ali Pasha was at various times courted by the French and the British, neither of whom trusted him. He had hoped, once Levkas had been captured by the British, that the island would have been handed over to him. This was at one time seriously considered by the British who were anxious for his help against the French on Corfu. George Foresti, then British Consul at Yannina, made it clear that this was completely unwarrantable as it would turn Ionian opinion against the British; the Greek Light Infantry was therefore instead left to garrison the island. As soon as it became clear that he could no longer hope for British support, Ali took over the fortress of St George. Although he denied it, this move was meant to be regarded as a threat to British communications. St George is probably Venetian by origin, although Ali is on occasion credited with being completely responsible for its construction. It is now abandoned. Our taxi-driver knew nothing of its origin, which he said was shrouded in mystery. It's an answer you will hear about many ancient sites.

The canal extends for about a mile and a half until it reaches the northern extremity of the island at the Fortress of Santa Mavra. The coastal road however winds inland through a forest of olive trees, some of them as spreading and almost as tall as oak trees. On reaching the edge of the forest, you come to citrus-fruit farms and small-holdings. Then suddenly you are passing the jumble of cafés, repair shops and booths which marks the town bus terminal and the beginning of the long street which is the backbone of Levkas, a little town of some eight thousand people. The street plunges straight down to the salt lagoons on the northern boundary of the town and continues along the causeway until it terminates opposite the Santa Mavra fortress. A chain-ferry takes vehicles at any time of the day or night across to the eastern side where the road runs round the long, grey, crumbling fortifications and across the sea marshes to the mainland.

17

Levkas—the Town

∽✺∾

Levkas, a grey, untidy town, always under repair, its shambling houses revealing the constant battering it has had over the ages from earthquakes, has a melancholy reputation. Leake, who was here in 1806 when it was occupied by the Russians, remarked that it much resembled Missolonghi, both because of its proximity to the lagoon and the structure of its houses. But unlike Missolonghi, Levkas faces due north and thus looks away from the sun. The light, seen from this angle, seems to emphasize the lifelessness of the grey, turgid waters of the lagoon, enclosed by the long neck of sand dune which separates it from the open sea.

The town seems to have turned its back on the lagoon, to have turned inwards on to its little squares and winding alleys. There is no pride of waterfront here as there is in Zakynthos and Corfu, nor any noteworthy buildings in the town except for a scattering of small, elegant baroque churches. These and the liveliness of the population, which quickly disperses any feelings of melancholy, make Levkas intriguing, almost beautiful when it comes alive on a fine summer's evening, enhanced by magnificent mountainous skylines to the south and east.

The old houses, tightly packed down the main street and along the little alleys which wind off it, were built with wooden frames on the ground floor into which bricks or stones were packed; where houses are of two storeys, the upper was made completely of wood and covered with stucco. In this way they have proved flexible under the stress of earth tremors. Villas in the process of being built today reveal the same wooden skeletons. Corrugated iron sheets, painted in pastel shades of blue, grey, green or russet, are then pinned over the walls to stop the hard core from falling out of the wooden frames when the tremors are severe. This way of building is said to have been

156

introduced by the British but as Leake described this same method four years before they arrived, it must date back at least to the Venetians. The British were certainly responsible for the neat patterns of paving stones which form the footpaths along the alleyways; these were necessary because the parts of the town nearest the lagoon are below sea level and many of the drains run through open gutters. Internal sanitary arrangements are however such that these gutters are not noisome. Here and there between the houses in the alleyways are little green, blossoming gardens, where vines, pomegranates, citrus trees and carnations flourish.

There is, in this least Ionian of towns, a strong feeling of the Epirus, of the towns of Yannina, Arta and Preveza. As you walk along the main cobbled street, you notice pungent smells of home-grown tobacco mingling with those from roasting maize and from sheep's intestines, twined together, being turned on a spit over a charcoal brazier. There is a mainland look about the faces of the people themselves, a more rugged, bonier structure in the features of the men and perhaps the handsomest girls in the Seven Islands. Visitors in the early nineteenth century remarked that the women here were far less confined than, for example, on Zakynthos where they endured an almost oriental seclusion. In the Epirus, on the other hand, women as well as men have been warriors in the age long struggle against the Turks.

This affinity with the mainland and especially with the Epirus is real. It is often argued that Levkas is not a true island but a peninsula. Its earliest known name, according to Leake, was 'Akte' or 'peninsula' and it was known in Homeric times as the 'peninsula of Epirus'. While a shallow fordable trough between the island and the mainland has probably always existed, the shifting sandbanks immediately to the north of the town long ago silted up any opening to the sea beyond, thus forming an isthmus. When the Corinthians founded a colony here in 640 B.C., they cut through this obstruction to ease communications with their colonies to the north, as the vast cliffs which run the whole length of the west coast offered no shelter to shipping. During the Peloponnesian Wars, when the island was devastated first by the Corfiots (or Corcyreans) in 436 B.C. and later by the Athenians ten years later because of its staunch loyalty to Corinth, the channel had obviously become silted up again as we read of boats being dragged across the isthmus.

Levkas must still have been joined to the mainland two hundred years later, when the Acarnanians had established their capital here.

This was reduced by the Romans in 230 B.C. during their campaign against Philip of Macedon. They re-opened the canal, and it was certainly open during the reign of the Emperor Augustus who won his decisive victory over Antony and Cleopatra off Acteion some nine miles to the north-east. Virgil, whose patron and friend Augustus was, probably had not visited the Ionian Islands when he wrote the *Aeneid*. As an elderly man he started on a tour of Greece with Augustus when ill-health forced him to return to Brindisi where he died.

He described the town of Levkas as a 'little city', as indeed it must always have been and still is today. Nevertheless it was important enough to have been the seat of a bishop who was one of the Fathers at the Council of Nicaea in A.D. 325. But from Roman times until the Napoleonic Wars, the island sank into obscurity. We know that a sister of one of the Palaeologue emperors founded a Byzantine convent here, the Ogithitria. Its ruins are to be seen about a mile south of the town, close to the bend in the road where the bus starts to climb into the mountains on the way to the large inland village of Karia. It is battered by earthquakes and now deserted; the frescoes on the church walls which appear neither old nor noteworthy are open to the skies and fading fast. A number of icons hang rotting on the walls but those of any value have been removed to the small museum in the centre of the town. Rambler roses and other creepers cover the walls and weeds are obscuring the paths. Within a few years, the only building of the Byzantine period on the island will be indistinguishable from a heap of rubble.

The fortress of Santa Mavra on the east side of the canal, opposite the end of the causeway across the lagoon, is said to have first been built by the Latins. We know that the Dukes of Lefkadia held court here. It was further developed by the Turks when they took over in 1479. They built the causeway into which the aqueduct, for supplying fresh water from the island to the fortress, was also incorporated. The Venetians in their turn used the fortress as their main stronghold; during this period many of the administrative buildings were inside the perimeter of the walls, at least at the beginning of their rule. Later, the civil authorities established themselves in the expanding town on the southern edge of the lagoon.

The Venetian administration of Levkas was far shorter than elsewhere in the Ionian Islands. After their capture of Crete in 1669, the Turks concentrated on expansion in Central Europe and in 1683 a vast Turkish host invaded Vienna. Its defeat by John Sobieski in that year was the turning point; from then onwards Turkish forces became increasingly on the defensive. One year after Vienna, the Serene Republic embarked on its great expedition to reconquer the Peloponnesos. Francesco Morosini, renowned throughout Europe for his valiant twenty-year defence of Crete, was appointed its commander. Today this Venetian campaign is best remembered for the destruction of the Parthenon. During the siege of the Athenian Acropolis, a Venetian cannon ball exploded the powder magazine which the Turks had stored in the temple, causing the ruin we see today. Morosini was given the proud nickname of 'il Peloponnesiaco' on his return to Venice in 1688 when he was elected Doge, but conditions in Greece necessitated his return there. He died in Nauplion six years later. Venice was again to lose all its mainland Greek possessions to the Turks in 1716 with the exception of their outposts of Butrinto, Parga and Preveza on the Epirot coast and of Vonitsa in the Gulf of Ambracia.

Morosini's first success in his campaign against the Turks was the capture of Levkas in 1684, which remained Venetian until 1797. To celebrate his victory he had built the little baroque church of Pantocrator which is situated half-way along the main thoroughfare. Thus began the great age of building in Levkas, if it can thus euphemistically be described, although it was later and on a much smaller scale than in Cephalonia, Corfu and Zakynthos. Nevertheless, in addition to Pantocrator, the churches of St Spiridion, St Minas, St Demetrius and St Nicolas are well worth a visit.

The church of Pantocrator, like the other churches of this period in the Ionian Islands, is built in the shape of a basilica. There is little decoration on the exterior apart from the well-balanced spacing of the main entrance and windows and the decorative carving around them. The ceiling however is painted in the Italianate style typical of this period. The iconostasis is unusual. Instead of an elaborately carved design, there are competent but undistinguished portraits of the twelve Apostles in two rows, six of them on each side of the central picture of Christ. In style they are completely Italian; the name of the artist I was not able to discover. Outside at the east end of the church is the tiny garden where lie the tombstones of the poet Valaoritis and his Typaldos wife.

The best-known church is undoubtedly that of St Minas, the patron saint of Herakleion (Candia) in Crete, near the southern end of the town. It has a magnificent golden iconostasis and fine painted ceiling, especially the portraits on it of the four evangelists and of the decapitation of St Minas painted by Nicolas Doxaras in 1761. All however badly need cleaning. At the rear of the church are three late eighteenth-century Italianate religious scenes by Spiridion Ventouris (1761–1835) of Levkas, perhaps the island's best-known painter. Outside, there is, instead of a campanile, a miniature Eiffel Tower standing detached from the church from which two bells are hung; several other churches have similar strictly utilitarian bell-towers like elaborate iron tripods, which cannot so easily be shaken to the ground by earthquakes as bricks and mortar are. Apart from its fine interior, St Minas is also a local landmark; now that one-way traffic has been introduced, all transport (including mules) coming into the town turns left at the little baroque church and passes the great modern hospital now in course of construction. It is a pleasant route, shaded by tall eucalyptus trees, which finds its way to the western edge of the lagoon.

The church of St Spiridion, which is not open to the public, is still privately owned by a Venetian ennobled family, in spite of the fact that it forms the west side of the small central square of St Mark. The design of the church is extremely simple, its finest feature being the elaborate iconostasis which is painted ivory white, not gold. This probably dates the church as late eighteenth century when the Republic was gliding into its final phase of poverty. St Spiridion is rather longer than St Minas and, since it is so central, deserves to be as crowded with the devout as the great church of St Spiridion in Corfu. Levkas, however does not possess the saint's bones. There hangs about its interior an air of mustiness and neglect, which its elegant simplicity does not deserve.

The smallest but perhaps the most noteworthy of the Levkas churches is St Demetrius, standing in a neglected position away to the east from the town centre. A few steps further and you are facing towards the mountains of Acarnania beyond the intervening waters. Its outward design is in simple good taste, its interior enriched with ample light which does full justice to the fine ivory and gold iconostasis. But the great treasures of St Demetrius are the paintings of 'Christ Crowned with Thorns', 'Christ Enthroned', 'St Demetrius' and 'St John the Baptist', all of them recognized by Procopiou as the work of Panayiotis Doxaras. They are in his later style, developed through his visit to Italy. The figures are rounded and soft, the expressions sensitive, the perspective exactly observed as laid down in his principles of painting. Especially fine is his 'St John the Baptist',

16
Post-Byzantine Cretan
icon of St John the
Baptist in Zakynthos
Museum

17
St John the Baptist by
Panayiotis Doxaras
(1662–1729) in church
of St Demetrius, Levkas
Town

18. Corfu Club

a wonderful dominating figure with giant eagle's wings, standing full length and dwarfing the sombre mountains in the background, painted after the manner of Leonardo da Vinci. Did he paint these works on the spot? The mountains could well be those of central Levkas. Perhaps the most impressive feature of this painting is the expression of the Prodromos or the Fore-runner of Christ. He is holding on a salver his own mortal head, grim and pain-wracked; but the expression of the risen saint is full of pity and understanding, not for himself but for the world.

The small two-storey building which houses the library and the art museum is only a minute away from the main square. It is unpretentious but houses a fine collection of icons saved from the island's ruined or neglected churches. Great pains have been taken to hang and light them to advantage.

The town of Levkas is small and confined and one soon longs for wider horizons. We were fortunate in our guide who, after a morning spent in visiting churches, drove us up to the monastery of the Phaneromene high up on the steep limestone hillside about two miles south-west of the town. It is an ancient site and the first monastery was built here soon after 1684. The present buildings however were erected after the 1948 earthquake and the church is lacking in appeal. An elderly monk lives here in isolation, consoled by his radio and by the wonderful views, which Edward Lear climbed up here to sketch. Immediately below is the great plain of olive trees stretching to the lagoon and to the outskirts of the spreading town. To the north is the golden ribbon of sand which starts where the western cliffs end and stretches in a great arc round the exterior of the lagoon until it meets the causeway opposite the Santa Mavra fortress. From this height even the lagoon reflects the blue of the summer sky.

The monks of the monastery must have had a wonderful view of the British attack in the spring of 1810 on the Santa Mavra fortress. The French had retreated to it from the town, then known as Amaxichi, or 'the place for wheeled carriages'. In command of the British expedition was General Oswald who had occupied the southern Ionian Islands in the previous year. First into the attack was the recently raised Duke of York's Greek Light Infantry under the command of Major Richard Church. As soon as the presence of Greek troops was known, some sixteen hundred Greek irregulars serving with the French deserted. The Greek Light Infantry, advancing along the sandbank round the outer edge of the lagoon, captured the first French redoubt. The French then dug in again further back and mounted such heavy fire that the Greeks in the next phase of the attack went to ground and could not be persuaded to advance further. A mixed body of seasoned British troops then attacked in strength; this enabled Colonel Hudson Lowe to advance with the Corsican Rangers along the causeway, but they in turn were halted because of the exposed terrain. The fortress was captured about a month later, but only after heavy artillery had been brought over from Sicily.

From 1810 until 1864, the Santa Mavra fortress was occupied by British troops. Apart from enforcing the unpopular policy of strict neutrality during the early years of the Greek War of Independence, they were rarely needed during the British Protectorate. There was a little local trouble while Sir Thomas Maitland was High Commissioner. Taxes were raised, among other things, to help open up the canal which was once more silted up. Communications between the government and people were bad; the official language was still Italian throughout the Seven Islands and remained so for many years. The peasants did not understand the reason for these taxes and were encouraged by local factions to rise in protest. Blood was shed and one or two executions followed in the peremptory fashion of those days. But during the remaining forty-five years of the Protectorate all was quiet. During the last fifteen years, Levkas was fortunate in its British Resident— Charles Sebright, who before taking service in the Ionian Islands had been in employment of the Duke of Lucca, who had ennobled him Baron d'Everton. Visitors to Levkas were impressed not only by his efficiency and his courtesy but by the fact that he had bothered to learn modern Greek. The fact that the canal had still not been cleared when the Ionian Islands were ceded to Greece was not his fault.

The road from the fortress stretches over the shallows and marshes to the barren coastal foothills of Acarnania, on the edge of which can be seen the high narrow fort of Tekia. Leake in 1806 talked of a 'Tekieh of Dervises' on the mainland opposite to the Santa Mavra fortress, no doubt a reference to this monastic fortification, its sloping roof and curving walls hinting at its oriental origin. The road into the interior passes immediately underneath its walls.

For about a mile and a half north-eastwards, parallel with the coast, run the flat exposed Plaka sandbanks. Here and there they are covered with rough grass and shaded by a few trees under which nestle one or two white cottages. Angelos Sikelianos, who was born in Levkas and who became one of the most distinguished of modern Greek poets, owned one of these and would retire here from time to time. He died in 1951 at the age of seventy-one.

Another literary figure born in Levkas was Lefcadio Hearn who is still remembered for his travel books and stories about Japan where he died in 1904. Born in 1850 of an Irish surgeon in the British Army who had married a Greek girl, he was christened Patrick Lefcadio, his second name commemorating the island of his birth. The islanders are, if anything, prouder of his memory because he is so intimately their own, than that of Sikelianos who belongs to the whole of Greece.

Some say the Greeks have no private life. As a generalization this is certainly true of the town of Levkas in summer. From about two until five in the afternoon, everything is hushed on account of the siesta, but after that the whole community emerges into the streets and squares where it often remains until after midnight. As the evening wears on and the town lights are lit, some go to one or other of the three open-air cinemas. Even meals are often taken at one of the many small restaurants scattered about the town.

An acquaintance was anxious to introduce us to a friend of his. There would, we were assured, be no difficulty in finding him. Gerasimos would be promenading in the main street. Having walked its full length, he was not there. Our friend then started questioning all mutual friends we met. Yes, said one, he had been seen going down to the lagoon. We went down to the lagoon, silvery grey in the evening light, where men were rowing out to their fish traps. He was not to be seen. We strolled along the pleasant path round to the northeast edge of the town where the waters of the lagoon mingle with the deeper waters of the canal, a favourite summer walk. We even visited two of the three open-air cinemas to ask if he had been seen going in. He had in fact been at the third, as we discovered when we eventually met him at his favourite restaurant at about half past ten. But never at any stage had there been any question of going to his home. This was the one place where he would most emphatically not have been.

Levkas is not yet on the foreign tourist map. While there are rumours that the island's tourist amenities are about to be developed, there are as yet no visible signs of this. Although crowded in summer, the visitors are usually expatriates returning home from Athens, Patras or further afield. There is excellent bathing and some pleasant tavernas outside the town but it is essential to have local friends to discover them. The one tourist feature is the annual Festival of Folk

Dance and Folk Music, held for a week in August. Founded only about three years ago, it has already attracted groups from as far away as Brittany, Scotland and Norway. On at least one occasion, Maria Callas has graced the occasion by giving a recital.

Part Five

CORFU

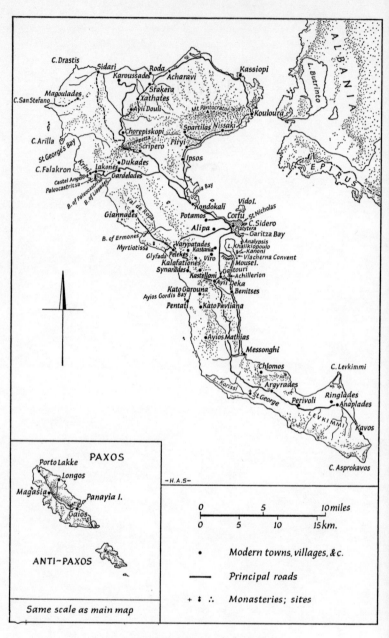

ALBANIA

L. Butrinto

C. Drastis
Sidari
Roda
Acharavi
Kassiopi
Karoussades
Sfakera
Magoulades
Xathates
C. San Stefano
Ayii Douli
Mt Pantocrator
Kouloura
Chorepiskopi
Spartilas Nissaki
C. Arilla
Strongili
Piryi
St George's Bay
Scripero
Krini
Ipsos
C. Falakron
Lakones
Dukades
EPIRUS
Castel Angelo
Gardelades
Paleocastritsa
Govia Bay
B. of Paleocastritsa
B. of Liapades
Vido I.
Kondokali
Corfu
St Nicholas
Giannades
Potamos
C. Sidero
Val de Ropa
Alipa
Platytera
Garitza Bay
B. of Ermones
Analypsis
Myrtiotissa
Varypatades
L. Khalikiopoulo
Kanoni
Glyfada Pelekes
Kastania
Vlacherna Convent
Kalafationes
Viro
Mouse I.
Synarades
Gastouri
Kastellani
Achillerion
Ayii Deka
Kato Garouna
Benitses
Ayios Gordis Bay
Pentati
Kato Pavliana
Ayios Mathias
Messonghi
Chlomos
C. Levkimmi
L. Korissi
Argyrades
St George
Perivoli
Ringlades
Anaplades
LEVKIMMI
Kavos
C. Asprokavos

—H.A.S—

PAXOS

Porto Lakke
Longos
Magasia
Panayia I.
Gaios

ANTI-PAXOS

Same scale as main map

0	5	10 miles
0	5	10	15 km.

•   Modern towns, villages, &c.

——   Principal roads

+ ⁞ ∴   Monasteries; sites

4, 5. Corfu, Paxos and Anti-Paxos

166

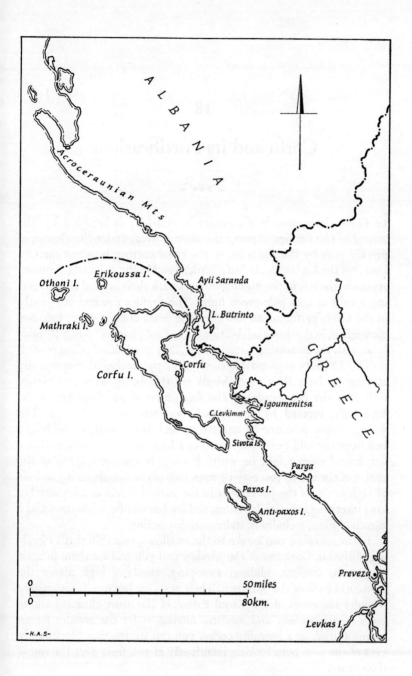

ALBANIA

Acroceraunian Mts

Othoni I.

Erikoussa I.

Ayii Saranda

L. Butrinto

Mathraki I.

Corfu

GREECE

Corfu I.

Igoumenitsa

C. Levkimmi

Sivota Is.

Parga

Paxos I.

Anti-paxos I.

Preveza

0   50 miles

0   80 km.

Levkas I.

-H.A.S-

18

Corfu and its Fortifications

～⚜～

In Corfu the approach of summer in mid-May is heralded by the arrival of the fireflies. Among the olive groves, under the clumps of prickly pear by the roadside, in the canal cutting between the Old Fort and the Esplanade, in leafy gardens and in the quiet tree-haunted spaces in the town, the night glimmers with their myriad tiny hovering sparks of cool pale-green light. The fireflies rise and fall gently in the warm perfumed air and the little gems of light glow, fade and glow again, in rhythmic celebration of the final phase of spring. By mid-June, with the increasing summer heat, they have entirely disappeared.

The Corfiots respond to these gay, pyrotechnical displays by staying up later than ever. Meals are still being served at eleven o'clock under the arcades of the fine group of buildings facing the Esplanade, erected by the French between 1807 and 1814. The young people continue to saunter up and down until the midnight bell from the Old Fort is accepted as a hint, at least by some, that a few hours' sleep might be worth having. If you are staying in the centre of the town, you may be conscious of the reverberating sounds of high-heels on the pavements in the narrow street or alleyway below, intermingled with laughter, sudden bursts of conversation and a snatch of song, melodious, Italianate, distracting.

In the morning you awake to the swallows, to a thin shrill vibrating in the air. Look out of the window and you will see them in their thousands, circling, gliding, swooping, climbing high above the terracotta roofs of the old town. Their nests are built indiscriminately —under the eaves of the Royal Palace, of the many churches and of houses both ancient and modern. Sitting under the arcades for an evening drink or a morning coffee, you can see the tiny black beady eyes of the new-born looking incuriously at you from over the rim of their nests.

Now that Venetian Zakynthos has gone and all the fine old buildings in Argostoli as well, Corfu is incomparably the loveliest town in the Ionian Sea with its palaces, churches, fortresses and parks, its terraces of tall houses, narrow alleys and broad thoroughfares, to which not only Venice but also Britain and France have contributed in varying degrees. Basically the old town has an Italian rather than an Hellenic look, largely because of its Venetian origins. But this impression is also due to the atmosphere itself and to the lushness of vegetation which springs from the heavy winter rain. The island of Corfu, which is the second largest in the Ionian group, has probably the highest rainfall in all Greece. The light itself no longer has quite the clarity to be found in the Aegean where the distant island is etched as clearly in the brilliant air as the little domed chapel a hundred yards away. Here among the northern reaches of the Ionian Sea, it is gentler, softer, more changeable. Sea mists, especially when the south wind blows, hang in folds over the inland sea and obscure the Epirot coast. The sunsets are richer, more varied in their colours, reminiscent of the Bay of Naples rather than of the Saronic Gulf. This is not entirely unexpected; Brindisi is nearer to Corfu than Patras and on a clear day you can see the coast of Apulia from the summit of Pantocrator.

Yet Corfu has never been anything but Greek within historical memory. The language of the island has always remained Greek in spite of the fact that, during the Venetian occupation, official communications of all types were in Italian and the aristocracy used among themselves the same dialect as spoken in Venice. It is this contrast between appearance and reality and the harmonious interweaving of different cultures that makes the Ionian Islands, and above all Corfu, so fascinating as a group.

The origins of the present town date back to when, sometime in the middle of the tenth century A.D., the Byzantine authorities began building on the promontory of the Old Fort. With the gradual decline of the Imperial power, raiding expeditions made the town of ancient Corcyra on the Palaiopolis peninsula near by too vulnerable. Some claim that the name 'Corfu' derives from a corruption of 'koryphai', meaning peaks or breasts, a reference to the twin peaks of the citadel. Today, the Greeks have reverted to Kerkyra, a variant on the original name of Corcyra, the name given to the Corinthian colony which was established on the island in 734 B.C.

The Old Fort is a wonderful landmark. Perhaps the loveliest

approach to it is from the north on the Brindisi ferry on a clear summer morning. The boat, moving peacefully through the calm waters of the Corfu Channel, swings from the entrance to Butrinto into the great inland sea. The length of the green hilly island stretches away south to the open sea, where Levkas lies hidden below the horizon. There standing out to sea in the middle distance, is the promontory with its great Veneto-British fortress. The high fortifications reflect a pale golden light from the early morning sun, in contrast to the darker gold of the town to the west and the harbour beyond.

When the site of the Old Fort was first occupied, the island was part of the Byzantine theme of which the centre was Cephalonia. Corfu was to remain Byzantine until the capture of Constantinople by the Fourth Crusade in 1204. This is not to say that all was peaceful. The island was twice captured by the Normans—first by Bohemund in 1083 who was joined by his father Robert Guiscard in the following year, and secondly by King Roger of Sicily in 1147—but on both occasions the Norman rule was short-lived.

Corfu was also on the Crusader's route to Asia Minor. Pisans on their way to reinforce the Latin kingdom of Jerusalem raided Corfu and other Ionian Islands in 1112. Ten years later, the Venetians besieged the citadel in vain for six months, having recently quarrelled with Byzantium over trading concessions. Richard Coeur de Lion landed here in 1192 on his return from the Third Crusade but hurriedly left in disguise to avoid capture by Byzantine officials; they regarded him as an enemy of the Orthodox Church as he had tried to persuade Saladin to latinize all the churches in Jerusalem.

Despite the Normans and Crusaders, the island was generally described as rich and fertile by visitors and was able to pay a considerable sum annually into the Imperial treasury. Villehardouin, here in 1203 with the Fourth Crusade, found Corfu a very fertile island and well supplied with food. No wonder Venice claimed it when the spoils of Byzantium were divided up among the Latin despoilers of the Imperial city on the Bosphorus.

Venice was not, however, to assert her full control until 1387. The Byzantine Despot of the Epirus gained the island from the Venetians in 1210, while agreeing to recognize their suzerainty, and in 1267 it became a possession of the Angevin Kingdom of Naples and Sicily. Under the Despots, the old Byzantine fortifications were further strengthened. Because of the insecurity of the times, the Epirots followed the Venetians in granting special privileges, such as exemption from taxes and freedom of worship, to the inhabitants of the Old Fort which then contained the town. The Angevins and the Venetians in due course were to do likewise. The Angevins however were responsible, as Roman Catholics, for exalting the Latin over the Orthodox Church. The title of archbishop was transferred to the chief of the Latin clergy, while the former Greek metropolitan had to be content with the title of Protopappas or chief priest. Even the churches, including the cathedral of St Arsenius, were taken over by the Roman Catholics. Fifteenth-century sketches show this cathedral as a three-nave church between the two citadels. Afterwards a tower appears to have been added. Today it no longer exists, as in 1718 a streak of lightning blew up the neighbouring powder magazine and the cathedral with it.

The town had probably begun to spill out from the Old Fort beyond what is now the Esplanade by the time the Venetians were invited in 1386 by a deputation of six Corfiots, representing the Greek, Italian and Jewish communities, to take over the administration and protection of the island; this they did in the following year. Even by the time of the first great siege, embarked upon by Suleyman the Magnificent in 1537, the fortifications were still confined to the Old Fort promontory. Although the siege only lasted twenty days, the Turks swept through the island with fire and sword and led away some twenty thousand into captivity.

The strength of the Old Fort was commented upon by two English travellers in the sixteenth century. Sir Richard Torkington did not stop at Corfu, but noted 'I trowe they had no where so strong as this in Greece', adding, 'they speke all Greke and be Grekes indeed.' John Locke stayed in Corfu in 1553 after the first great siege on returning from Jerusalem, and wrote in similar vein about the fortifications which had now been baptized by fire.

It was only after a highly destructive raid by the Turks against the suburbs of Corfu in 1571, the same year as the defeat of the Turkish fleet at Lepanto, that the Venetians decided that further fortifications were necessary. The New Fort, which towers over the outer harbour from where the ferry boats depart for Igoumenitsa was erected between 1577 and 1588. At the same time, strong fortifications were built across the town from the New Fort in a straight line to Garitza Bay, ending close to where the Corfu Palace Hotel now stands. There were three gates through these fortifications; the Spilia Gate close to the harbour, the Royal Gate on the road to San Rocco and the

Raimondo Gate where the road from the Esplanade descends to the water front of Garitza Bay. There was a fourth gate at the little harbour of St Nicolas just to the north of the Palace of St Michael and St George. All these gates have now disappeared.

The final fortifications were not raised until after the second great Turkish siege of 1716, which marked the end of a two-year campaign whereby the Turks regained almost all that they had lost to Morosini at the end of the seventeenth century. The Venetians, very well aware of this impending attack on the Ionian Islands, the last of their overseas possessions, had appointed Count von der Schulenburg to command the garrison. Thanks to his energy in putting the fortifications into serviceable condition and to his bravery in leading the defence of the New Fort, at one stage severely breached by the fury of the Turkish assault, the attack failed. After 1716, the Provveditore Grimani was responsible for the erection of further strong fortifications on the two hills of San Salvator, between Garitza and the airport, and on Mount Abraham to the west; both of these were hotly contested by the opposing forces in 1798–99, when Admiral Ousakov with his Russian and Turkish troops, together with Albanians sent over by Ali Pasha from the mainland, attacked the French who were then holding Corfu.

At the end of the Napoleonic Wars, the defence system of Corfu was immensely strong. The French, at the end of their second occupation of 1807–14, were forced to surrender not through military defeat by the blockading British but because of Napoleon's collapse. The Old Fort was then still very much as it had been under Venice. Here was the palace of the Venetian governor-general, the 'Provveditore-Generale del Levante', and the offices and homes of his civil and military officials together with churches, schools and a hospital. Much of this the British were to convert during their fifty years of power into a purely military headquarters, pulling down the old Venetian buildings and replacing them with up-to-date barracks. We gain some idea of what the Venetian barracks were like from Private Wheeler who was stationed there in 1823. 'Our barracks are any thing but comfortable,' he wrote home, 'by day they are alive with bugs, fleas, and mosquitos. . . . Scorpions and centepedes are very numerous and we often find them on the walls in the rooms. We have a remedy against the bite or sting of these reptiles, it is simple and every company is provided with it. A bottle of rum is kept, into this every venemous reptile that can be caught alive is put. If anyone should get stung you have only to wash the part with the liquor, the relief is instantaneous and cure certain.'

What you will see if you visit the Old Fort is largely British. The best time to go is at about six o'clock in the evening cool, because to reach the higher of the two citadels, the one nearer the land, involves a considerable climb. You enter the Old Fort from the road that divides the Esplanade or Spianatha into two, crossing by bridge over the canal, built after the first siege in 1537, which separates the Old Fort from the Esplanade. Just in front of this entrance, which is flanked by two Venetian cannons dated 1684, is the statue to Schulenburg, high on his dais, an elaborate period extravaganza which gives little impression of what the field-marshal was really like. Of Saxon origin, this fine professional soldier fought with distinction under the Duke of Marlborough at Tournai and Malplaquet. After his victory over the Turks, he retook Levkas and Butrinto, captured Preveza and Vonitsa and drew up plans for the systematic strengthening of the Ionian defences, including the Corfu citadel after the explosion in 1718. His sister was one of the mistresses of George I, who created her Duchess of Kendal.

From the citadel you look west over the fortifications and canal to the Esplanade, across the roofs of the old Venetian town to the New Fort which dominates the middle distance. Note how all the roads leading into the Esplanade are at right angles to allow cannon from the Old Fort to fire straight down them in event of an attack. Immediately below, on the right, is the little enclosed harbour where the Venetian galleys were berthed. The Provveditore's palace used to be immediately above it but was pulled down during the British Protectorate to make way for the barracks you now see there. To the northwest, just below the Palace of St Michael and St George, is the little port of St Nicolas, complete with tiny chapel and a bathing place. We occasionally hired a boat to row out to the eastern end of the Old Fort to enjoy secluded, excellent bathing under the ramparts. Beyond St Nicolas is the great curved Bay of Ipsos and Pantocrator dreaming in the evening light.

To the north, lying a short distance out into the inland sea, is the flat, wooded island of Vido which proved on at least one occasion to be the key to the defence. The Russo-Turkish forces in 1798–1799 besieged Corfu from the west but even with the blockade exercised by their fleet made little headway until a certain Commander Stuart, R.N., on a friendly visit from Sicily, pointed out the importance of

Vido. The allies then made a successful attack upon the little island which the French had thought impregnable. As a result of its capture, the Old Fort came under direct fire from the Russian guns. Soon after this General Chabot capitulated. During the British Protectorate Vido was further fortified, as was the massive New Fort which covers an area as great as the Old Fort. Above Vido in the far distance are the Acroceraunian heights of Albania, snow-capped until early summer. East and north-eastwards is the Epirot coast and inland the great Pindus range.

On the south side of the Old Fort is the chapel built in Doric style by the British as a garrison church and dedicated to St George. Now Orthodox, it still serves the same purpose. Restored in 1951, it is unusually light and airy inside and has a fine iconostasis. The Pargiots when they sought refuge in Corfu from Ali Pasha, who was allowed by Maitland in 1819 to occupy Parga, placed in this church the sacred icons and relics from their home; these were eventually taken back to Parga in 1913 by descendants of the original refugees, after the Greek liberation of the Epirus in the first Balkan War.

When Britain ceded the Ionian Islands to Greece in 1864—an act of unheard-of generosity during the height of empire—she was forced by the protecting powers of the United States of the Ionian Islands, and particularly by Austria, to demilitarize the Ionian fortifications, in spite of the fact that their importance had long since dwindled. At first the Austrians insisted on the dismantling of all fortifications throughout the Seven Islands, but eventually this was made to apply only to Corfu and Paxos; in addition, the Old Fort was spared. The last Lord High Commissioner, Sir Henry Storks, was however limited either in his ability or his willingness to communicate the situation as it really was to the Ionians who for a time thought that these fortifications had been built exclusively from the taxes they had paid—although their cost had been borne equally by the British taxpayer—and that the demolitions were made at the instigation of the British alone.

Since 1864, the Corfu fortifications have been useless. The Old Fort is now an infantry training centre. The New Fort was used after the First World War as the headquarters of a British Police Mission to help train the Greek urban police; the Italians fired a shell through the British commandant's bedroom during their 1923 bombardment of Corfu, where they also landed troops, as a reprisal for the Greek Government's supposed involvement, quite unfounded, in the murder

of the principal Italian delegate on the Greek-Albanian frontier de-
marcation commission. A part of the New Fort is now occupied by the
Greek navy but in the main it is empty and neglected although still
structurally sound. The Lion of St Mark still stands over the entrance
off the harbour.

The island of Vido was occupied during the First World War by
those Serbian troops who survived the disastrous retreat at the end of
1915 in the face of the overwhelming Austro-Bulgarian advance.
Today it is a reformatory.

19

Venetian Corfu and St Spiridion

A stroll westwards from the Esplanade down Nikophoros Theotokis Street and then north towards the harbour reveals the heart of Venetian Corfu; it also gives some idea of what the Plateia Rouga of Zakynthos looked like before 1953. Much of it is arcaded. The houses vary from two to six stories with all windows above the ground floor protected by wooden slatted shutters which are usually painted green. Public buildings of the Venetian period were sometimes built of stone but bricks are made very cheaply on the island and were used for domestic architecture, overlaid with stucco. These houses have both grace and strength. They are occasionally enlivened with decorative ironwork round the balconies and with carved stonework round the doors. One house on the north side of Nikophoros Theotokis Street, built by a Cretan after the fall of Candia, has gargoyles above the arches of its arcade whose grimaces of anger or despair reveal how heavily the great house rests upon them.

Between Nikophoros Theotokis Street and the sea wall to the north, there rises a hill over which spreads the district of Campiello, built in a huddle of alleyways and tiny squares. Wells were sunk for water; one of the most elegant wells is that of Kremasti, carved in marble and dated 1699. The alleyways between the tall houses form narrow canyons into some of which the sun barely penetrates. Yet as you mount and descend the stepped alleys, there is warmth from sunbaked walls beneath whose crumbling stucco can be seen the pale pink bricks. It is perhaps as well to forget about the lack of amenities in many of these picturesque old houses—one tap of running water only, the only lavatory in the kitchen, and the resulting tuberculosis and dysentery with which their inhabitants were until recently plagued. These matters are now being put right.

There is no pattern about the way the alleys run and it is almost

19. Bell-tower of Church of St Spiridion, Corfu   20. Entrance to New Fort, Corfu

21
Palace of St Michael and
St George, Corfu

22. French architecture
in Corfu

impossible to come direct upon a particular point you wish to reach. They twist under archways, move past tall whitewashed walls, which hide a little garden or a private chapel, and into unexpected open places created by bombing in the last war. Here grass has sometimes grown sparsely and you come upon a donkey grazing, firewood which its master has brought in from the country piled high upon its back.

Towards the more patrician east side it is a quiet place, but on the west towards the harbour, artisan families live tightly packed and clouds of washing hang above you on lines stretched from side to side of the passageways. Here under arcades or awnings are shops with baskets of fruit and vegetables, water melons piled high on wooden ledges, and strings of garlic. Many of the ground-floor interiors are workshops where furniture and coffins are made and wrought-iron is twisted into decorative shapes for balconies or gates; the sounds of sawing and hammering re-echo at every twist and turn.

Once the fortifications from the New Fort to the Bay of Garitza had been built, the inner town grew rapidly. 'It is not a hundred years, since this City was nothing but the Old Castle and the present suburbs of Castrati (now Garitza),' wrote Sir George Wheler in 1675. 'But now it is a good large city and well fortified. . . .' With the fall of Crete, Corfu became the headquarters of the remaining Venetian possessions in the Ionian and Aegean Seas. As such it again became a haven of refuge, as it had been after the fall of Constantinople, this time for Cretans.

But a much older settlement had long been established in the old town. There were many Jewish communities scattered throughout Greece when Benjamin of Tudela wrote an account of them towards the end of the twelfth century, but he reported that there was only one Jew in Corfu. Under the Angevins a colony was encouraged to develop and a ghetto complete with synagogue was established in Campiello. This first settlement was Greek speaking and the earliest known example of demotic Greek prose is said to be the translation of the Book of Jonah made for this synagogue. The Jews were not then popular in Corfu for religious reasons and even today damaged household crockery is occasionally put on one side to be thrown out of the window on Good Friday morning as a symbolic stoning of Judas. Certainly the constant repetition of edicts both under the Angevins and the Venetians insisting on their proper treatment indicates that conditions were far from good.

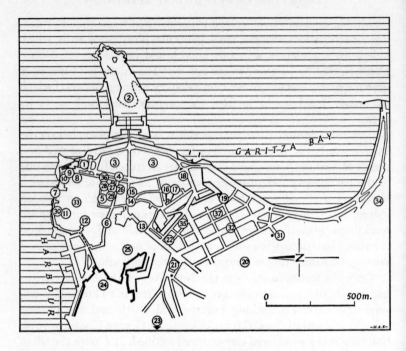

CORFU TOWN

1. Palace of St Michael and St George
2. The Old Fort
3. Esplanade
4. French Arcade
5. Church of St Spiridion
6. Nikophoros Theotokis Street
7. Arseniou Street (Mourayia)
8. Corfu Club
9. Nomarcheion (Prefecture)
10. Palace of Metropolitan (Archbishop)
11. Campiello District
12. Metropolis (Orthodox Cathedral) of St Theodora
13. Voulgaris Street
14. Town Hall
15. Catholic Cathedral of St James and St Christopher
16. Ionian Parliament Building
17. British Vice-Consulate
18. Site of Ionian Academy (destroyed)
19. Museum of Antiquities

20. British Cemetery on site of San Salvador Fort
21. San Rocco Square
22. Opera House
23. Mount Abraham and Platytera Monastery
24. New Fort
25. Synagogue
26. Church of St John of the Cisterns
27. Church of Panayia ton Xenon
28. Church of St Eleftherios
29. Ionian Bank Square
30. Tourist Office
31. Tomb of Menekrates
32. Alexandras Street
33. Well of Kremasti
34. Anemomilos Village
35. Post and Telegraph Office
36. Capodistrias Street
37. Tennis Courts

The strength of the community was illustrated by its representation of two in the deputation of six which visited Venice in 1386.
Later, a second ghetto was established in 1540 between the harbour
and Voulgaris Street for refugees from the persecutions in Spain and
Portugal at the end of the fifteenth century and from Southern Italy
some fifty years later. When, by the decree of 1572, all Jews were
banished from Venetian territory, the Corfiot communities were alone
exempted. They were allowed to practise as advocates and, forbidden
to own land, came to monopolize all trade, banking and money-
lending. Count Marmora, whose *Della Historia di Corfu* was published
in Venice in 1672, remarked that the Jews would have been rich if
they had been left alone.

But left alone they rarely were. They were likely to be seized for
the galleys or, worse, made to act as executioners with gallows erected
in their cemetery. They were made to wear a badge of the Star of
David unless, of course, a payment was made in the right quarter.
They also had to provide the carpets which were laid in the streets
when a newly appointed Provveditore-Generale del Levante made his
stately procession on arrival from Venice.

Nevertheless the community continued to survive. It fought well
against the Turks during the 1716 siege and one of their number was
promoted captain. Schulenburg recommended the Venetian Senate
to grant a general permission for Jews to settle on Corfu on payment
of a tax. Ansted estimated that they amounted to a third of the town's
population during his visit in 1863.

Then came the German occupation. In June 1944—only three
months before they evacuated the island—the Germans forced the
local authorities to collect together those Jews who had not already
escaped with local help. They were herded into the Old Fort—the
sick, the old, pregnant mothers, lunatics—where they were kept for
three days without food or sanitary arrangements. Afterwards, they
were thrust into ships and taken away to an unknown destination.
Several mothers threw their infants into the sea to end their suffering.
Now about two hundred have returned. The ghetto walls were pulled
down during the British Protectorate, but the present small community is concentrated round their synagogue, where the second ghetto
was situated.

The Venetian administration was oligarchic and based in the
Ionian Islands on the Greek and Italian aristocracy, those 112 noble
families whose names, according to Marmora, were inscribed in the

Libro d'Oro; if an aristocratic family became extinct, one from the burgher class was elected to take its place. All these were eligible for the General Assembly which met once a year to elect a Council of one hundred and fifty members. This latter body was responsible for choosing who should fill the minor administrative offices. The Baillie, who was the chief civil administrator of the island, and his two councillors were of course appointed from Venice. The Corfiot aristocracy was debarred from trade and compelled to reside in the town if they wished to play a part in the General Assembly, so that agriculture too became neglected. The only work open to them was legal or in the administration but this afforded limited opportunities. No wonder there was so much gambling.

If the basis of the Venetian administration was the aristocracy, its aim was to raise money. Although a Catholic state, La Serenessima became more tolerant, especially after the fall of Crete, of all religions —as we have seen in their attitude towards the Jews. In any case tolerance towards the Orthodox Church was essential because of, among many good reasons, St Spiridion, the Orthodox patron saint of Corfu, who has saved the island from two major epidemics of plague, relieved it from a major famine in the sixteenth century and brought about the defeat in 1716 of the besieging Turks. On this last occasion, the Ottoman camp was suddenly swept by an enormous storm; during the confusion, the panic-stricken Turks saw a number of acolytes with lighted candles approaching them, urged forward by an elderly bishop, staff in hand, who could only have been St Spiridion himself.

Spiridion's origins were remote from Corfu. He was born in Cyprus where, according to Butler's *Lives of the Saints*, he combined the care of sheep with the cure of souls. He became bishop of an obscure rural diocese. Nevertheless, he attended the Council of Nicaea in A.D. 325. On his way there, accompanied by his deacon, he met with a group of bishops travelling in the same direction. Such was his rustic simplicity that his colleagues felt that his presence at Nicaea might compromise the cause of orthodoxy. Accordingly, they instructed their servants to cut off the heads of the mules of Spiridion and his deacon so that they could not continue their journey. When Spiridion discovered this on getting up just before dawn, he was in no way disconcerted but told his deacon to put back the severed heads of the mules upon their bodies; this being done, the heads and bodies grew together and the mules lived. When the sun rose, they found that a mistake had been made in the dark, for the white mule now had a brown head and vice versa. In this way the journey was successfully completed. Spiridion lived to be well over ninety and when he was buried in Cyprus, his tomb exhaled sweet odours and put forth sprays of red roses.

At a much later stage his embalmed remains were moved to Constantinople and then, after 1453, taken by easy stages to Corfu. At that point they belonged to one Kalochairetis, a priest who also owned the embalmed body of St Theodora Augusta. He is said to have packed each in a sack and to have carried one on each side of his mule. In 1460 he settled in Corfu, where Spiridion provided him and his descendants with an excellent revenue. Eventually the saint's body came, as a marriage dowry, into the distinguished family of Voulgaris. In 1589 the great yellow-washed church was built whose bell-tower, surmounted by its red onion-shaped dome, is one of the most prominent landmarks of the town. The Voulgaris family administered the church and its revenues until as recently as 1925, when full control was handed over to the Greek Orthodox Church. A member of this family was Evyenios Voulgaris, renowned as a pioneer of modern Greek towards the end of the eighteenth century, after whom the thoroughfare is named. He worked for much of his life in Yannina, then a great centre of Hellenic learning.

Wheler remarked on the fine silver lamps hanging in the church and one of gold 'given by a Gentleman of Corfu, who by his Will, left five thousand Cichins (which amount to about three thousand pounds sterling) to buy it'. One of the finest silver lamps was tactfully dedicated by the Venetian Senate to St Spiridion for his major role in defeating the Turks in 1716.

At the east end of the church is a great white marble iconostasis shaped like the entrance to an Italian baroque church, and surmounted by a hexagonal dome. In the little chapel through the door on the right-hand side of this screen is the elaborate silver casket of the saint. The priest (in his 'undress' uniform of long royal blue tunic and without his cylindrical hat) showed us some of the treasures of the church, including the grave full-length portraits of saints by Contarini and Tzanes in the elaborate majesty of Orthodox ecclesiastical vestments, and the scholarly Italianate paintings by Spiridion Sperantzos (1740–1775) at the west end.

The great glory of St Spiridion was its ceiling, painted by Panayiotis Doxaras towards the end of his life. Apart from portraits of the four evangelists, one in each corner, the ceiling was divided up into thirteen scenes of the life and posthumous miracles of the Saint. Together with the now destroyed roof of the Phaneromene church in Zakynthos, the ceiling of St Spiridion was the finest achievement of this small, remote school of eighteenth-century painting.

The ceiling you see today however was not painted by Panayiotis Doxaras. In the second quarter of the nineteenth century, the Voulgaris family decided to have these scenes replaced with a fresh version. Perhaps the colour of the original paintings had faded, perhaps they had become blackened from candle smoke. Nicolas Aspiotis, a well-regarded and skilful religious painter who did much work in Montenegro as well as in Corfu, was commissioned to copy the Doxaras works. According to Spiridion Lambros, who wrote a monograph on Doxaras in 1871, Aspiotis' work fell far short of the originals. For many years, the Doxaras paintings were known to have been stored in stables near the town; then they vanished, sold perhaps to itinerant merchants who cut up the canvases for re-sale.

There is a constant movement of the devout about the church, going from icon to icon, each of which is reverently kissed, and ending at the shrine of the Saint. The demands upon his powers are never-ending. He is still given shares in all sorts of local enterprise, especially where ships are concerned, and their resultant successes have rewarded his church accordingly. His powers in recent years were never better shown than in the recent war. The church was packed during the bitter fighting between the Germans and Italians in 1943 and during the bombing which created much havoc in the vicinity; never once, however, was the church in any way damaged. No wonder that every caique, bus, lorry and taxi carries a facsimile of Spiridion.

As the island's most prominent citizen, the Saint has been accorded the fullest honours by the occupying or protecting powers—by the Venetians, by the Russians, even by the British. Only the French who arrived in 1797 showed any disrespect, inspired as they were by the New Order of the Revolution; it is perhaps significant that their first occupation was quickly over.

For centuries the Saint has gone in stately procession round the Esplanade four times a year. Private Wheeler described in 1823 how, before the start of the procession, the Saint was taken out of his coffer and placed upright by the grand altar at which moment the guard presented arms, the band, somewhat inappropriately perhaps, played 'God Save the King' and a near-by battery let off a Royal

Salute. The Saint was then carried in procession by four British colonels. It is sad to think that as the British Protectorate moved towards its close, British officialdom took less and less part in the Saint's procession, until the Saint and the Lord High Commissioner were barely on bowing terms, Spiridion in his stately perambulation hardly bothering to stop outside the Palace of St Michael and St George to receive the Lord High Commissioner's briefest nod from the terrace.

The procession today has changed little over the centuries except for the uniforms and the nationalities of the guards, now consisting of the Greek services. Otherwise the route, the vestments of the clergy and the enthusiasm of the Corfiots are the same. Emerging from the church, the procession proceeds eastwards into Capodistrias Street and then south round the Esplanade. The Saint's upright casket, part of which is glass-encased to enable him to see out, becomes a sedan chair and is borne aloft on the shoulders of four priests; over them an awning is carried for protection against the sun. Extra protection is now provided by a lace shawl over the casket. In front of the Saint walks the Archbishop of Corfu, complete with pastoral staff, wearing his splendid silk-embroidered vestments and a great jewelled ecclesiastical crown. Behind him come the leading civil and military dignitaries of the island. This central group is preceded and followed by long lines of priests. Guarding the procession on the outside, soldiers and sailors march in slow time to the florid music of Corfu's two brass bands, resplendent in their plumed and gleaming helmets. Sick are laid in the middle of the road for the Saint to pass over; if they have sufficient faith they will be cured.

Having circled the Esplanade, the procession winds back down Capodistrias Street, turns right into Nikophoros Theotokis Street, crossing the square in which stands the Ionian Bank, and so up the steps to re-enter the church on its south side. The square was a few years ago dedicated to the 'Heroes of the Struggle for Cyprus' but is universally known as the 'Ionian Bank Square', or, more simply, 'i plakatha t'Ayiou' ('the paved space of the saint'). In its centre stands a statue of George Theotokis, the most distinguished Corfiot politician since the union of the Ionian Islands with Greece.

The Theotokis family, which settled in Corfu from Byzantium after 1453, has produced landowners, writers and statesmen who have figured prominently in the annals of the island and, since 1864, of Greece as well. George Theotokis was four times Prime Minister during the first decade of this century. Nikophoros Theotokis, after whom the street is named, was one of the two great pioneers of modern Greek towards the end of the eighteenth century together with Evyenios Voulgaris.

20

The Venetian Decline and the French

⟨∿⟩

Arseniou Street, better known as the Mourayia, starts just beyond the Palace of St Michael and St George and runs on top of the sea-wall down to the harbour. Morning, while the sun is still rising and a faint golden mist softens the contours of Pantocrator and the distant Albanian mountains, is the ideal time to stroll along its length.

Close to where the road swings north above St Nicolas there are two buildings of note. One is an elegant Venetian house with stone steps mounting to a fine stone-arcaded entrance on the first floor; the windows under the staircase are protected by wrought-iron grilles. This is the Corfu Club and Reading Centre. Of particular note is its library which contains a great many works of historical interest about the island. Here also is a copy of the *Libro d'Oro* of the Corfiot aristocracy, originally compiled during the Venetian supremacy and continued into the twentieth century.

The other is the Nomarcheion or Prefecture, which stands close by; it is a fine neo-Classical building by Chronis, the island's leading architect in the nineteenth century. Its inspiration is Roman rather than Greek; you are left in no doubt about its official character, but the design is not pompous. Chronis was also responsible for the Ionian Bank building.

On the Mourayia itself is the Metropolitan's palace, a simple two-storied white stucco building which is said to contain many fine icons. Further along is the grandiose building, part of which houses the island's official tourist organization. At the bottom end are a number of shipping offices and cafés. Edward Lear lived in rooms here for some time.

At the top of a flight of steps, set well back from the harbour square, is the Metropolis or Cathedral, although it has no exterior splendour to distinguish it from the other churches of Corfu. The roof is of plain wood, and inside there is a simple white iconostasis with some undistinguished icons. Here is none of the golden richness which was so characteristic of the churches of Cephalonia and especially of Zakynthos. On the south wall are two vast canvasses, but they are difficult to see because they are badly hung and covered with dirt. Even the tomb of St Theodora appears to be neglected as if all concerned are much disappointed with her inability or unwillingness to rival the exploits of St Spiridion, her travelling companion from Constantinople. It is his church and not the Metropolis which has the highest belfry in the old town.

The Orthodox churches of the post-Byzantine period in the Ionian Islands rarely attempt to impress by size or decorative effect. They were built, most of them, in the seventeenth century or the first half of the eighteenth when the Ionian Islands were at their most affluent. They are simple and neat in style and stand, not elaborately apart, but shoulder to shoulder with houses and shops, thus emphasizing that they are not for special occasions only but for everyday use.

In the Ionian Bank Square are two very popular churches. On the south side is St John of the Cisterns, named after the water tanks which once stood in the square, which goes back to at least 1520. The priest, who takes much interest in his church, pointed out the rather gloomy ceiling by Aspiotis and the frescoes, thought by some to have been painted by Damaskinos. He would have liked, he said, to have claimed so distinguished a painter for his church—but frankly, he did not think they were up to Damaskinos' standard; in any case, he only spent part of 1583 in Corfu. His greatest pride were the paintings by Emmanuel Tzanes who came to Corfu from Crete in 1646 at the age of thirty-six, and painted many lovely icons before continuing to Venice in 1659. Perhaps the finest here is his portrait of St Demetrios, shown in intricately wrought breast-plate and greaves and holding a spear and a shield. The figure is full-length and occupies the whole of the canvas in Byzantine style but apart from this and the Greek inscription on the golden background, the feeling is closer to the west than to Byzantium. It is in St John's that the few Russians who died in Corfu during the years of the Russian Protectorate (1802–1807) are commemorated.

The other church is the Panayia ton Xenon (The Madonna of the Foreigners), opposite St John's. Its windows face south and its spacious interior is usually flooded with light. The iconostasis is of gilded wood but the detail is over-elaborate and the paintings framed by it appear to be inferior works of the nineteenth century.

Just off Capodistrias Street—its north wall in St Spiridion Street—is the little church of St Eleftherios. Originally a private chapel belonging to the Vervitsiotis family, it was subsequently enlarged with the curious result that its altar is now at the south end. A portrait of the benefactress in the gallery was pointed out to us by an enthusiastic priest who produced a notebook in which his predecessor had written down the principal points of interest. The ceiling had originally been painted by Sperantzas but it had been completely ruined by bombing during the war; the present restored ceiling of wood is painted blue. The iconostasis is one of the finest in Corfu—the finely-carved ivory-coloured wood picked out in gold—and there are several fine paintings, including one of twelve scenes from the Creation by Panayiotis Paramythiotis. There is a Holy Family and three indifferent scenes from the life of St Eleftherios by Sperantzas and a fine full-length portrait of St Kerkira, notable for its treatment of the garments, which the parish priest thought was painted either by Contarini or by Tzanes.

Although there are few Roman Catholics left in Corfu today—even during the Venetian ascendancy they were always heavily out-numbered by the Orthodox—there are several Latin churches still in existence. The most important is that of St James and St Christopher, built in 1658, which became the Latin Cathedral after the destruction of St Arsenius in 1718. It stands opposite the Town Hall which is of the same period. All that remains of it is its façade because the interior was destroyed by a bomb in the last war, but it is now being rebuilt. Its façade is elegantly baroque and, although surmounted by a spire and not a dome, might have served as a model for the iconostasis in St Spiridion and in the tiny Orthodox church of St Antony at the harbour end of Nikophoros Theotokis Street. Its small congregation consists mainly of Corfiots of Maltese descent.

The Maltese first came to Corfu as masons for the construction of the Palace of St Michael and St George in the years between 1819 and 1824, for the palace, like parts of the new Roman Catholic Cathedral at Liverpool, is built of Maltese stone. Other Maltese were encouraged to settle and open market gardens to supply the British colony with vegetables. The Maltese community was still sufficiently integrated before the war for Sir Harry Luke, then secretary to the Maltese government, to visit it in 1937. He found them proud of their origin although able to speak only Greek. Today, in spite of inter-marriage and assimilation a few Maltese still exist.

The Town Hall was built between 1663 and 1693. Small, elegant and with a well-preserved exterior, it was originally designed as a meeting-place for the nobility. Subsequently it was fitted out as a theatre and used as such until 1903 when its place was taken by a large opera house; the latter stood, until wrecked during the war, on Voulgaris Street just beyond the old Royal Gate. In the basement of the Town Hall is the font in which Frederick North, later Lord Guilford, was baptized in 1791 into the Greek Orthodox Church. On the east wall is a trophy, now in battered condition, which was erected in honour of Morosini, the conqueror of the Peloponnesos. The Venetian Senate on principle did not allow the servants of the Republic to have monuments and statues erected to them by their subject peoples. Morosini and Schulenburg were the only exceptions to this rule in Corfu.

The Venetians kept an outward show of magnificence until the very end but during the last few years the decay was rapid. Their officials were drawn almost invariably from the poorer gentry, known as Barnabotti, who came to their colonies in order to make fortunes or to recoup them. As often as not, the offices were bought. Arrogant and intractable, they used their privileges to extort as much as possible from the local population. The Provveditore-Generale, who held all power in his hands, lived on a grand scale. It was customary for him to be escorted everywhere by four liveried servants and for an orchestra of three to play when he dined. He gave several official banquets annually but those invited were expected to leave under their plate a promissory note for so much olive oil.

It was the same at all levels; the Provveditore-Generale's secretary, known as chancellor, did well by blackmail and anonymous denunciations, as a result of the information he was in a position to acquire. Even the troops had to beg or work at some trade in their spare time in order to survive, since pay was rarely forthcoming. The Venetian garrison at this time consisted of some nine infantry regiments. There were, however, a great many dead men on the payroll. Woe betide any soldier who had to go into hospital where only public charity stood between him and starvation. The navy had to pay its way by undertaking commercial transport. Because the old cruelties of the Roman code were still accepted, such as cutting out tongues and putting out eyes, it was easy for the judges to extort money. Another weapon was that of excommunication; in return for a consideration, it was not unusual for a priest, either Catholic or Orthodox, to excommunicate a whole village until a certain sum had been surrendered.

In these circumstances, it is understandable why the Ionian Islands proved a drain on, rather than an aid to, the Republic. It is equally understandable why the French were at first warmly welcomed when they arrived in 1797 as the inheritors of the Republic's territories. Yet the last Venetian Provveditore-Generale, Widmann, had perhaps the warmest welcome of any when he arrived at Corfu. His successful administrative career in the navy and his very honourable record gave the Corfiots hope that at last a real attempt was to be made to end corruption. Certainly there was no ostentation in his means of transport. Instead of arriving with the customary escort of a Venetian naval squadron, all that could be spared him was a small frigate.

His first discovery was that the Ionian treasury was empty. Immediate steps had therefore to be taken to raise funds; inevitably this fell on the Jews. The individual islands were promised, in return for immediate contributions, relief from further taxes for several years —but even then funds were difficult to raise because of poor currant crops for several previous years. Widmann finally pledged his own fortune, thus living up to his reputation as a man of honour.

In the meanwhile the days of La Serenissima were drawing rapidly to a close. In 1797, after a brilliant campaign in Northern Italy terminating in the Treaty of Campio Formio, General Bonaparte gained control of Venice and her overseas possessions; never again was the ancient Republic to be an independant state. Bonaparte quickly realized the importance of the Ionian Islands, especially of Corfu. A French fleet was hastily combined with a Venetian convoy which was taking relief to the Ionian Islands; although placed under the command of the French General Gentili, it sailed under the Venetian flag. The first Widmann knew of the French presence was when messengers came ashore from the fleet when safely at anchor in Corfu harbour. No opposition was possible, because he had no troops capable of fighting and scarcely any powder.

The French were not then popular in Corfu because of the ill-mannered behaviour of a party of French sailors towards St Spiridion earlier in the year; their slovenly appearance had also told against them. Soon after the French occupation of Corfu, however, Bonaparte was able to write to the Directory in Paris a most enthusiastic account of the way General Gentili, another Corsican, had been greeted. Gentili had issued a proclamation in French, Italian and Greek, promising that the French would help the Greeks to revive their ancient glory and this had made an excellent impression. 'An immense crowd', wrote Bonaparte, 'were on the seafront to welcome our troops with cries of happiness and enthusiasm, now that they have regained their liberty. At the head of the crowds was the "Papa", or chief of the religion of the country, a learned man already well advanced in years. He approached General Gentili and said: "Frenchman, you will find in this island a people ignorant of those sciences and arts which make nations distinguished, but do not despise them for that reason. They are capable of becoming again what they once were. Learn to appreciate their worth by reading this book." ' The book proved to be the Odyssey.

The islands of Zakynthos, Cephalonia and Levkas, according to Bonaparte, showed the same enthusiasm for their new-found freedom. Trees of liberty were planted in all the villages and everywhere there was hope, so he wrote, that with the help of France, the arts, the sciences and commerce which had previously decayed under the tyranny of oligarchy, would be revived. The future emperor saw the conquest of the Ionian Islands as a stepping stone to India and to establishing French supremacy in the Levant; his report was even more expressive of his own enthusiasm for his latest acquisition than that of the islanders for their new rulers.

Some enthusiasm there undoubtedly was at first, but the French proved too radical, too unsympathetic to local traditions, too narrow in their applications of the principles of the French Revolution for this to last for long. Soon after the burning of the Venetian flags and the coats-of-arms of the nobility, disillusion set in. The French, whom the islanders had hoped would end Venetian corruption and relieve the heavy burden of taxation, were found to be as penniless as their predecessors and equally anxious to raise funds. Gentili's explanation that liberty could not be had for nothing was received with some reserve. When, barely a year after the French takeover, the Russo-Turkish force under Admiral Ousakov progressively invaded the Ionian Islands from the south, they were greeted everywhere as liberators. The French, when they returned in 1807, after the Tsar Alexander had ceded his protectorate of the Ionian Islands to Napoleon at Tilsit, came as straightforward masters, without any promises of fraternity and equality, and were all the more acceptable as such.

Between the collapse of Venice and the arrival of the Russo-Turkish expedition, the social balance in the islands changed hardly at all. The aristocracy maintained their grip, even though titles were theoretically abolished; Count Spiridion Theotokis became president of the reconstituted town council and Count Andreas Sordinas was elected as deputy for Corfu, now that it was one of the three Departments of the French Republic into which the Ionian Islands had been divided. The Orthodox Church not only retained but even strengthened its position. It was the anger of the Orthodox clergy at religion being replaced by philanthropy, at the introduction of the ten-day week whereby Sunday was ignored and, above all, the French disrespect in Corfu towards St Spiridion which roused the peasantry so violently against them. In spite of the imaginative measures which the French planned for bettering education, the installation of the first printing press in 1798, their substitution of Greek for Italian as the official language, the Venetian way of life in effect lived on for many more years.

What, therefore, was the Venetian achievement in the Ionian Islands, bearing in mind the arrogance of her officials and the poverty and corruption at the end? The Venetians are still blamed for many local shortcomings, but there is also a positive side. First and foremost, Venice provided long periods of peace, interrupted only by the two sieges of Corfu, which were separated by nearly two hundred years. The attacks of the corsairs continued, but to a much diminished extent because of the Venetian fleet. By the encouragement of the olive and the currant vine, Venice brought prosperity to the islands as well as to herself. Through tolerance, the local arts and crafts flourished freely; this tolerance was further illustrated by the decision of the Venetian Senate in 1550 to allow Greek schools to exist; from that date no restrictions were imposed on them. While her cultural influence grew, especially after the fall of Crete, it at no time imposed restrictions either of religion or of language, so that the development of post-Byzantine painting into what became virtually a regional school of Italian art was a natural one. This happy blending of two cultures into something unique is seen in the simple baroque architecture of the churches with their Byzantine screens. By allowing the Greek Orthodox Church to maintain its traditions and the peasantry its customs, Venice allowed the Ionian Islands to retain their unique identity as Greeks. By keeping open the door to the West through which the Ionians, even if only the aristocracy, could go to Padua for their education and thus obtain a wider picture of Europe, its arts and thought, Venice made possible the development of what was basically a contemporary Greek culture, which became one of the corner-stones of the modern Greek state when it emerged from the Greek War of Independence. Finally, Venice left as an inheritance the civil and ecclesiastical architecture which have made Corfu and Zakynthos amongst the loveliest towns on the edge of the Mediterranean, a large proportion of which still exists in Corfu today.

Capodistrias and Maitland

❧❦❧

The Esplanade or Spianatha is the social centre of Corfu. It is in two sections: the upper part is grass-covered and has many luxuriant horse-chestnut and lime trees; the lower part which faces the French arcaded buildings, and the cafés shaded by elms and acacias, has a gravel surface and is used both for cricket, still played in Corfu alone among the Ionian Islands, and as a car-park. (For an exciting account of cricket as played in Corfu—and many other good things as well— see *Corfu—Venus of the Isles*, edited by John Forte, British vice-consul in Corfu.)

The Esplanade has always been a place for entertainment. In the eighteenth century, touring groups of actors and acrobats from Italy set up their booths here. During the Russo-Turkish siege of the town in the winter of 1798–1799, the only people allowed to remain within the French defences after all Ionian suspects had been evicted, were a few townspeople and an Italian troupe whose job was to keep up morale. During the British Protectorate, concerts were given here and another British legacy is the elegant wrought-iron bandstand, worthy of Bournemouth or Torquay.

The Esplanade is also the most delightful and informal guide to the history of the island from the eighteenth century onwards. We have already met Count von der Schulenburg outside the bridge leading to the Old Fort. At the southern end of the Esplanade stands the statue of Count John Capodistrias, the first president of modern Greece and perhaps the most distinguished Ionian since Odysseus. Executed in marble by the very able Ionian sculptor, Prosalendis, a pupil of Canova, the statue faces the distant Palace of St Michael and St George at the northern end of the Esplanade; that his right hand is raised in admonition and his face slightly averted from the official residence of the British Lord High Commissioners may

193

be symbolic of the antagonism which developed between him and Sir Thomas Maitland who was responsible for building the Palace.

Capodistrias' origins are typical of many Ionian aristocrats. His family moved from Istria to Corfu in the fourteenth century and their name was inscribed in the *Libro d'Oro* as early as 1471. He himself was born in 1776 and grew up when the intellectual ferment, which developed in France in the middle of the eighteenth century, was spreading far and wide. Although he probably went to the Franciscan monastery school of St Augustine in Garitza, he was a devoted member of the Orthodox Church, perhaps because of his mother who came of a substantial Epirot family.

Like many young Ionian aristocrats, Capodistrias went to Padua University, where he studied medicine from 1794 to 1797 and returned to Corfu during the first French occupation. During the siege of 1798–1799, he was imprisoned because of his refusal to pay taxes but he managed to escape and worked in the Turkish military hospital.

John Capodistrias became a great favourite of Mocenigo, when he came to Corfu as Russian minister in 1802, and was appointed first secretary in the local administration. From this time onwards, he became passionately concerned with the national aspirations of the Ionian Islands and later with those of Greece, but considered that in practice it was essential for a small country to depend upon the protection of a great power. This was one of the reasons why he joined the service of Russia whose aristocratic and ecclesiastical traditions were similar to his own.

Before leaving for Russia, he gained valuable military experience in defending Levkas from the clutches of Ali Pasha. He showed considerable powers of leadership; not only did he obtain assistance from Cephalonia, Zakynthos and other of the Ionian Islands but also from the mainland Klephts; these were armed bands of warriors, often organized on a clan basis, who were in a state of semi-continuous resistance against the Turkish authorities and who maintained themselves by cattle-raising—the word *klepht* implying both heroism and theft. It was here that he achieved friendship with such chieftains as Colokotronis and others, which was to stand him in such good stead when he later became Greek president.

Once in the Russian service, Capodistrias rose steadily in position. He was particularly involved in furthering Russia's aspirations to be the protector of the Orthodox subjects of the Porte. His success led to the Tsar Alexander I appointing him one of his principal secretaries for foreign affairs at the end of the Napoleonic Wars. There is a fine portrait of him painted by Sir Thomas Lawrence at the Congress of Vienna, which hangs in the Waterloo Room at Windsor Castle.

Capodistrias recognized in 1814 that British and Austrian suspicions of Russia were too great to allow her to return as the protecting power over the Ionian Islands. He therefore favoured Britain, in preference to Austria, who had some claims as the heir of Venice. He scotched a rather curious proposal to hand over the islands to the Knights of the Order of St John who had been turned out of Malta by Napoleon, because as Roman Catholics they would be unpopular with an Orthodox population and as a crusading organization they would be hostile towards the Turk.

Capodistrias' support for Britain was not unconditional. Lord Bathurst, the Colonial Secretary, would have been happier if the islands, which were already occupied by British troops, could have passed completely under the British crown. Thanks to Capodistrias' efforts, Britain was given a protectorate only over what was declared to be an independent state with the title of 'The United States of the Ionian Islands'. But Bathurst need not have worried. By appointing Sir Thomas Maitland as the first Lord High Commissioner in 1815, as complete a command was exercised over the islands—at least during the first half of the British Protectorate—as if they had in fact been a crown colony.

Maitland was a man of robust but unattractive character who was known as 'King Tom' to his staff, because of his autocratic methods, and as 'the Abortion' to the Corfiots, because of his supercilious attitude towards them. William Miller writing of him, said that Maitland, 'if able and honest, was a rough soldier, who looked like a bulldog, whose language surprised the elegant Ionians by its coarseness and whose convivial habits disgusted a naturally abstemious people.'

He was born in 1760, the second son of the seventh Earl of Lauderdale. He had a varied career, after being called to the Bar in his early twenties—fighting in India; a radical M.P. in association with Samuel Whitbread and Richard Brinsley Sheridan, when for a time he championed the French Revolution; disentangling British troops from San Domingo during the negro uprising under Toussaint l'Ouverture; and then, in 1806, his appointment as Governor of Ceylon. Here he succeeded Frederick North, the future Lord Guilford. Both of noble birth, both bachelors, both to end their lives in the service of the Ionian Islands, no two men could have been more dissimilar in character. North took the greatest and kindliest interest in the people among whom he found himself and invariably gained their affection. Maitland was not interested in the affection of subject peoples; he was however interested in sound administration, in the proper use of financial and other resources and, above all, in the superiority of Britain to all other nations.

In 1813, Maitland became Governor of Malta. When, in 1814, Corfu capitulated to General Sir James Campbell (who was extremely popular with the Ionians) he, Maitland, successfully pressed his claim to the post.

The Treaty of Paris recognized the United States of the Ionian Islands as a 'free and independent state'. Article Four, however, stated that the 'Lord High Commissioner of the protecting power should regulate the forms of convocation of a Legislative Assembly, of which he shall direct the proceedings, in order to draw up a new constitutional Charter for the States.' Maitland used this clause to draw up a constitution consisting of a Legislative Assembly of forty members and a Senate of five, all of whom were appointed directly by the High Commissioner or from an approved list. At the head was a President, appointed by the Crown on the advice of the High Commissioner, who held the title of 'Highness' and was granted military honours. The High Commissioner appointed a Resident as his Representative on each island and the Senate appointed Regents as heads of the local municipal councils.

Each assembly was elected for a period of five years. It met in Corfu only every other year and then for not more than thirty working days, so that business was usually left unfinished because so much time was spent in picking up threads from the previous session. It had no real power. Any measure that it passed was sent up to the Senate for approval; afterwards it had to receive the sanction of the Lord High Commissioner who had the power of veto.

Maitland's contempt for the organization he created is well illustrated by a story reported by Napier, who said that it was too like Maitland to leave much doubt of its correctness. 'The senate having been assembled in the saloon of the palace, waiting in all form, for his Excellency's appearance, the door slowly opened, and Sir Thomas

23a. b, c, Count von der Schulenburg; Count John Capodistrias; Sir Frederick Adam—all three on Esplanade, Corfu

24. Rotunda erected in memory of Sir Thomas Maitland, on Esplanade, Corfu
25. Church of St Jason and St Sosipater, Corfu

walked in, with the following articles of clothing upon him, namely:
One shirt, which like Tom O'Shanter's friend, the "cutty sark".
"In longtitude was surely scanty".
One red night cap.
One pair of slippers.
'The rest of his Excellency's person was perfectly divested of garments. In this state he walked into the middle of the saloon with his hands behind him, looked round at the assembled Senators and then said, addressing the Secretary of the Senate. "D— them, S—y! tell them all to go to h—ll!" and walked back to his room with a grunt.'

It became at once apparent to the Ionians that they had no substance of power. When Capodistrias returned to Corfu in 1819, he found considerable bitterness against the British. There was a strong pro-Russian party who hoped that Capodistrias would be able to use his influence to improve the situation. Capodistrias later that year went to England, while still in the Russian service, to protest against Maitland's interpretation of the Treaty of Paris. Castlereagh on this occasion upheld Maitland who came to hate Capodistrias in the way he hated all opposition.

Unattractive as Maitland was, he was determined to introduce sound government. On his arrival he found, according to Henry Jervis, 'a peasantry ground down by the usurious loans of their landlords, judges openly bribed, and a treasury containing but three obolis. Soon after the assembling of the first Legislative Assembly, the mortgages were converted into simple contract debts, and the system of advances from landlord to tenant was discontinued; by these measures, the peasantry was released from the bondage in which they were held by their signori, a great blow was struck at the wholesale system of perjury, which was at the disposal of the landlords, while the higher classes had no longer the control of the courts of justice. To free the courts of law from any indirect influence, he kept the executive, the legislative and judicial authorities distinct from one another; and to correct party decisions he established at Corfu a Supreme Court of Justice, consisting of two British and two Ionian judges; to whom an appeal might lie from the several local jurisdictions.'

One of Maitland's greatest achievements was to put Ionian finances on a sound basis. As a result, the Seven Islands were able to bear the cost of the British troops stationed there, the construction of new roads and the repair of the churches and other public works. He increased the salaries of local officials and thus diminished the temptation of bribery; in addition he created new posts in the administration to give wider opportunities for intelligent young Ionians to find employment under the Crown.

What, surprisingly, Maitland did not do was to replace the use of Italian in the courts of law, a language which the peasants did not understand, with Greek. The official *Gazette*, the only newspaper for many years during the Protectorate, was printed only in Italian. Greek did not become obligatory in the administration until 1852.

In 1824 when Maitland died of apoplexy in Malta, while there on an official visit and where he is buried, he left the Ionian coffers well filled. His funeral oration was pronounced by Count Spiridion Voulgaris and the pretty little stone rotunda with Ionic columns on the upper Esplanade, within view of Capodistrias, was erected by Ionian well-wishers. Charles Napier summed him up in these words, Maitland's rule 'was sagacious and on the whole beneficial', but . . . 'He was only fitted to govern under peculiar conditions; he had talent, but not of the first order. Narrow-minded, he saw many things under false lights, was constantly drunk and surrounded by sycophants who thought him a god because he had more intelligence than they.'

Maitland died three years before Capodistrias reached the peak of his career. By 1827, the antagonism between the various Greek parties involved on the mainland in the War of Independence against Turkey had enabled the Turks to regain most of what they had lost. At a meeting of the dissident parties in Troezen in that year, there was a feeling that peace would have to be negotiated, on the condition that some degree of autonomy remained. Capodistrias, as the most distinguished Greek diplomat who was in addition close to the Tsar, was accordingly elected President of Greece on the initiative of Colokotronis.

Between his election and his arrival, the whole situation had been transformed by the destruction of the Turkish fleet at Navarino and the withdrawal to Egypt of Ibrahim Pasha and his troops from the Peloponnesos. Capodistrias' task was therefore to create the administration of the new Greek state emerging, which he did with considerable success. He however failed, as a Corfiot aristocrat and a former Russian diplomat, to appreciate the pride and independence of those whom he was called upon to lead. The appointment as Commissioner of Aegina of his elder brother, Viaro, who behaved as a petty despot, was particularly unpopular. But it was after the successful conclusion of the war against the Turks in September 1829 that real opposition arose. Capodistrias' increasingly autocratic methods, coupled with his reliance on Russian forces to suppress any open assistance, only encouraged further opposition. He was assassinated at Nauplion in October 1831 by members of the Mavromichaeli clan whom he was trying to suppress.

John Capodistrias was succeeded by his younger brother, Agostino, as president. Unfortunately, he blindly followed his brother's policy and showed no desire for the reconciliation which circumstances demanded. As a result, there were soon two rival authorities again, a situation which persuaded the European powers of the need of a foreign prince as distinct from a native president. The choice fell on the Bavarian Prince Otho.

The remains of John Capodistrias are buried in the Platytera Monastery, on the upper road leading to the north of Corfu. Now in good repair and standing on the slopes of Mount Abraham, it was first built in 1744 through the efforts of a monk from Levkas. The French destroyed it in 1798, presumably during the fierce fighting which took place hereabouts against the Turks and Russians, who were joined by reinforcements from Ali Pasha. It was soon rebuilt and the bell-tower, similar in design to that of the church of St Spiridion, added in 1864 to celebrate the union of the Seven Islands with Greece. The inner courtyard is reminiscent of a quadrangle of a smaller Oxford college except that the wall of the chapel, which forms the far side, is painted bright blue and intersected by pillars painted in imitation pink marble. The interior of the chapel, which has windows on the north side only, is dark and cool. The iconostasis and the many icons can only be seen when the electric lights are turned on. The iconostasis, ivory-white painted wood entwined with golden vine tendrils and leaves, frames icons of Italianate apostles painted by Koutouzis. Over the entrance are two large, careful, competent paintings by Kandounis, one of them the 'Washing of the Feet' and the other the 'Last Supper'. On the ceiling is painted a pleasant if uninspiring composition in late eighteenth-century style.

The most interesting pictures however are in the little entrance lobby at the west end (where electric light is again essential if they are to be properly seen). Firstly, there is a fine Tzanes, showing pilgrims, bearing crosses, struggling uphill towards Christ, who is surrounded by the blessed who have reached Him. The pilgrims on the lower slopes are being offered distractions such as wine, women and song and the comforts of the earthly city at the bottom left of the canvas from which they have set forth. Devils with pigtails are standing by to seize any that fail. It must have been painted sometime between 1646 and 1659, a period which coincides with Cromwell's Protectorate and only a few years after John Bunyan wrote *The Pilgrim's Progress*. According to Procopiou, Tzanes was recognized by his contemporaries as well as by historians of post-Byzantine art as the most delicate, the noblest and the most spiritual of Cretan artists.

The 'Fountain of Life', a popular theme with artists of the period, which hangs close by, is also thought to be by Tzanes. It depicts the Virgin and Child arising from the bowl of a fountain. Above them hovering angels form a gothic arch, while round the base stand captains and kings in armour, holding spears and lances. In the top right-hand corner is the domed city of Jerusalem. This picture has a more Italianate feeling about it than that described above.

Perhaps the most distinguished and, in style, the most Byzantine painting here is that of the Apocalypse by Theodore Poulakis. Born in Crete in 1622, he in due course came to Corfu where he died in 1692, He may have travelled to Venice as there are paintings of his there also. Poulakis was distinguished not only by the richness of his imagination but by his ability to paint both in the primitive style of the Cretan school and in that of Italian baroque. This painting is in the former, and shows the inhabitants of the world, rank upon rank of them, standing before Christ in Majesty. Closest to Him are the Twelve Apostles, next the Saints, bishops and martyrs, then the kings and princes and equally important, the monks, and finally the ordinary people who have found salvation. Below in the bottom left-hand corner is the judgment hall where the good are being sorted out from the wicked who are seen departing downwards to the devil and his kind. Finally there are those waiting to be judged; over these there is a strong air of suspense, the families and friends clinging to each other in case they are about to be parted forever.

The tombstone of John Capodistrias is in a little sky-lighted corridor through a door to the right of the iconostasis. It is in Italian marble because at the time it was carved, there were no Greek marble quarries in working order nor any masons either. It is in the simplest good taste, merely recording his name, dates and the word 'Kivernitis' or 'President'. Close by is the tombstone of Photos Tzavellas (1774–1811), a famous Suliot chieftain who fought valiantly in the Epirus against Ali Pasha.

22

The Lord High Commissioners

∽∾∿∽

From our balcony we looked down on to the west side of the Palace of
St Michael and St George. The roof is largely covered with corrugated
iron strips owing to lack of funds. Outside the entrance to the inner
courtyard, Evzone sentries stand guard, complete with long tasselled
soft red caps and the pomponned slippers which, although picturesque, make precision-marching somewhat difficult.

The palace, which was built between 1819 and 1824, stands at the
northern end of the Esplanade. Its main façade faces south and is
flanked on each side by a great triumphal archway, known as the
Gate of the Archangel Michael and the Gate of St George; these in
turn are connected by a Doric portico of twenty fluted columns, in the
centre of which is a broad flight of steps leading into the palace.
Rising above the portico are two upper floors surmounted by an
ornamental parapet on which the emblems of the Seven Islands are
sculpted in stone. Crowning the façade was the figure of Britannia
seated in a barque but she withdrew when the islands were ceded to
Greece; now only the barque remains. The whole gives the impression of a fine neo-Classical building which might well have been built
in England at the end of the eighteenth century for some nobleman or
rich East India merchant, except that the shaded portico is a conces-
sion to the greater intensity of the Mediterranean sun. Behind the
main façade is a courtyard, enclosed by two architecturally unpretentious wings but open to the north and its magnificent scenery.

The palace was erected by Sir Thomas Maitland. He had quickly
realized that a sound way of developing the loyalty of influential
Ionians to the British crown was by the creation of an order of knighthood. 'Hence to gratify the desire for distinction common to man-
kind,' wrote Napier, he 'created an Order of Knighthood called the
Order of St Michael and St George. Surrounded by "stars" which

sparkled in their eyes from every country in Europe, the Ionians had no hope of such honours but from Russia. Their religion which in all other countries was an impediment or a stigma, formed in Russia the merit and the hope of the Greeks; and there, assisted by Capodistrias, they looked forward to honours and emoluments. Maitland saw the necessity of countering this source of influence, which a concurrence of circumstances had opened to Russia.'

The foundation of the Order was approved by the Prince Regent in 1818, its purpose being to provide a means of conferring a mark of royal favour on 'natives of the Ionian Islands and of the island of Malta and its dependencies, and for such other subjects of His Majesty as may hold high and confidential situations in the Mediterranean'. After the end of the British Protectorate, the Order was completely remodelled to do honour to British subjects who distinguished themselves in the service of the Crown overseas. Nevertheless the insignia has remained unchanged. In the centre of the collar is an imperial crown over two winged lions, each lion holding in his forepaw a book and seven arrows. The lion is the Lion of St Mark, acknowledging the Venetian connection and the seven arrows symbolize the Seven Islands. The Star, which is worn on the mantle, likewise has seven silver rays. The colours, now as then, are Saxon blue and magenta.

The first Grand Master of the new order was Maitland himself. When the Senate of the Ionian Islands proceeded to vote him a diamond star of considerable value, he suggested that a suitable edifice be built instead which could serve as a Residence for the Lord High Commissioner, as Treasury for the Order and as a legislative chamber for the Ionian Islands. He may also have had in mind the idea of creating a building which would be at least as impressive as the arcaded buildings put up by the French between 1807 and 1814 on the Esplanade.

The lovely golden stone employed for the palace was imported from Malta in order to associate that other island of which Maitland was Governor with the new Order. Corfu in winter is much wetter than Malta and the stone has suffered somewhat from the weather. The architect was Colonel, later Sir George, Whitmore, R.E. He encountered a number of difficulties, including lack of funds; he was only told about the proposal to use the building as a legislative chamber well after the construction had started. Moreover, he had to rely upon comparatively untrained staff, employing a sergeant and a corporal of his Corps as his house carpenter and his Clerk of Works respectively.

The palace suffered some exterior damage during the bitter fighting between the Italians and Germans in 1943 after the collapse of the
Mussolini regime. When in December 1944, the resistance troops of
General Zervas were transported from the mainland to Corfu by the
Royal Navy, because of overwhelming mainland Communist forces,
many refugees were sheltered in the palace, some of them no doubt
descendants of those Souliots who had fled to Corfu to escape from Ali
Pasha some six generations earlier. Considerable damage to the
interior arose as a result. The present excellent state of repair of the
state rooms first of the Order and afterwards of the King of Greece is
due very largely to the late Sir Charles Peake. When he was Ambassador in Athens in 1952 he conceived the idea of having the state rooms
restored to their original condition as a memorial to the British connection with Greece and as a notable example of the English architec-
tural style of the period. Mr John Collas, the distinguished Corfiot
architect, was responsible for the restoration which was carried out
with the greatest attention to detail.

Visitors to the palace normally enter through the courtyard to the
east wing, on the ground floor of which is the public library and along
whose corridors hang the arms of the local aristocracy. On the first
floor there is an exceptionally fine collection of Chinese and Japanese
ceramics, collected by a former Greek ambassador to Japan; in addition, beyond the central staircase, there is also perhaps the finest
collection of icons in the Ionian Islands, including full-length portraits
of St Cyril of Alexander and St John Damaskinos by Emmanuel Tzanes
and John Tzenos respectively, a 'Fountain of Life' by John Moskos
from the beginning of the seventeenth century and a portrait of St
John the Baptist by Theodore Poulakis. There are also some fine
ancient mosaics from the now battered church of Ayia Kerkyra on the
Palaiopolis Peninsula.

The state rooms on the first floor and the Senate Room on the
ground floor are not normally open to the public. We were however
enabled to visit them. The Senate Room is off the grand marble-paved
entrance hall which is reached from the main entrance on the south
side. It is a simple room, its only embellishment being full-length
portraits of presidents of the Ionian Senate.

At the far end of the hall, which is flanked by Ionic columns, is a
staircase of considerable elegance, supported by a fine wrought-iron
balustrade, which leads to a spacious upper hall. From here the two
great state rooms, the Throne Room and the State Dining Room, are

reached through a rotunda-shaped anteroom. In the Throne Room, the ceiling is decorated with the emblems of the Order. On the wall facing the windows are over-dramatic paintings of the two saints of the Order, while in between them is a copy of Sir Thomas Lawrence's full-length portrait of George IV. The State Dining-room has a vast Regency mahogany dining-table capable of seating at least thirty people, together with chairs of the period. Regency-type wallpapers have been used and the floors laid out in gleaming herring-bone parquet. The great polished mahogany doors gave us special pleasure.

It was here that Maitland entertained the members of the Order. 'The crafty Old Man', Napier wrote, 'laughed in his sleeve when he opened ostentatiously the "Halls of St Michael and St George" and saw the Corfu "galaxy" glittering in all the brilliant decorations of chivalry.' Napier goes on, in his somewhat boisterous, schoolboy humour, to describe a further sartorial embellishment designed by Maitland. This was a 'blue and yellow "*Ionian uniform*"; and a pair of bright yellow breeches became "*the houries of the happy*" at Corfu; a taste which, for a time, infringed upon the laws of decency, for many an "*ambitieux*", whose inexpressibles had passed their grand climacteric, and whose thirst for the distinguished "*unmentionables*" was "*ardent as first love*", dangled between *snip* and *glory*, till hope and repairs delayed, so ordered matters, that to be "*covered with glory*" and *yellow breeches* became physically, morally, and fundamentally desirable on all parts! By these means the desire of honours was fully gratified, without recurrence to Russia'.

The palace was officially opened on St George's Day, 1823, when a grand ball was given. Private Wheeler, who was on guard there, described the fireworks and the blaze of lights from the palace. The dancing continued until five in the morning when Baron Theotokis, then President of the Senate, was escorted home by the military bands and all the colours of the different regiments in the garrison.

Maitland was succeeded as Lord High Commissioner by Sir Frederick Adam (1781–1853), who had previously been the Deputy High Commissioner. His statue in bronze, by Prosalendis, stands in Roman robes on its plinth in the little garden in front of the palace. Of distinguished Scottish ancestry, Adam commanded the light infantry brigade which at the Battle of Waterloo attacked the exposed flank of the advancing Imperial Guard and then routed them, thus giving Wellington the opportunity of a general advance and victory. Perhaps his greatest achievement in Corfu was building the aqueduct

26
Portrait of Dionysios
Solomos, in the possession
of Mr and Mrs
Charalambos Zois,
Zakynthos

27
Bust of Frederick
North, fifth Earl of
Guilford, in public
gardens, Corfu

28
Campiello District,
Corfu

29. British Residency,
Gaios, Paxos

seven miles from above Benitses to Corfu, to provide ample water supplies.

Adam was a handsome, cultivated, rather vain and easily flattered man who enjoyed entertaining lavishly and living grandly. Napier accused him of wanting a guard of lancers and of purchasing a special gold coat at the cost of £300 at the public expense because he was too grand to wear a more ordinary garment on state occasions; unfortunately it was ruined by rain the first time he wore it. 'The Greeks', wrote Napier, 'said that "while Corfu kept the Lord High Commissioner, Cephalonia paid his tailor, and Zante his coachmaker."' Adam was fond of Corfu society and married into the Palatianos family. He and his wife created a brilliant Anglo-Ionian circle of which Dionysios Solomos became the star. This toned down considerably the pro-Turkish bias among the British, which had developed under Maitland and upon which Müller had remarked severely when passing through Corfu in 1821. Adam was perhaps the most popular of all the Lord High Commissioners. Unfortunately having inherited ample funds from his predecessor, he left the administration in debt. In spite of this he was delighted to be voted by the Senate the statue which faces the Esplanade from the Palace of St Michael and St George and in addition the sum of £2,000 for the purchase of a diamond star.

Adam's departure from Corfu in 1832 coincided with the acceptance of the throne of the newly-created Hellenic kingdom by Prince Otho of Bavaria who arrived in Greece in the following year. Now that an internationally recognized Greek state actually existed, the desire of the Ionian Greeks to be united with their fellow countrymen on the mainland began to develop. The sound, if somewhat restrictive, administration of the British and the prosperity it brought in its wake were no real compensation for the lack of political freedom. Subsequent High Commissioners found it increasingly difficult to rule through the constitution drawn up by Maitland and were forced more and more to govern by decree.

Adam's immediate successor, Lord Nugent (1832–1835), was a liberal politician who promised a number of reforms. The Ionian parliament however was too precipitate in making further innovations and was dissolved on instructions from London. Nugent, although he ruled despotically in council, according to Kirkwall, is remembered affectionately by liberals to this day.

Sir Howard Douglas (1835–1841), perhaps the soundest administrator of all, is commemorated by an obelisk on the sea-front of

Garitza Bay on which are recorded his many useful acts. A conservative man and a believer that the islands were not yet ready for full constitutional self-rule, Douglas nevertheless wrote to the Colonial Minister that 'the internal state of the country, the moral and physical state of the people have not been benefited by the British connection so far as to protect us hereafter from the reproach of having attended less to their interests than to our own.' He insisted on his officials learning modern Greek.

One very considerable achievement of Douglas was the creation of the Ionian Bank in 1839. The idea originated from the grant of a state loan in 1833 by Nugent to finance the currant and olive growers who were facing ruin through a general slump in commodity prices, which had begun soon after the end of the Napoleonic Wars, and through the enormous rates of interest charged by moneylenders. Nugent's scheme that loans made from surplus funds in the Ionian Treasury at six per cent—instead of twenty-five to thirty per cent demanded by the moneylenders—should be established on a permanent basis was summarily rejected by the Treasury in London. One of Nugent's aims was to encourage the circulation of money instead of hoarding of coinage as a safety measure. This coinage included not only British gold sovereigns but gold Venetian sequins and silver Spanish, Imperial, Roman and Neapolitan dollars.

Douglas, realizing the importance of Nugent's scheme, persevered towards the establishment of a National Bank to be financed first within the Ionian Islands and later, when this effort had failed through lack of local support, through funds raised in Britain. The prospectus pointed out that the 'Ionian Islands are so advantageously situated with respect to the Mediterranean, the Adriatic and the Levant, that the operations of the Bank are capable of easy and advantageous extension over a wide range, and thus the project established may be the nucleus of a great and important undertaking.' In fact, the Ionian Bank was to expand in due course into Greece, Cyprus and Egypt. It quickly gained strong Ionian as well as British support and the reliance placed on its issued notes was a great stabilizing factor during the British Protectorate and afterwards. Today, the Ionian Bank, London, has become completely independent of the Greek branches, which in 1957 were incorporated into what is now the Ionian and Popular Bank of Greece.

Little is remembered of Mr Mackenzie who succeeded Lord Nugent in 1841, except that he was a liberal, well-liked locally for that reason, and the only High Commissioner after Maitland whose revenue was greater than his expenditure. Mackenzie's successor, Lord Seaton, came to Corfu in 1843 from long service in Canada where he had ended as Governor-General. As Sir John Colbourne, he had commanded the 52nd regiment in Adam's brigade at Waterloo and is generally credited with the initiative for the brigade's successful attack on the Imperial Guard. Tall, exceedingly handsome, of immense dignity and courtesy, he was personally very popular with all. For a time the Duke of Cambridge served on his staff. He took a great interest in local conditions and opinion. His administration was at first conservative; this was however a period when King Otho in Athens was being forced to grant a more liberal constitution, which was keenly noted by the Ionians, whose wish for union with Greece became the stronger.

Then came 1848, the year of revolutions throughout Europe, with the disturbances in Cephalonia. Seaton thereupon immediately decided to introduce a highly liberal constitution, including freedom of the press and of election despite the doubts of Earl Grey, then Colonial Minister. As a result of these reforms, which Kirkwall and others thought hastily conceived, the popular movement for union with Greece developed rapidly. The newly created free local press at once began a vituperative attack against the British as oppressors. Seaton, strongly criticized by those who wanted a continuation of British rule, firmly defended himself in the *Edinburgh Review* of January 1853, by saying that after the liberal reforms granted all over Europe in 1848, it was not possible to maintain a constitution which all knew to be a mockery. In any case . . . 'the prospect is scarcely more delightful than that the islands of the Ionian Sea should form a district of Greece, as soon as ever a prosperous and powerful Greek nation shall come into existence.'

Sir Henry Ward, who succeeded Seaton as High Commissioner from 1849 to 1855, had to carry the full brunt of increased Unionist activity which arose from these reforms, not only in the Cephalonian uprising, which took place soon after his arrival, but at the centre of government in Corfu where he had to prorogue the Ionian parliament and rule by edict. It was during this period that the Assembly moved from the palace to the Ionian Parliament Building at the corner of Zambelli Street, quite close to where the British vice-consulate is now situated.

Sir John Young, Ward's successor, was a man remarkable for his

THE LORD HIGH COMMISSIONERS

mildness and gentleness rather than for his aggressive qualities, yet the opposition grew ever more vocal and now completely controlled the Legislative Assembly. The public galleries of the Chamber were crowded with rabble who made it impossible for anyone to voice sentiments with which they were not in agreement. Young became involved in quarrels with the local municipal authorities which were reported back to the Colonial Minister in London. One of these was that he had failed to show sufficient respect to a procession of St Spiridion.

The Colonial Minister did not give as much support to Young as some felt he deserved and then, in November 1858, announced the appointment of Mr W. E. Gladstone, 'whose renown as a Homeric scholar will justly commend him to the sympathies of an Hellenic race', as a special commissioner to inquire into 'the causes which obstructed the good government of the Islands; and into all matters affecting the well-being and contentment of the inhabitants thereof.' Young found himself in the unenviable position of entertaining a future prime minister, who proceeded to advocate Young's recall and himself to accept the High Commissionership, which he resigned two weeks later because of English political commitments. Gladstone, who visited all the Ionian Islands except Kythera, and Athens as well, had a number of useful political reforms to recommend, but he could not understand that it was not reform that the Ionians wanted but union with Greece.

The last High Commissioner, Sir Henry Storks, a soldier, succeeded Gladstone. Edward Lear found him a sympathetic personality, but Kirkwall had little to say in his favour. Certainly Storks seems to have behaved generally like a despot and disgracefully over the case of Sir George Marcoran. Marcoran was one of the two Ionian supreme judges, who were inexplicably not reappointed to positions—which in Marcoran's case he had held for nearly twenty-five years—thus losing a well-merited pension. Storks implied that the two Ionian judges had led their two English colleagues astray in their appreciation of the political situation, notwithstanding that both the latter were exceptionally intelligent.

In 1861, the British government of which Gladstone was a member was still insisting on maintaining the *status quo*. In 1862, however, the expulsion of the increasingly unpopular King Otho from the Greek throne and the search for a successor changed conditions. Although warned by Britain that for international reasons an offer of the Greek throne to Prince Alfred, Duke of Edinburgh, could not be accepted, even if supported by a plebiscite, Greece voted overwhelmingly in his favour. Britain maintained her position but promised to help find a suitable candidate. At the same time she agreed to the union of the Ionian Islands with Greece.

Prince George of Denmark proved finally acceptable to all concerned and Britain proceeded to carry out her promise of ceding the Ionian Islands to Greece. Even at this stage there was a small party, mainly men of property, who wanted the British connection to remain. They were forgotten however in the universal rejoicings, so also was the understandable disaffection over the destruction of the fortifications and over British Treasury insistence that Ionian government pensions not only of Ionian but also of British personnel should be taken over by the Greek government. On June 6th, 1864, the youthful King George of the Hellenes landed in Corfu, four days after the departure of the last Lord High Commissioner, and immediately proceeded to St Spiridion to celebrate a Te Deum.

23

The Ionian Academy

❧

Christian Müller described Corfu during the first decade of the British Protectorate as completely Italian, 'Italian manners prevail in the interior of the houses, in the public amusements and in the language; in fact they have been adopted by all, except the lower orders of the people . . . If you go into the interior of the families, you find as little relish for society and domestic pleasures as in Italy. All their affections are turned abroad towards public assemblies, the theatre, promenades, and coffee houses.'

Müller went on to suggest that the manners of the English did not compare with those of the Venetians, Russians and French; he obviously felt that they had a superiority complex. He was compelled to admit however that the city of Corfu gained in many respects through the British. 'It has become much cleaner and better lighted. Houses, colonnades, and palaces have been built; in the neighbourhood of the city, gardens, parks and country-seats have arisen.' Here Müller must have been thinking of the development of the suburbs of Garitza, where there are Kensington overtones. 'Many English shops have been opened, and for ready cash every luxury and comfort of life may be procured. The British only purchase what comes from Old England. They even extend this patriotism to the votaries of Aphrodite Pandaemes, although I could not learn whether their custom-house officers class them among the articles of luxury. Once a whole cargo of these naiads were imported from the Thames.' An unusual sidelight, if true, upon recreation facilities available in this pre-Victorian era, presumably for the troops.

Certainly the contrast between the British and the Ionians was often a subject for comment. Aubrey de Vere, the Victorian poet, visited the Ionian Islands where his brother's regiment had been posted; and subsequently described his travels in *Picturesque Sketches of Greece and Turkey*, published in 1850. 'From Zante I sailed to Patras in an English steamer and have seldom been more amused than by the contrast between English manners and those of the islanders among whom I had lately been sojourning. The unceremonious vitality of the Greeks makes even a lively Frenchman look dull by comparison. Judge then of my astonishment when I find myself in the midst of Englishmen, and of Englishmen recently come from home. I could never sufficiently admire their sublime tranquility, or, rather, that wonderful *vis inertiae*, which seems sufficient of itself to keep the ship steady in a storm, and which would, no doubt, have made even sea-sickness a dignified condition. I gazed almost with awe at their smooth-brushed hats, which the Aegean breezes hardly dared to ruffle,—their unblemished coats and immaculate boots, on which several of them gazed more attentively than they would have done at the Leucadian rock. Happen what might, their magnaminous indifference to all chances and changes, not connected with business or duty, preserved them from "all astonishment". Had a whale risen close beside us and spouted its foam in their faces, they would, I believe, have contented themselves with observing that "it was not in good taste". To one of them I spoke, by way of experiment, of Sappho's leap and the Leucadian rock; "Yes", he replied, "I have heard that it was the scene of a distressful accident." I must say, however, in justice to my new acquaintances, that they appeared thorough gentlemen.' De Vere was not incorrect in referring to the Ionian Sea as the Aegean as this name was generally used at that time to describe all the seas around Greece.

Napier had hard words to say about the way the officers pampered themselves. 'A pretty sight, truly, to see officers unable to show their noses without parasols. I do not say that an officer is never to use an umbrella, but it is very unsoldier-like to see officers on duty with parasols while the private soldiers are exposed to the sun or the rain— these are things all should take in common.' But this was the age of umbrellas and Murray, in his 1854 guide to Greece, recommends 'a large and stout cotton umbrella' as protection against rain and sun. 'A white umbrella should be purchased at Corfu or Athens in hot weather.' An English shooting jacket and wide-awake was, he added, the most respectable and respected travelling costume throughout the Levant.

Professor Ansted, who visited Corfu in 1863, reported that 'the habits of the English at Corfu are somewhat monotonous; and our countrymen do not mix much with the natives. There is, of necessity, a considerable amount of official and formal division into sets—the civil and military departments keeping, in some measure, apart. Few of the residents or officers take interest in anything beyond the ordinary occupations of their respective professions.' No wonder Edward Lear, who loved the beauty of the island and lived there for long stretches, wrote to Chichester Fortescue, later Lord Carlingford, in 1858, 'just figure to yourself the conditions of a place where you never have any breadth or extent of intellectual society and yet cannot have any peace or quiet.' Again, in 1861, he wrote, 'Everybody was overwhelmingly hospitable, from the Palace downwards:—but as the balls, and small monotonous whist or tea-parties are wholly out of my line in this very very very small tittletattle place, and as moreover night walks from this side of the city to the other don't suit me, not to speak of the late hours and a multitude of new and uninteresting acquaintances, I decline all visiting on the plea of health and antiquity ... this tone of social life bores me even worse than total loneliness ...'

Yet life, if humdrum, must have been pleasant however undemanding. The late afternoon was spent in strolling to Kanoni and back. For the officers and senior officials there was good shooting in season, especially at Butrinto on the Epirot coast, now part of Albania. There was a race track just beyond Mandouki on the coast where meetings were often held. The absence of foxes did not deter the officers of the garrison. Instead they had paper-hunts. A bold rider went ahead across the country, dropping pieces of paper at intervals. 'The field,' wrote Ansted, 'then follows; and it becomes a kind of steeple-chase, everyone endeavouring to take the leaps and ride over the difficult ground that the leader has marked out. As the whole country is un-enclosed, and there are plenty of small difficulties, the sport is often very exciting; but, not unnaturally, the cultivators complain that their crops are injured, and their land cut up by this wild romp.' And, of course, there were picnic parties to Paleocastritsa, to Kassiopi and elsewhere.

Towards the end of the Protectorate, Lear remarked on how local politics were affecting society. 'Society is far less amalgamated than in former years. . . . And so, the aspect spiritual of this little piggy-wiggy island is much as a very little village in Ireland would be—peopled by Orangemen and papists—and having all the extra fuss and ill-will produced by a Court and small officials—more or less with or against a resident crowded garrison.'

Visitors to the islands then were plentiful. Many families took rooms or villas for the winter or spring to escape the harshness of the English winter, although this custom seems to have died out with the Protectorate. It was on these rather than on the Ionian families that the resident English came to depend for entertainment. It was not only the question of politics; it must also have been to some extent the question of language. The Ionians are gifted linguists and so were the English in earlier days when a knowledge of French and Italian was normal among the educated classes. With the development of empire, however, the gift for languages seems to have disappeared and, therefore, the ability to communicate became that much less easy. But there were other reasons as well. Ionian women had not taken their full place in society, certainly not as in the west. Again the Ionians are abstemious, preferring ginger-geer, which they still brew, to beer and, according to Kirkwall, 'the want of large and even of considerable fortunes, is another impediment to the pleasures of society . . . But,' he continued, 'the Ionians are *naturally* an agreeable, quick and hospitable people. If they cannot give champagne dinners to the English it is for want of something less easily obtainable than good will.' And so, with much courtesy no doubt upon both sides, the two groups went their own ways.

This emphasis on the monotony of life in the British colony by various writers is oddly in contrast with the development of Corfu, not Athens, as the principal Greek literary and intellectual centre throughout much of the nineteenth century. This started with the exceptionally pleasant Anglo-Ionian society under the leadership of Sir Frederick and Lady Adam. They had adopted as their own daughter a niece of Lady Adam, Margarita Alvana, who later, as Margarita Alvana-Migniati, became a well-known writer and patron of the arts in Florence; her husband, a member of the respected Migniati family of Cephalonia, was a painter of some competence. We read of Edward Lear being offered the directorship of a School of Art to be established in Corfu during the High Commissionership of Sir John Young, a post which he refused, and wonder whatever happened to the School of Fine Arts founded in Corfu in 1805 by Prosalendis, later to be re-established during the second French occupation and again in 1815 by the same artist.

The French, during their second occupation of Corfu, had started to cultivate the considerable intellectual ferment, developing in Zakynthos as well as in Corfu, by the creation of an Academic Society. Its purpose was that its members should publish works every six months on their researches into agriculture, manufacturing and other subjects of particular interest to the Ionian Islands. It also set out to run a number of courses on such subjects as elementary physics, political economy and criminal law. This Society disappeared with the collapse of the French. The arrival of the British, however, contributed further to the development of the intellectual life of the Seven Islands, by providing a sound economic basis to enable it to flourish and particularly through the creation of the Ionian Academy by Lord Guilford. A marble bust of him, by Prosalendis, stands in the little public garden off the Esplanade overlooking the canal and the Old Fort. The long distinguished features of the great Philhellene are somewhat chipped and it is difficult to form an impression of his personality from this work.

Maitland, as we have seen, torpedoed the Ithaka site and then delayed all further progress in Corfu. The project suddenly came alive again after his death in 1824, when the Senate passed a resolution for the establishment of the University or Academy with the four faculties of theology, jurisprudence, medicine and philosophy. By this time the Palace of St Michael and St George had been completed, so the now vacated Venetian palace of the Provveditore-Generale became the university's home. At the end of the first academic year in 1825, the number of students enrolled amounted to two hundred and eleven and the staff of professors to fourteen. This was the only university to exist among Greeks until the foundation of Athens university in 1837. Guilford was throughout lavish with his own treasure and unsparing in his efforts to get others to contribute as well, which many did. By the end of 1827, the library contained as many as twenty-one thousand volumes, many of them of great value from Guilford's own library.

Part of the funds, however, came as a subsidy from the local administration which was always less sanguine than Guilford himself about the results to be achieved. There was understandably little enthusiasm for his proposal to found a Chair of Sanskrit and there was unfortunately an element of ridicule in the customs and costumes which he encouraged. Napier described him in a letter written in 1819, 'Lord Guilford is here, a queer fish, but very pleasant. He dined with Sir Thomas, and entered the room at the head of twelve men, professors in black, with powdered heads, bandy legs, cocked hats under their short arms, and snuff-boxes in hand—brimful with snuff, and Greek. ... All the Greeks would speak Italian, the Italians English, the English French and Italian mixed, and the French all the five languages together. . . . Babel and confusion of tongues. Lord Guilford was very pleasant, addressing every person in a different language, and always in that which the person addressed did not understand.'

Napier again met him in 1825, 'Lord Guilford is here again . . . He goes about dressed up like Plato, with a gold band round his mad pate and flowing drapery of a purple hue. His students' dress is very pretty, and said to be taken from ancient statues.' The academic dress consisted of a tunic and chlamys. The students had their hair bound in the manner of Hermes and were shod in buskins of red leather which reached to the knee. Faculties were distinguished by the colour of their garments—a citron tunic and orange chlamys were the colours of the medical faculty, while law for example was distinguished by a light-green tunic and violet chlamys.

Guilford unexpectedly died after a short illness in England in October 1827. The Ionian Official *Gazette* of November 3rd recorded, 'Letters have lost in him one of their most powerful protectors, England one of her most erudite peers, Society one of its most beneficent and honourable members, the youth of Greece its most loving father and benefactor.' And with his death the more grandiose aspects of his plans collapsed. Napier, in spite of his teasing references to Guilford in personal letters home, appreciated what he was trying to do and blames Frederick Adam for what followed. A solicitor, acting on behalf of Lord Sheffield, Guilford's heir, wrote to the Secretary-General of the Ionian Senate, ordering the return to London of Guilford's collection of manuscripts—and the instructions were carried out! The solicitor wrote again, demanding the return of the library, and most of this was likewise sent to London, including many volumes which had been donated by such well-wishers as the King of Denmark and Count Mocenigo. A codicil to Guilford's will, whereby all the treasures were to become the property of the university on condition that the local government endowed it with £3,500 yearly, was ignored.

Adam eventually announced plans for a much-reduced scheme for the Academy, which nevertheless continued to play a valuable role in the Ionian Islands. In 1837, it was moved from the palace in the Old Fort, which was pulled down to make way for new barracks, to a corner site at the southern end of the Esplanade, close to the statue of Capodistrias. Further developments took place especially under Sir George Bowen, who became Rector in 1847, soon after leaving Oxford. But as there was no encouragement for students to study at English universities, Ionians continued to go to Padua, Pisa and, after its foundation, to Athens University to obtain the broader view. When Ansted visited the Academy in 1863, he found that the number of students in each faculty rarely exceeded twenty. After 1863, it was closed and its faculties merged with those of Athens University. 'In consequence,' says Professor Romilly Jenkins in his biography of Solomos, 'the valuable and characteristic civilization of the Ionian Republic became merged and lost in the new cultural centre of Athens.'

The library which Guilford founded, even after a large part of it had been sent back to England, survived and many valuable books and manuscripts were added to it. A great tragedy of the war was the destruction which took place in the savage fighting between Germans and Italians in 1943; not only were fourteen churches with precious examples of the Ionian School of painting destroyed but this irreplaceable library completely burnt out.

The Ionian Academy, while being the centre of intellectual activity, was not the only creative body which came into existence during the Protectorate. There was an association founded by the President of the Senate, Count Emanuel Theotokis, for the encouragement of the Greek language and a society whose chosen task was to translate the Bible into demotic Greek. Other associations were started, such as that for the encouragement of music by Nicolas Mantzaros, a composer best known because he wrote the music of the Greek National Anthem; the Philological Society which provided a reading room and opportunities for debating and, in 1851, the Ionian Association to promote agriculture, industry and the arts.

These associations merely reflected the existence in Corfu of an exceptionally talented group of writers, whose first and foremost was Dionysios Solomos, protégé of Sir Frederick and Lady Adam. The patronage of the arts continued under Adam's successors. Lord Nugent founded a literary periodical called *The Ionian Anthology* to which Solomos contributed. Lady Douglas and, much later, Sir Henry and Lady Ward were equally appreciative of the poet, even though by this time he was as often drunk as sober.

If Solomos was the brightest star in the constellation, there were other highly talented men whose creative abilities were to now flourish —historians, such as Mustoxidis, Ionnis Romanos, Emanuel Theotokis and Spiridion Lambros, and poets like Valaoritis, Kalvos, Mavilis, Markoras and Polylas, most of whom taught or studied at the

Ionian Academy. Vretos wrote, 'What would have been the condition of learning in Greece when she became a kingdom, I know not, if there had been no Earl of Guilford, and if he had not founded a university in Corfu which gave instruction to nearly all the doctors, lawyers, professors, teachers, and civil functionaries of the present kingdom.'

24

Palaiopolis

~~~

Every year, on the day after Ascension Day, a feast is held at the village of Analypsis on the highest point of the Palaiopolis Peninsula beyond Garitza Bay. These church festivals are popular rural occasions, at which quantities of lamb are eaten washed down with buckets of local wine, to the accompaniment of dancing and music, but the feast or 'panayiri' at Analypsis is one of the most celebrated in Corfu and is always crowded with Corfiots and tourists. Today Analypsis—whose name means 'Ascension'—consists of a handful of whitewashed cottages and ancient olive groves high above the sea with distant views of Epirus. It is also the site of the acropolis of the ancient city of Corcyra.

We know from Thucydides that the Corinthians colonized the island in 734 B.C. to secure their lines of communication with Magna Graecia and Sicily. The prosperity of the colony must have grown rapidly, because it was able to stand up to the mother-city, against whom the first recorded sea-battle in Greek history was successfully fought in 665 B.C. Subsequently we hear of Corinthian despots ruling the island and of the despicable act of Periander in sending off to Asia Minor three hundred boys belonging to leading Corcyrean families to be made into eunuchs. Herodotus recounts how they were able to take sanctuary in a temple of Artemis in Samos; here they were aided by the inhabitants who surreptitiously fed them until the Corinthian guards got tired of waiting for them to be driven out by starvation and left the island.

By 435 B.C., when the islanders were again independent of Corinth, trouble arose inside the colony of Epidamnus, the site of modern Durazzo, and Corcyra and Corinth, each of whom regarded herself as the city's founder, supported opposing factions. Corinthian reinforcements for their party in Epidamnus were met by a Corcyrean fleet off the Sivota Isles and defeated, the Corinthians losing fifteen warships. The Corcyreans now had temporary control of the Ionian Sea and ravaged Levkas, always a loyal supporter of Corinth, and the port of Kylline opposite Zakynthos.

This situation did not last long. Corcyra, rightly fearing a return of the Corinthians, sent envoys to Athens to negotiate a treaty. The Corinthians did likewise, as Athens was then the leading naval power in Greece. The Athenians sided with Corcyra and sent a squadron into Ionian waters to counterbalance the massive Corinthian fleet which had been built up to subdue Corcyra. Another great sea-battle was fought off the Sivota Isles in which the Corcyreans would have been defeated had they not been supported by ten Athenian warships which were reinforced by a further twenty half-way through the battle. The immediate results were inconclusive, but Corinth now had a grudge against Athens—and the long and disastrous Peloponnesian War had started.

The Corcyrean fleet was then among the three largest in Greece, which implies excellent harbour and boatbuilding facilities on the island. The main harbour was in the bay or lagoon of Khalikiopoulo, over whose shallow waters the airport has been built from the rubble of war-scarred Corfu. Then it must have been much deeper and its narrow entrance protected by fortifications. Timber must have been plentiful, judging by the density of coniferous trees on the Palaiopolis peninsula; these, like the Cephalonian firs, would have been ideal for shipbuilding. There was however a second port, described by Thucydides, as 'facing towards the mainland'. This was in Garitza Bay, immediately to the north of the peninsula, where the village of Anemomilos is situated.

The Peloponnesian War had tragic effects upon Corcyra which was split into two warring factions as Epidamnus had previously been. On the one side were the aristocrats, supported by the Spartan alliance and on the other, the democrats who favoured the Athenian cause. Trouble started with the return of prisoners released by Corinth who had been bribed or brainwashed to win Corcyra away from Athens. Both sides behaved brutally and ruthlessly. Overall, the democrats triumphed. Thucydides, although naturally sympathetic to the Athenian cause, does not whitewash the democrats in Corcyra who put their enemies to death, ostensibly in defence of democracy but in fact on grounds of personal hatred, or because this was an excellent way of wiping out a debt. 'There was death in every shape and form. . . . People went to every extreme and beyond it. There were fathers who killed their sons; men were dragged from the temples and butchered on the very altars; some were actually walled up in the temple of Dionysus and died there.' This breakdown of law and order which first occurred in Corcyra spread throughout the city-states embroiled in the war.

Nevertheless the aristocratic party in Corcyra managed to survive the first holocaust and continued to cause trouble, raiding the town and surrounding countryside from a strong point situated either on Ayii Deka or Pantocrator. Eventually these exiles, when surrounded by Athenian forces, laid down their arms on agreed conditions. The democrats however, seized them by a trick, using agents provocateurs to make them break their agreement, and butchered them all, except for those who preferred to take their own lives; their women were sold into slavery.

Through most of the war, the Corcyreans were active at sea and together with contingents from Cephalonia, Zakynthos and Kythera, joined the Athenian expedition to Sicily in an attempt to gain control of the main source of Corinthian revenue. It was probably in Garitza Bay that the great fleet assembled before setting forth. After the disaster at Syracuse, however, we find no further mention of Corcyra in Thucydides' account of the war.

The story is then taken up by Xenophon. An aristocratic party again emerged in Corcyra with a policy of neutrality, but fell under Spartan domination at the beginning of the fourth century. In 377 B.C. however it joined the second Athenian confederacy. As a result, Corcyra was besieged by a powerful Spartan fleet under Mnasippos and would have fallen if the Spartan mercenaries had not revolted through lack of pay. The islanders made a successful sortie, Mnasippos was killed and the siege lifted. The main interest arising from this episode is Xenophon's references to the wealth and fertility of the island; so well did the troops live off the land that they would drink only wines with a good bouquet.

Corcyra was involved in the turbulent conditions of the fourth century B.C. which saw the rise of Macedon and the decline of Athens. For most of the third century, the island was ruled first by Syracuse and then by King Pyrrhus of Epirus until it came under Roman control in 299 B.C. Thus ended the island's independence. Corcyra then became the principal naval base for the Roman expansion into Macedonia and Greece, and was inevitably embroiled in the various power struggles during the Roman Republic and afterwards. The island no doubt thrived commercially because of its fertility and as a port of call between Rome and Greece. When the Roman Empire was divided into two, the Ionian Islands were ruled from Constantinople until the beginning of the thirteenth century.

The heights of Analypsis must always have been a fortified stronghold until the move to the Old Fort took place at the end of the Byzantine period. From the wireless station, there is a sweeping view over the wooded park of Mon Repos—the summer retreat of the Greek royal family—to the Old Fort with Pantocrator away to the north-west. It is from here that a steeply sloping path, partly stone-flagged, twists down through luxuriant vegetation to the ancient Kardaki Spring, which was used for watering the Royal Navy during the British Protectorate. Just to the north of the spring is a little jetty where the Navy came ashore. Above the spring, just inside the park of Mon Repos, is the site of the temple of Kardaki, which dates from the sixth century B.C. It was discovered in 1822, when British engineers were putting the spring into good repair; only a few stones remain on the site which is however quite clearly marked. The Kardaki Spring itself has special qualities. If you drink of its waters, you will always return to Corfu. Although we needed no such incentive, we cupped our hands together and drank, finding it slightly rusty in taste, but suffered no ill effects.

Today, the remains of the ancient city which covered a site larger, until recently, than that of the modern town have almost completely disappeared. Sir George Wheler wrote in 1675, 'It [the ancient city of Palaiopolis] stood on a promontory to the South of the present City, separated from it by a little Bay of about a mile or two over. The abundance of Ruins and Foundations, which are to be seen there, do sufficiently demonstrate it to have been so. The ground it covered is almost an Island, and therefore anciently called Chersopolis. It had on the South-West a good large Port for Vessels of those days; but now has hardly water enough for small Shallops. . . . Besides abundance of Foundations of Temples, Arches, Pillars and Marble Inscriptions have been dug up here and employed to build the new Fortifications of the present City.' Here, then, is the explanation. The ruins of the ancient city were used to build the New Fort and later the defences of Mount Abraham and San Salvator.

A few remains however have been found in addition to those at Kardaki. During the second French occupation, General Donzelot decided to add to the town's southern defences by opening up the ancient moat which ran from Lake Khalikiopoulo to the far end of the Bay of Garitza, just before the road turns inland towards Kanoni. As a result, traces of the Temple of Artemis were discovered. Also revealed was a small section of the northern walls of the ancient city which proved to be of ancient Greek origin with Byzantine additions; this stands at the edge of Lake Khalikiopoulo.

The most dramatic discovery made in Corfu, however, was that of the famous Gorgon's pediment of the Temple of Artemis which dominates the main hall of the new Corfu Museum of Antiquities in Garitza. The terrifying central figure of the Gorgon, over nine feet high, is shown in a running position with her eyes and tongue protruding. Twisting serpents form her hair and serve as a belt for her tunic, which would originally have been painted in red, the entwining snakes in blue. Either side of the main figure are two reclining beasts, part lioness, part panther. The work dates back to the beginning of the sixth century. Here are intimations of that earlier, more archaic period before Zeus replaced the Great Goddess as the principal deity. The pediment was dug up as recently as 1911 during an excavation financed by Kaiser Wilhelm II who summoned Dörpfeldt to supervise it and who eventually published an account of its discovery in 1924 from his home of exile at Doorn, Holland. Of the same period is the recumbent lioness of Menekrates, found near Marasli Street in Garitza, not far from the obelisk to Sir Howard Douglas. This beast has a naturalness which is lacking in the Gorgon's panthers.

If the pre-Roman remains are few, those from the Roman period are even fewer. Close to the moat, and behind the Olive Cultivation Institute, the foundations of some Roman baths have been discovered together with fragments of a fine mosaic pavement; the quality however does not compare with the mosaics at Nea Scala in Cephalonia. There are also a few fragments of a fine mosaic pavement in the garden of a village house at Benitses, the little fishing village on the east coast of the island under the heights of Ayii Deka.

Christianity was brought to the island during the reign of the Emperor Caligula by Jason, Bishop of Iconium, and Sosipater, Bishop of Tarsus, who were martyred by being burnt to death inside a bronze bull. They were afterwards canonized. The lovely Byzantine church which bears their names—the only one of this period in the Ionian Islands—is in the village of Anemomilos, but out of sight from the road to Kanoni. It stands within its own gardens which in summer are ablaze with roses. The priest is renowned locally as an enthusiastic gardener and, we were told, corresponded with the Royal Horticultural Society. We asked him about this while enjoying a little sweet cake which his wife kindly insisted that we tasted; his face lit up and, after rummaging in the drawer of a table, produced a packet of Carter's seeds.

The church was built in the twelfth century. It is in the shape of a cross and surmounted by an octagonal domed tower. The walls are built from great blocks of stone into which are sunk low, narrow windows under Romanesque arches. Inside, the vestibule is separated from the body of the church by three pillars which originally formed part of a temple, two of them of black and the third of white marble. Here are two fine full-length icons, one of each saint, by Emmanuel Tzanes. The interior of the church is partly whitewashed and partly covered by wallpaper simulating marble—a tasteless feature found in many churches, including the Corfiot Metropolis—but in the northeast corner behind the iconostasis are signs of frescoes which must originally have covered most of the walls.

Two important refugees from Byzantium after 1453 are buried here—Catherine Zaccaria, wife of the Despot Thomas Palaiologus, a brother of the last Emperor, and George Phrantzes. Catherine preferred to stay in Corfu rather than continue to Rome with her husband, whose unruliness in the Peloponnesos had weakened the Byzantine cause; the purpose of his journey was to sell to the Vatican for a considerable reward the head of St Andrew the Apostle, one of the great treasures of the Greek Orthodox Church, now recently returned to the Archbishop of Patras. Phrantzes had been the faithful secretary of the last Emperor and had carried out a number of diplomatic missions on his behalf. After imprisonment by the Turks he and his wife eventually escaped; both took religious vows, he himself joining the monastery then attached to the church.

At the far end of Anemomilos, opposite the gates of Mon Repos, are the remains of Ayia Kerkyra, the oldest church on the island, tucked away behind a private house so that it can only partly be seen from the road. Only the facade stands as the church was gutted by a bomb during the recent war. The site was originally that of a temple, dating back to the fifth century B.C. The Romans subsequently built here. In the fifth century A.D., a Christian basilica was erected which was subsequently burnt down by Saracen raiders. Two further churches were built during the course of centuries, the second of which was badly damaged by the Turks during the first siege of Corfu. Again restored, it lived on until 1943.

The villa of Mon Repos, belonging to the Greek Royal family, is not visible from the road. A solid late Georgian building with a pillared portico, it stands in a pleasant well-wooded park. It was originally built for Sir Frederick Adam and his Corfiot bride, who is best remembered because of Private Wheeler's description of her, 'her complexion is dark, features regular, eyes black as sloes so is her hair, but the beard of her upper lip would ornament an huzzar'. The house, originally called 'Casino', was meant for a country retreat but was much too close to the town for that purpose and was apparently rarely used as such. For a time during Sir Howard Douglas' rule, it was placed in the control of the Ionian Senate for use as a religious college, but later re-occupied by Mackenzie, the fifth Lord High Commissioner. The Empress of Elizabeth stayed here before she acquired the site of the Achilleion. Prince Philip, Duke of Edinburgh, was born here.

At the southern end of the peninsula is the One Gun Battery at Kanoni with its justly famous view. From thickly wooded slopes which drop steeply to the sea below, you look south down the green eastern flanks of the island. To the right is Lake Khalikiopoulo with the villa-dotted hills of Perama beyond which used to supply ancient Corcyra with water. The magic of the scene derives particularly from the two tiny islands, on the nearer of which is built the whitewashed Convent of Vlacherna with its fine example of an Ionian belfry. The Convent island is connected with Kanoni by a causeway but it is a steep climb down to sea level and the buildings themselves are generally said to be uninteresting. We prefered to relax over a drink at the fine Tourist Pavilion just above the car-park.

The further island is known as Mouse Island because of its shape. Those who believe that the harbour of the Phaeacians was situated in Lake Khalikiopoulo accept it as the ship turned to stone by Poseidon in revenge for taking Odysseus home to Ithaka. Tall cypresses surround the two or three houses on it. The German romantic painter, Boecklin, who spent some time on Corfu, is said to have been inspired by Mouse Island when painting 'The Isle of the Dead'. The spirit of this heavy German extravaganza is so remote from anything on Corfu that it is hard to imagine that this is true.

25

Paleocastritsa

∾

The best time to explore the island is in early morning, so as to avoid the midday heat. Accordingly we had left Corfu town for Paleocastritsa soon after eight o'clock. We drove along by the port, with its long line of moored yachts, then bumped over the narrow road through the sepia-stuccoed suburb of Mandouki, the home of the fishermen and brick-makers—rough, independent, intransigent. The French in 1798 razed the village to the ground because of the persistent enmity of its inhabitants. Beyond the abbatoir, the road improves; here on the seaward side, was situated the race-course during the British Protectorate. The road, after it joins that from the Platytera monastery, is wide and well-made and Corfiots drive down it at an alarming speed. The number of cars on the island has increased rapidly in recent years and elaborate petrol-filling stations are now in evidence between the town and the Gouvia crossroads, beyond the pretty little village of Kondokali.

The waters of Gouvia Bay are completely sheltered except for the east side and, because of this, they were used by the Venetians as a repairing base. The great boathouses where the galleys were laid up are now roofless skeletons; in the summer a holiday camp for poor children is pitched here. Beyond, through an elegant Venetian gateway, was the site of the arsenal and of various administrative buildings, now long since disappeared. According to the date on an inscription by the gate, they were built as late as 1770, only twenty-seven years before the extinction of the Republic. Gouvia was also a seaplane base for Air France, who built a hangar here just before 1939. A little whitewashed chapel stands on an islet in the bay.

Beyond Gouvia, the road for Paleocastritsa swings inland towards the west and, after passing the excellent Lucciola (Firefly) Inn, which can provide the best food on the island, enters upon the real Corfiot countryside. The road was built by a British regiment, as indicated by the familiar old British milestones along the route, because Frederick Adam, who was anxious to obtain easier access to Paleocastritsa, of which he was very fond, hit upon the ingenious idea of establishing a convalescent home for British troops there. Napier, the originator of this story, naturally thought that Assos in Cephalonia would have been a far healthier site. Corfu must nevertheless be grateful to Adam for this lovely road which winds through verdant peaceful country, first meadows and then unending olive groves with glimpses of the slopes of Pantocrator beyond, which start swinging round to meet it near the branch road to Dukades. Passing the large village of Gardelades which stands on a little ridge just to the south, the road starts twisting down through olive groves under great limestone slopes. Suddenly, between the gnarled trunks of the olive trees come glimpses of the sea, incredibly blue against the dramatic grey-white and green mountainside of Mount St Angelos, where the western flank of Pantocrator sweeps down into the Mediterranean. The road twists in corkscrew fashion through the olive groves, past occasional cottages, and then climbs up round the base of the mountain and back to sea-level near the little sandy beach of Alipa. On this last stretch there are several modern villas, well-designed and unobtrusively sited so that the coastline is not spoilt.

The bay of Paleocastritsa itself is only about two hundred yards further on. In 1945 it had basically not changed since Edward Lear included a drawing of it in his *Views of the Seven Ionian Islands* which was published in 1863. A deserted sandy beach enclosed by the two rocky peninsulas, the more northerly of the two mysterious with dark entrances to deep caves and crowned with the monastery of the 'Panayia' or Virgin. Today, there are three hotels and several restaurants all of which specialize in crayfish or lobster which are caught locally and kept in tanks in the sea under the cliffs. In addition, there are several recently built villas so that there is now little room for further development. Behind rise the lower slopes of Mount St Angelos, covered with vines and olive trees, facing views as dramatic and lovely as those from One Gun Battery at Kanoni.

The little road climbed up under pines and cypresses to the gateway of the monastery, which was built mainly in the seventeenth century. Leaving the car we mounted the steps into the little stone-flagged courtyard, with its white-walled, green shuttered cells for the monks on one side and, on the other, the monastery church with its walls washed an apricot-parchment and framed in white. Inside there is an elaborate but rather undistinguished painted ceiling, in the midst of which is a representation of the Tree of Life carved in wood. The white iconostasis is shaped like an elaborate Ionian belfry with icons in the arches.

Through the open door on the south side is a little stone-paved open verandah with breath-taking views of Paleocastritsa bay, the rugged coastline extending south and the blue empty sea stretching to the western horizon. Somewhere below it, several hundred miles beyond, is the Calabrian toe of Italy and Sicily. There are no views in the other Ionian Islands comparable to this.

Just to the north of the monastery peninsula, the slopes rise steeply for nearly fourteen hundred feet to Castel Angelo. Edward Lear included an excellent drawing of it in his book from the beach just north of the road to the monastery. You cannot reach the castle from here but must take the steep but well-made road up to Lakones which branches off from the Paleocastritsa road soon after passing the turning to Dukades. The road corkscrews up under olive trees until it levels out just before Lakones. Here there is a café in a wonderful belvedere position—and is as far as the tourist coaches go. Not only can you see the whole panoramic view of Paleocastritsa but by looking south-east along the flank of the mountain you can see back to the town of Corfu. From heights such as these you realize how luxuriantly green, how untypical compared with most of Greece, is this fantastic island. But then there is three times more rainfall here than, for example, in Athens and from mid-October you can expect up to forty days of cloud and rain without a glimpse of the sun. In summer, how-ever, there is nothing to fear beyond the occasional thunderstorm during August and September, accompanied for a few hours by torrential rain.

To reach Castel Angelo we continued through the little village of Krini and over a bumpy track to the far end of an olive grove, where the track began to slope steeply down the terraced hillside to the beginning of the great fist of rock on which the castle perches; from here we continued on foot. Although it was barely nine o'clock, the perspiration was already beginning to course down our faces.

Venice was not strong enough after the Fourth Crusade to hold all her gains. In 1210, she allowed Michael 1st. Angelos, who had taken over the Byzantine administration of the Epirus and founded a Despotate with its capital at Arta, to control her interests in Corfu. He built Castelo Angelo to guard against Genoese pirates, one of whom, Vetrano, had himself briefly held Corfu between the departure of the Fourth Crusade for Constantinople and his capture and execution by a Venetian squadron in 1206. Genoese attempts to seize Corfu continued into the fifteenth century; as late as 1403 they made an unsuccessful attempt on Castel Angelo and were soundly beaten by the island militia near Dukades.

Castel Angelo's greatest trial of strength was during the Turkish invasion of the island when, apart from the Old Fort, it was the only stronghold which held out. The garrison flung back the Turks four times, spurred on by the fact that three thousand refugees had taken shelter within its walls.

We clambered up the steep path and through the entrance into the outer keep. The inner keep is higher still; at the top are the ruins of the commander's house—a very small shelter only—and a water cistern. In the limestone rock there are several carved tombs. It is difficult to imagine so small an enclosure holding so many refugees plus a defence force. Hunger and disease, rather than the besiegers, must have been the principal enemy. At the cliff edge is a tiny chapel; from here there is a sheer drop into crystal dark blue sea some fourteen hundred feet below. To the north-west lie the three islands of Othoni, Mathraki and Erikoussa, the last north-western outposts of Greece in the central Mediterranean. Further still the long lines of the Acroceraunian Mountains stretch away up the Albanian coast.

Before returning to Krini, we descended to another little chapel in a cave in the rock. Here, as in the chapel at the summit, were icons which were mouldering away with age. We could not see the quality as we had neither match nor candle. Edward Lear in 1862 described the utter beauty and peacefulness of the scene on Easter Sunday and remarked on the 'scores of asses male and female', referring to his compatriots, who would be invading the scene on Easter Monday. From Corfu and back must have meant at least seven hours in the saddle, a healthy reflection on the toughness of our ancestors in search of pleasure.

Paleocastritsa has other fascinations. Was the capital of the Phaeacians here? It is generally accepted that the island of Corfu was Scheria, the land of the Phaeacians: Thucydides did not doubt this, nor did Strabo in his turn. We know that Odysseus, to reach Scheria, sailed on his raft for eighteen days in an easterly direction, keeping according to Calypso's instructions the Great Bear constellation

always on his left. Ernle Bradford, in *Ulysees Found,* favours Malta as
Calypso's Isle, from where it would have taken approximately this
time to drift eastwards to Corfu.

'So for seventeen days he sailed on his course,' says Book Five of
the Odyssey (E. V. Rieu's translation), 'and on the eighteenth there
hove into sight the shadowy mountains of the Phaeacian's country
which jutted out to meet him there. The land looked like a shield laid
on the misty sea.' Most of the west coast of Corfu is rugged, but where
it is at its rockiest, where the mountains jut out into the west with
the greatest magnificence is between Cape Falakron, some two miles
north of Castel Angelo and the Bay of Liapades, immediately to the
south of Paleocastritsa. Odysseus' journey, judging by the reference
to 'shadowy' mountains and the 'misty' sea, must have been made in
summer, the time when south from the Adriatic comes occasionally
the sudden raging storm called the Bora which is what, under the
direction of Poseidon, seems to have smashed into Odysseus' raft.
Approaching from the south-west, the heights of Castel Angelo and
the great mass of Pantocrator behind would look very much like a
shield.

Odysseus eventually struggled ashore in a little bay into which
flowed a river. This must have been somewhere further south, because
Athene, intervening on his behalf, checked all winds except a strong
breeze from the north, 'with which she beat the waves down in the
swimmer's path, so that King Odysseus might be rescued from the
jaws of death . . .' The only place which answers to the description is
the little Bay of Ermones, about seven miles down the coast. We went
there from Castel Angelo by car, twisting down the wooded slopes
back on to the Corfu-Paleocastritsa road and then back to the Gardelades fork which leads into the Val de Ropa. The road is an exceedingly
rough one, like most Corfiot roads, and we proceeded with the ut-
most caution. On the fringe of the plain outside the village, there were
several clumps of cypress trees amidst the olive groves and some
intensely cultivated fields. As we progressed further into the plain,
which is as flat as a billiards table, the cultivation became less and there
were no trees except around the occasional farmhouse.

The Val de Ropa is fringed on all sides by low-lying hills, those on
the western side enlivened with little golden-cream villages on their
eastern flanks. At the southern end of the plain rises the great hill of
St George with the village of Pelekes on its south-east flank. The
village was built in the seventeenth century high up from the sea to

avoid Saracen raids. Pelekes means literally an axe and the inhabitants
are known as Pelikates or the people of the axe. Below, at sea-level, is
the wonderful sandy beach of Glyfada, fringed by pines, and reached
by the worst road in the world. A number of villas are nevertheless
being erected there. Below also are 'The Bride's Rocks' about which
a sad story is told. Saracens suddenly fell upon the village once during
a wedding and snatched the bride away, who was later killed by being
flung onto these rocks. The watchman who should have given warning
did not do so because he had been jilted by her. One of the favourite
drives of Kaiser Wilhelm II was up through the colourfully washed,
vine-entwined village, its verandahs glowing with roses, carnations
and geraniums, to the peak of St George from which there is the most
wonderful view of the island north to Pantocrator, east to the Epirus
and Albania and south to the Ayia Deka range. The ideal time to come
here is at sunset.

We eventually emerged from the Val de Ropa on to the road which
connects Corfu town to the village of Giannades, off which a rough
track runs down to the little Bay of Ermones. The river which rises
on the southern slopes of Pantocrator flows through the Val de Ropa
and cuts its way through low hills to reach the sea. Homer described
the river as 'noble . . . with its neverfailing pools, in which there was
enough clear water always bubbling up and swirling by to clean the
dirtiest clothes.' It is more like a bubbling moorland stream, swift,
clear and more cooling to look at than the intense blue sea beyond. We
drove over an ancient bridge, over a low rise—and there below was
the little beach cupped by the bare hills. There were no trees and the
only shade was under some great rocks on the beach, partly washed
by the sea.

After a bathe, we had a simple meal at the little taverna, the only
building in sight. The proprietor, a peasant, went over to his small
market-garden by the river to cut a cucumber for our luncheon. I
asked him about his wine, which proved to be strong, rough and red;
he described it merely as 'topiou' or 'from nearby'. There were two
other small parties on his wooden verandah and several puppies which
were badly infested with ticks. The meal if simple was perfectly
adequate. Afterwards, we returned to the beach and slept in the shade
of the rocks, close to where Odysseus must have taken shelter to
recover from his ordeal.

Where, however, was the city of Alcinous, King of the Phaeacians?
Victor Bérard was convinced that it was sited at Paleocastritsa.

According to him, the acropolis was built on the southern of the two peninsulas, which has a harbour on each side, in keeping with Nausicaa's description. The palace of Alcinous was, in his opinion, built where the monastery is now sited. The distance from Ermones to Paleocastritsa is about seven miles, a journey of around three hours—certainly not exhausting for Nausicaa, as she and the dirty washing went in a mule-cart while her handmaidens followed on foot. I can think of no lovelier place to own a palace, as several well-built villas testify. But would any seafaring people have built a harbour on so wild a coast, exposed to the open sea? The ancient Greeks, as their descendants today, always sought the maximum shelter, which in the Ionian Islands means keeping to the east side.

One answer to this is that the Phaeacians were not Greeks, but possibly Phoenicians, who were perhaps more adventurous and skilful seafarers than the ancient Greeks. Nevertheless, even if this were so, which I doubt, the Phoenicians were also traders and would not risk the loss of valuable cargoes unnecessarily. It happens that Palaiopolis on the eastern coast is scarcely further away from the bay of Ermones than Paleocastritsa and the journey as easily negotiable. Palaiopolis, as we have seen, has both an acropolis and a harbour on each side. The neighbourhood is well-wooded with a variety of trees, a clump of which would have been sacred to Athene where Odysseus paused in prayer before going up into Alcinous' palace. Surely it was from here, and not from Paleocastritsa, that the long black vessel, manned by fifty-two sturdy young oarsmen, set off with Odysseus that evening for Ithaka, seventy-odd miles to the south? They would have had a better chance of doing the journey in ten hours between dusk and dawn in the inland sea than off the west coast.

All arguments are inconclusive. Paleolithic and neolithic remains have been found in limestone caves on the west side of the island. Traces of man on Corfu therefore go back some twenty to thirty thousand years, but no evidence has so far been found to show that these ancient inhabitants were of Phoenician origin. As there have been no Mycenean discoveries to compare with those in Cephalonia and Zakynthos, the inhabitants were probably not Achaean but perhaps from Illyria. More than that we do not yet know.

26

A Southern Tour

The square of San Rocco is the terminal for communications with the south and west of the island. From here buses depart punctually for Gastouri, Benitses and the large, prosperous agricultural villages of Levkimmi in the far south. The square itself is situated at the far end of Voulgaris Street, about a hundred and fifty yards beyond the half-completed opera house. In its original design—it was first built at the turn of the century—this opera house was the temporary home of the Serbian parliament during the First World War and it was here that the Pact of Corfu which brought into existence the Kingdom of the Serbs, Croats and Slovenes was signed in 1917. Unfortunately the building was badly damaged in 1943 and the attempt to rebuild it has come to a halt through lack of funds. Its half-finished modernistic concrete structure does nothing to dignify this wide, dusty shopping street nor the equally dusty square beyond.

The roads leading out of San Rocco Square—down, past the garage and showrooms of the enterprising Manessi brothers, to Garitza Bay; west across the waist of the island to Pelekes; round to the Platytera Monastery and onwards to the north-west; past Lake Khalikiopoulo southwards and to the south-west—are partly cobbled, partly macadamized and sometimes badly in need of repair.

The road to the south leaves from the south-west corner of the square, past the large garden and buildings of the lunatic asylum. The gardens are fenced by high iron railings and shaded by eucalyptus trees. Built during the British Protectorate, it is now one of the principal asylums in Greece and said to be exceptionally well run.

On the left, although not visible from the main road, is the British cemetery, on the site of the San Salvator defences, which once protected the southern approaches to the town. The entrance is through a handsome wrought-iron gate. It is large and spacious with green lawns, intersected by well-kept paths and handsomely wooded with pines and cypress trees. Its haunting peacefulness, said an English friend, is a perfect setting for *Les Sylphides*. Here are graves from the earliest days of the British Protectorate up to the mining of three British warships by Albania in October 1946 at the northern end of the Corfu Channel.

The road to the south leads on between hedges of prickly pear past the neat little airfield, now capable of taking jet aircraft, which has been built over part of Lake Khalikiopoulo, the rest of which is now mainly reed-covered marsh. As the road begins to rise above the level of the lake, there is a road junction; the main road leads on to Gastouri but the left-hand fork continues round the lake to Perama on the coast, opposite Kanoni, and so to the pretty little fishing village of Benitses. There is however a third fork to the right, just before that to Perama. This leads to the village of Viro and the old Venetian country house of Kothoniki, which has belonged to the Sordinas family for centuries. Next to the house is a great stone tithe barn, partly sunk into the ground. During the Venetian era, the Sordinas family gained the right to give sanctuary to fugitives from the law. In return, those who were given sanctuary were made to pay heavily for the privilege, which brought in a handsome income.

The need for sanctuary implies the existence of lawlessness. The conditions described by Grasset de St. Sauveur in Zakynthos can be matched by the observations of Wheler towards the end of the seventeenth century. He wrote, 'The inhabitants of Corfu are of a very revengeful nature, never forgetting any injury done; which is often the ruin of whole Families . . . There happened a quarrel between two families upon no great occasion at first; but at last was brought up to such a height, that several persons were killed on both sides; especially on his side, who was the principal party offended. This man, dying, left only a young son; to whom, when he came of age several years after, it was proposed, that he should Marry a daughter of his Father's enemy, that so all differences might be ended, and a lasting peace made between the two families. After much sollicitation he agreed to it, so that a Dowry was concluded on and Married they were, with a great deal of seeming joy. But not long after, having carried his new-married wife back to his house and having thither invited her Parents, Sisters, Brothers and other Relations of hers, he persuaded them to stay all night, and barbarously Murder'd every one of them, Wife and all.' I cannot remember any reference to the vendetta in any account written by Englishmen during and after the British Protectorate.

The Perama road winds like an English country lane through green slopes rich with flowering fruit trees. By the time it reaches the coast, the olive trees have taken over, but the little whitewashed, red-roofed villas are wreathed in bougainvillea and vine, the gardens gay with canna flowers and geranium. They are mainly used as summer retreats by townspeople. They are not ideally situated because they are too close to the road which twists so violently round tiny rocky bays and over the little headlands, that drivers use their horns with enthusiasm, especially as there is barely room for two vehicles to pass.

The road meanders on through the olive groves until it coasts down to the rocky fringe of the sea's still waters and under the stone arch of the Kaiser's Bridge; this connects a little jetty to the grounds of the Achilleion, hidden high up in the densely wooded slopes above. Here the Kaiser used to land on arriving at the island. A little beyond, a road climbs up to Gastouri through luxuriant woods to where the Achilleion stands at the apex of the village.

The Achilleion was originally built for the Empress Elizabeth, the beautiful, ill-fated wife of the Austro-Hungarian Emperor Franz-Joseph. She belonged to the brilliant but unstable Wittelsbach family of Bavaria—a cousin had been Otho, the first King of Greece and another the mad King Ludwig of Bavaria. Married to an unimagina-tive and over-conscientious authoritarian, she found official life onerous. Her first visit to Corfu was in 1861 on returning by sea from Madeira whither she had gone to recuperate from an illness. Queen Victoria had lent her the *Victoria and Albert* for the occasion. This first visit was for a day only, but, estranged from her husband, she returned later that year with her brother-in-law, the Archduke Ferdi-nand Maximilian, who later accepted the Mexican throne and was subsequently executed. The Emperor managed to arrange a reconcilia-tion and came to Corfu to fetch her home. He was far more interested in the fortifications and English regimental drill than the scenery. Kirkwall recalled how a young officer, seeing a civilian too near to where he was drilling his troops, galloped up to him to ask him to move. 'As he approached the tall upright individual in a white hat, it suddenly occurred to him that it was the Emperor, whom he had not yet seen, but of whose presence on the island he was doubtless aware. He, however, with great presence of mind, continued his course, and asked his Majesty if he had any orders to give.'

Elizabeth's desire to have a home in Corfu came much later and the little rose-coloured Brailla villa at Gastouri was eventually chosen. The plans for conversion were elaborate. 'I want a palace with pillared colonnades and hanging gardens, protected from prying glances—a palace worthy of Achilles, who despised all mortals and did not even fear the gods', she wrote. Every whim seems to have been gratified; there were marble baths piped with warm sea-water, Roman style couches covered with leopard skins, fine copies of Greek and Roman statuary brought from Italy for the gardens. The result was supposed to represent a Phaeacian palace, but visitors today to what is now a casino will be intrigued by the lack of taste, which certainly cannot be blamed entirely on the German Emperor, Wilhelm II, although it was he who had engraved on the base of the statue to the wounded Achilles the words, 'To the greatest of the Greeks from the greatest of the Germans'. The building of the Achilleion lasted from about 1888 to 1891, but almost before it was completed, Elizabeth was bored. In 1890 there had been the scandalous death of her son, the Crown Prince Rudolf, at Mayerling and she became increasingly restless for the rest of her life. She shunned society and on her visit in 1892 virtually her only companion was Christomanos, a hunchback Greek, whose duties were to teach her Greek. They made a strange pair, the tall, slender Empress and her dark limping companion, walking at great speed through the olive groves. Her last visit to Corfu was in 1896, two years before her senseless assassination in Geneva.

Tales about her are still told on the island. She was well-liked and went everywhere without pomp. On one occasion, a peasant woman, to show her affection, spat on the Empress, adding 'may you flourish like my pig'. Peasants will never make a direct compliment as this is sure to lead to disaster. Another story tells of the Empress's visit to a woman who lived with her daughter in the trunk of a large plane tree at the edge of the village. By contrast most of the ochre-washed houses which lead up to the Achilleion are rather more substantial than those found elsewhere.

The gardens of the Achilleion and the views from there are its finest features—wide stone terraces and gardens with flower beds intersected by paved walks. Once, before it became a casino, we entered the gardens through a gap in the hedge off the Benitses–Gastouri road and wandered up a gravel path, densely overhung with trees and covered with pine needles and rustling brown laurel leaves, to come suddenly upon the elegant marble rotunda in which stands a statue of the Empress, romantic but somewhat characterless. The Kaiser erected it soon after he bought the property in 1907. Originally the rotunda had sheltered a statue of her favourite poet, Heinrich Heine, but this was cast forth, only to turn up later in the public gardens at Toulon. The Kaiser visited Corfu nearly every year between 1907 and the outbreak of war in 1914. He is still remembered, dressed always in white naval uniform and driving everywhere in a cavalcade of red motor cars.

The Manessi family, who own the enchanting villa of San Stefano, the rose-red walls of which can be glimpsed high up above the road to Benitses, possess his signature in their visitor's book.

Benitses itself is a little fishing village, built, in spite of the danger of Saracen raids, on the shore. It consists of some twenty houses in solid Venetian style, mostly of two or three floors, in good unpretentious style, facing the tree-shaded road and the sea beyond. The little church of Ayios Demetrios has fifteenth-century wall paintings. At its southern end, where the buses stop, are several cafés. Close by is the jetty to which the fishing boats, each with a large acetylene lamp at the stern, are moored during the day. From about midnight until dawn however, they will be working out at sea and the pom . . . pom . . . pom . . . of their engines can echo disturbingly across the still waters. The other fishing system is by means of an enormous net, owned by a local syndicate, which is dragged out at least a hundred yards to sea each evening and pulled in the following morning. The catch seemed remarkably small for the effort involved, but the Eastern Mediterranean is said to be overfished which accounts for the high price of fish in restaurants. Further along the beach beyond Benitses is the simple, pleasant little Avra Hotel with its tables for meals outside under trees and a vine trellis.

Inland and uphill on the edge of the village is the source of the water supply which Sir Frederick Adam arranged to be conveyed to the town by covered aqueduct. A stone inscription commemorates this. Sir Frederick was wont to drive out here in his carriage to entertain his friends; a special service of plate was kept in the village for this purpose. From here, there is a pleasant walk through pine woods up to the village of Ayii Deka, which gives its name to the limestone range forming the southern skyline of the town.

Ayii Deka is spread out along the road which twists uphill towards Makrata and the narrow inland plain beyond through which the road continues to the south. Its name—the ten saints—commemorates ten Cretan soldiers in the Roman Army who were martyred for their faith during the Christian persecutions. The two-storey houses are washed in a pale ochre colour, each with its own vine trellis. The village faces across the valley towards Gastouri and there are splendid views of Corfu town, Pantocrator and the remoter Acroceraunian mountains. It was founded as the result of the discovery of an icon of the Virgin. A family in Gastouri was led to it by a light high up on the slopes of the Ayii Deka range. A church was erected on the spot and round the church grew up the village. The discovery of miraculous icons is not uncommon. A similar story is told about Myrtiotissa, just south of Ermones bay where the church was built for similar reasons. Such icons are usually found near the sea; they were probably carried as their most precious possession by refugees from Saracen raiders or the Turks and then stolen or lost.

After Ayii Deka, the road passes through straggling villages until a long valley, dominated by the large village of Ayios Mathias, about a thousand feet up on the western coastal hills, comes suddenly into view. In June the grass is still green and the olive trees covered with their delicate creamy flowers. Cypresses stand round solid, unpretentious farmhouses and golden broom flourishes by the roadside. A travelling journeyman passed, his mule laden with carpets and bales of dress material.

The road eventually joins the pretty coastal road from Benitses near Messonghi, beautiful with its great olive groves. Once over the little river, however, the countryside becomes much flatter. On the east side are some low coastal hills with the large village of Chlomos which can be better seen from the sea. On the left is the long shallow lake of Korissi and the sandy beaches of St George, about a mile off the road to the west. Here amid pine woods is the little monastery church of St George painted turquoise blue with a plum-red onion dome. The beach is usually quite empty and ankle-deep with dried seaweed at the water's edge.

In the south, in the Levkimmi area is a group of large villages—Argyrades, Perivoli, Ringlades and Anaplades—situated in a rich agricultural area. These villages are densely populated and there is about them an air of frugal prosperity. Some of the land is leased to tenants but most of it is owned by peasant proprietors. Where the land is leased, agreements are made whereby part of the rent is paid in kind. Many peasants when cultivating on a tenant basis still bring the owners an annual token of the agreement—a basket of potatoes, of oranges or of lemons. The road comes to an end a little beyond Kavos, from where there is a caique service to Paxos. This area as a whole has few tourist attractions, although it is one of the mainstays of the island's economy. The great salt pans of Levkimmi lie to the north of these villages. Here the Corcyreans erected a trophy to commemorate their first defeat of the Corinthians.

There is another group of unspoilt prosperous, well-ordered villages in much prettier surroundings in the well-wooded country to the west of Ayii Deka, among them Kastellani, where Lord Seaton attempted unsuccessfully to establish an agricultural college. Here the older women still wear their traditional costume and apart from the occasional bus or taxi, mules and donkeys are the only form of transport. A road winds up into the hills to end eventually at the village of Pentati. This spot offers splendid views of the sea, which are also enjoyed by Ano (Upper) Pavliana and Kato (Lower) Pavliana. In Kato Pavliana lived the Corfiot scholar and poet Polila, who translated Shakespeare's *The Tempest* into demotic Greek. Further inland, near Kato Garouna, in the limestone hills, there is said to be a bottomless pit or a series of tunnels through the rock, reminiscent of the system linking the water from the sea-mills near Argostoli with the caves near Sami; dogs thrown down this cavern have been known to appear on the western coast three miles away. Other caves now occupied by countless bats, may eventually reveal further evidence about prehistoric man on the island.

Another road leads to the large village of Synarades from which the great golden beach of Ayios Gordis Bay is reached—as lovely and as inaccessible as Glyfada. From Synarades there is an even worse road through olive groves and fields to Pelekes, standing on its hill to the north, its lower slopes covered by a profusion of fruit trees, cypress and olive trees, vines and cacti.

There are other pretty villages between here and the town— Kalafationes, Varypatades, Kastania—the ending 'ades' corresponding to that of 'ata' in Cephalonia, meaning 'place' or 'village'. One of the loveliest, Kombitzi, is about three miles from town on the road from Pelekes, situated on a densely wooded hill. The hamlet is named after a Cretan who sought refuge on the island after the fall of Candia. He built himself a small country house in Venetian style and gratefully endowed a church to the glory of God. Then suddenly his beloved young son died; as a result the father lost his reason and tried to burn down the church, but the walls were much too solid for this to be completely successful. Gently terraced stone steps lead down to the village spring where water gushes through lions' heads and the basins for washing clothes are made of marble.

The men of the village told us one evening about the reptiles of the island. Vipers we knew of and the long brownish-green grass snakes, both of which we had seen. We had also met with the tortoises and a variety of lizards, in particular one with a brilliant green body over a foot long near Pelekes. We recognized from their description the non-poisonous 'tiflitas'—brown, thick and about three feet long—and the venomous black thin 'gapokia', both of which we had seen near Scripero. Now in addition we heard about the mottled black and white 'astritas', about two feet long, which climbs fig trees and is said to be very poisonous, and the equally venomous very short grey 'kolovo'. Sophisticated friends in town doubted the existence of either of these but their peasant maid said they certainly existed, although she had never seen them.

27

A Northern Tour

❧

There was no exact time for the start of the ceremony—merely that
it would begin that morning when all had arrived. The channels for
the foundation of the villa had been dug into the rocky soil and the
workmen from the local village were already there when we arrived
with the owners and the architect. The priest came last, riding on his
mule and wiping his brow under his black stove-pipe hat as the
morning was already hot. Having dismounted, he first selected a
well-leafed switch from an olive tree and then started to rattle off
prayers from his breviary.

It was a ceremony of blessing the foundations—one as old as house-
building. Each of the four corners where the cornerstones were to be
sunk, was blessed with wine and water sprinkled from the olive
switch and a coin buried there for good luck. In addition, a hen was
sacrificed at each corner by having its throat cut and the blood
allowed to soak into the ground with the wine and water. A sudden
screech, a swooning flutter of feathers and the corpse was seized by
one of the workmen to be made ready for an evening feast among
themselves. Then the ceremony was over and the local deities, the
local priest and the villagers propitiated. It was now our turn to raise
glasses of wine to wish the owners health and happiness.

The June midday heat was beginning to veil the inland sea and the
bays of Dassia and Ipsos under a mile to the east. The town of Corfu,
some six miles away to the south-east, would only become visible
again in the cooler evening air. The view to the north was dominated
by near-by Pantocrator. The hillside, on a spur of which the villa was
being built, was abundantly covered with trees—olives, fruit trees,
pines, cypresses—so that the ground, even at the hottest time of the
year, never became completely parched and in spring was a riot of
wild flowers. The Ipsos road was invisible but passing traffic could

occasionally be faintly heard in the still air as could the band from the Dassia beach restaurant at night.

The road for Ipsos branches off the Paleocastritsa road at the Gouvia junction. It passes through well-wooded estates, including that of the Club Méditerranée at Dassia before twisting down to the little village of Ipsos and then running level with the shore for a mile to Piryi where the slopes of Pantocrator begin.

The sea here is shallow, the sea-bed sandy and in places covered with weed. There are several pleasant, simple hotels, restaurants and villas by the road. In summer the water can be, if anything, too warm for invigorating refreshment. Sailing dinghies skim over the still surface and caiques from Corfu town, bearing tourists *en route* for Kassiopi in the north, chunter across the bay to Piryi to pick up further passengers from the comfortable Bogdanos Hotel and others in the vicinity.

Even in these tranquil waters, disaster can strike. The last poem written in Greek by Solomos, entitled 'Porphyras' (sea monster) was based on the death of a young British soldier who was killed in these waters by a shark. The poem describes the youth swimming at eventide in a calm sea, a thousand stars reflected on the water around him from the night sky and a nightingale's song encircling him with the wonder of her voice. As the young man penetrates and is enhanced by all this beauty, as he comes to a full appreciation of the joy and harmony of nature, the sea monster strikes. The magic of the night sea, especially of the calmer waters between Corfu and the mainland, has never been more beautifully described. A similar incident took place almost exactly a hundred years later when a shark killed a beautiful young girl who was swimming far out in Ipsos bay. Sharks, however, are extremely rare in these waters and another century could pass without anyone coming to harm in this way.

At Piryi the road climbs steeply up the flanks of Pantocrator and for the next ten miles, until well beyond Kouloura, stays at two or three hundred feet above sea-level. The only exception is when it runs along the edge of the sea for a short distance through the Barbati estates. A road branches uphill to Spartilas from where a rough track leads onwards towards the summit of Pantocrator, close to which there is a monastery. Here on August 6th takes place one of the island's most celebrated panayiri.

The road along the coast for several miles to Nissaki is in excellent condition but after that, in spite of much effort, it becomes exceedingly bumpy and in a light car is very slow going. At Nissaki, with Pantocrator towering magnificently above, there is a pleasant beach restaurant and a number of villas, which have been built in the last few years. Stroll a little way northwards through the olive grove on the edge of the sea and you will find excellent rock pools from which to bathe—although beware of sea-urchins. Here and there are deliciously refreshing cold water streams which flow out underwater from the descending limestone formation of the surrounding slopes.

Here, at the beginning of the Corfu Channel, the mainland coast of Albania approaches within five miles but is at its closest opposite Kouloura, where the distance across is barely a mile and a half. Looking down from the road, you can see the old grey Venetian villa of Kouloura with its great sheltered verandah at the water's edge, surrounded by a profusion of cypress, pine and eucalyptus trees and with its little curved jetty at which one or two caiques are usually moored. Opposite on the mainland is the entrance to the great lake of Butrinto, part of which you can see in spite of the coastal range of hills which contains it.

The history of Butrinto is as old as legend itself. Aeneas in his travels after the fall of Troy came here. Known to him as Buthrotum, it was a hill-city built above the harbour of Chaonia on the Epirot coast. This was the Trojans' first port of call after leaving Levkas where they had wintered. Walking up from the harbour towards the town, Aeneas chanced upon Andromache, Hector's widow, who was engaged in pouring sorrowfully a drink-offering in a ritual sacrifice to Hector's ashes. Her shock was extreme when she saw advancing towards her a warrior in Trojan uniform. Aeneas quickly revealed himself and the story he learned from her was indeed a strange one. Andromache after the fall of Troy was taken as wife by Pyrrhus, a son of Achilles, who ruled Buthrotum and the surrounding district. Pyrrhus was slain by Orestes, whose wife he was plotting to steal, and was succeeded by Helenus, a son of Priam, the late king of Troy, who had legal claims on the throne although his subjects were Greeks. Helenus promptly married Andromache, no doubt to consolidate his position by marriage to the wife of the former king, but also because she was a Trojan. It was Helenus, with his power of prophecy, who warned Aeneas not to land on the nearer shores of Italy, which were already colonized by the Greeks, but to proceed further afield beyond the bay of Naples to found his own city.

Helenus and Andromache entertained Aeneas and his companions well and loaded them with gifts. On his departure, Aeneas was moved to declare that, if he ever reached Tiber's estuary, 'we shall create by our mutual sympathy kindred cities having close ties with Epirus'. Perhaps Mussolini remembered these lines from the Third Book of the Aeneid when he invaded the Epirus in 1940; if so, deep must have been his disappointment at the reception he received. A more sinister legend, current among the Crusaders who passed through these narrow pirate-infested waters, was that a deserted castle in this area, called Butentrost or Butrinto, had been the birthplace of Judas Iscariot.

During the thirteenth and fourteenth centuries, Butrinto was held at various times by the Angevins of Naples and the Despots of Epirus. Later, the Venetians regarded it as the 'key to Corfu' and maintained its fortifications. Its strength was not, however, sufficient to deter Suleyman the Magnificent from pitching his tents here in 1537 before the first great siege of Corfu. Commercially the lake of Butrinto was famous for its fish and was farmed out at a high price to a Corfiot.

Butrinto became part of the Ottoman Empire only after the French were evicted from the Ionian Islands by the Russo-Turkish expedition in 1799. It became Greek briefly for about eighteen months as a result of the advance of Greek forces into what was then known as Northern Epirus in 1913 during the first Balkan War. International power politics however decreed the establishment in 1914 of an independent kingdom of Albania under Italian protection which included those southern districts which even today have a large Greek Orthodox population.

Throughout the British Protectorate and up until 1939, the lake of Butrinto was well-known to British sportsmen because of the great variety of game birds in the area. They were perhaps first introduced to these when Ali Pasha, during the negotiations over Parga in 1819, entertained Maitland and his suite to a great shoot on these waters. Today the lake, completely undisturbed, must be a paradise for wildfowl.

The road bumps painfully onwards, but Pantocrator here begins to retreat from the coast where the shore becomes less precipitous and there are several little bays, including San Stefano—the Italian version is still used quite frequently—which can be reached down rough cart-tracks. It is however a relief to reach the little northern port of Kassiopi, about two miles to the west of the Corfu Channel, a straggling cluster of white houses surrounded by trees. Now a small tourist resort, there are several simple restaurants under the plane trees near the little quay where there is anchorage for yachts. Just above it to the west are the ruins of what was obviously once a great fortress but now is almost completely destroyed. Built during the late thirteenth or early fourteenth century by the Angevins of Naples, it was destroyed by the Venetians soon after they gained control of the island in 1387, for fear that it might be seized by their hated enemies, the Genoese. Strange legends developed locally about it; one was that it had become deserted because a fiery dragon had poisoned the inhabitants with his breath. A walk round the site reveals what must have been its strategic importance in guarding the entrance to the Corfu Channel.

Although there are no indications left, Kassiopi was during the Roman occupation of considerable importance, as illustrated by the fame of the Temple of Jupiter on whose site the village church is said to be built. The most distinguished visitor during this period was probably the young Emperor Nero. Greek civilization and its artistic achievements appealed as strongly to the Roman upper classes as to their English counterparts in the eighteenth and nineteenth centuries, and there was a steady flow of Greek sculpture and pottery from Greece to Rome; witness the great shipment of Greek treasure discovered early in this century in the Roman wreck off Anti-Kythera. Nero himself started his Hellenic studies by arranging for Greek statues to be collected for his palace; then in A.D. 66, anxious to display his manifold histrionic talents before Greek audiences, the only ones capable in his opinion of fully appreciating his accomplishments, he crossed to Kassiopi where he gave a song recital before the altar of the temple, the first no doubt of many performances which he gave in Greece.

During the first hundred and fifty years of Venetian rule, before the powers of St Spiridion became fully recognized, the most famous shrine in the island was that of Our Lady of Kassiopi, to which returning sailors paid homage. John Locke in 1553 described this church as new. A market, free from all dues, grew up round the church and was said to be much frequented. Towards the end of the seventeenth century however, the travellers Wheler and Spon found the village to be merely a ruin. About the only inhabitants were three or four monks in charge of the church.

The church nevertheless was still noted for a miraculous icon of the Virgin, no doubt the same which had made Kassiopi famous over a hundred years previously. Wheler, who was both inquisitive and of a sceptical nature, decided to test its powers. 'Strangers', he wrote, 'that have a mind to know whether their Friends are alive or dead, go to the Picture and dab a piece of money upon it, thinking of some friend. If the person they think of be alive, the piece will stick fast, but if dead, it will drop into a sack placed underneath; so that alive or dead, the Priest is sure of the money. I applied some farthings which I had, to try how, and where they would stick; but had no other thought, nor end, being well satisfied that it was but a rediculous juggling. Some of them indeed stuck, but all to one and the same place; those that were clapt on elsewhere falling still to the ground. The Picture is painted up on the walls and is very smooth and shining, so that I Attribute the sticking to some clamminess of the varnish; which they take care, shall never be wanting in some places of it.' We were unable to identify this particular icon, but the little church is well cared for and there are several fine icons and offerings for salvation from shipwreck.

To the north-east lies the little Albanian port of Ayii Saranda or Forty Saints—note the Greek name—standing in its valley where the Acroceraunian Mountains turn inland from the sea. The legend itself dates back to the fourth century A.D. when forty young soldiers of mixed nationality, stationed at Sebastea in Asia Minor, refused to become apostates when the Emperor Licinius ordered in A.D. 320 a persecution of the Christians. They were thrust naked into a frozen pond where they remained for three nights and days; those who survived this treatment were flung into a furnace. These martyrs became very popular throughout the Eastern Roman Empire and their relics taken to many cities. I have never, however, heard that any relics were taken there. In any case, although not more than three miles away, Ayii Saranda is behind the Iron Curtain and as inaccessible as Lhasa.

Although a much longer road, it is as quick to return to Corfu town by going west along the northern coast road as far as Sfakera and then inland, climbing up into the western foothills of Pantocrator and joining the main Corfu–Karoussades road at Chorepiskopi. For the first few miles, there is a complete absence of shade on the bare coastal hills, but by the time Acharavi is reached the road is winding through ancient olive groves and then on into pleasant open country. The road climbs upwards from Sfakera and the sea and the Acroceraunian Mountains, remote and placid, come into view. This gracious and pastoral country is well-watered and rich in fruit trees as well as olive groves. Here and there we passed the occasional farm-house or cottage but these are the empty, unspoilt parts of the island with little likelihood of development because of their distance from the beaches and the absence of electricity and telephones. The villages like Xathates and Ayii Douli are clean, well built, the larger houses obviously dating back to the Venetian period. From Chorepiskopi, the road climbs to the saddle of Trompetta and so down to Scripero, which possesses some of the finest village houses on the island, and back to Corfu town.

From Sfakera, it is also possible to return to the coast along a rarely frequented road to Roda, a little fishing village in the centre of a scattered farming community. A little wooden pier runs out to sea; here you can eat under a rough awning to protect you against the sun. The outline of a small temple has been discovered close by and the area is thought to be rich in antiquities, but the funds needed for digging are not so far available.

The largest village in the area is Karoussades, reached from Roda by a very rough road which runs inland parallel to the coast. Here is a fine old country-house belonging to a branch of the Theotokis family. The church of Ayii Katerini is sixteenth-century with some interesting wall-paintings. Near by at Kavalouri is an old Venetian house belong-ing to the Giallinas family, the best-known member of which was the late nineteenth-century painter whose delicate water colours are to be found in various private houses.

At the western end of the north coast is Sidari, a scattered village of little consequence except that the sea has worn away the sandstone dunes into the most fascinating shapes; in one place it is possible to swim right through a cavern if the sea is not too rough. Some now almost invisible fortifications stood on one of the dunes and we found an abandoned cannon in the long coarse grass, stamped with the Russian imperial eagle.

Some of Corfu's sandiest beaches lie between Cape Drastis, imme-diately to the west of Sidari and the bay of St George with Cape Arilla at its northern end. These beaches are difficult to reach because of the almost impassible tracks; and, if you manage to win through, you are unlikely to find anyone else except the occasional fisherman from a nearby hamlet. One of the loveliest points is Cape San Stefano with a little chapel standing on its edge.

When we arrived back in the early evening, little wood fires had been lit in the alleyways of the town and children were leaping through the flames. It was St John's Eve towards the end of June and the enactment of this ancient rite from time immemorial was ensuring good crops and happiness for another year.

Part Six
PAXOS

28

Paxos

About six and a half miles long and up to a mile and a half wide, Paxos—remote, serene, content—lies ten miles south of Cape Aspro-kavos, Corfu's most southerly point. The island is barely known to history. No famous cities or temples have been built on its rocky shores, no despots or philosophers have brought renown to its name. Vulnerable to pirates and slavers, the only protection for its few in-habitants—today probably no more than about three thousand altogether—has been its remoteness from the highway of events, its almost conscious acceptance of obscurity as a way of life.

Ask a Corfiot about getting to Paxos and the answer may be vague. The fact of the matter is that, although Paxos has traditionally been administered from Corfu, Corfiots never go there. There are however daily boats in summer. You can either sail direct to Gaios the capital, in about three and a half hours or call at the tiny Paxiot ports of Lakke and Longos as well, which means a five-hour journey. The large motor caiques leave from a jetty, close to the quay used by the Corfu–Igoumenitsa ferries. On one occasion in early June, we chose the longer route. We were told that the boat would leave at half past ten. When we boarded at a quarter past ten, three oxen and half a dozen sheep were being tied down amidst deck machinery, sacks of vegetables, bales of cloth and the inevitable round baskets. The last items to be loaded were great slabs of ice for the cafés and but-chers of Paxos. This was still in progress at eleven o'clock when the skipper strolled across from a near-by café to supervise the final arrangements. At a quarter past eleven our boat was nosing its way round the Old Fort towards the south.

At Kavos, the southernmost village of Corfu, we stopped to unload ice into a little rowing boat from the café which stands under olive trees on the beach next to a wooden pier; from here there are daily services to Paxos for travellers from the rich agricultural district of Levkimmi, of which Kavos forms a part, and for those who prefer to travel this far from Corfu by bus. Opposite, near the mainland, are the Sivota Isles close to which the two naval battles between Corcyra and Corinth were fought.

The voyage down the Corfu Channel is usually calm but once south of Cape Asprokavos and into the open sea it can be quite choppy if there is a west wind. It is only now that Paxos comes into sight, lying on the sea like a sleeping cat. As the distance narrows, the eastern coastline proves to be rockier and the central ridge higher than at first imagined. You come unexpectedly upon the narrow entrance into the wide shallow bay of Porto Lakke. One side of this entrance is formed by a rugged limestone cliff. The little port itself is on the south side of the bay with excellent anchorage for yachts. The village street runs inland for some eighty yards and then disappears out of sight. Altogether there are no more than thirty houses.

The surrounding slopes rise steeply and are covered with olive trees, wave after wave of them, alive with the dancing, sparkling light of the sun, reflected by myriads of tiny, glossy, grey-green leaves. The oil from these trees is about the finest in Greece and the island's only export. Apart from oil, fish and the wine, which is grown on Anti-Paxos, nearly all meat, vegetables and wheat have to be brought in from Corfu or the mainland.

Most Paxiots returning to Gaios catch the island's only bus for the twenty-minute journey from Lakke. We preferred to continue the journey by sea, sailing down the east side of the island. It is a deserted coast, the only sign of life being the occasional sunbaked cottage or ruined tower, still keeping watch over these once pirate-infested seas. Perhaps they stood when the great Andrea Doria, the only Christian admiral thought capable of standing up to Kheyr-ed-din Barbarossa, defeated one of the latter's lieutenants in a battle before daybreak in 1537 and carried twelve Turkish galleys in triumph to Messina. In reply to this insult, Barbarossa sailed up the Ionian Sea, first to ravage Apulia, while Doria lay helpless in the Messina roads with a far inferior fleet, and then to launch the first great Turkish assault on Corfu. On the failure of this siege, Barbarossa undertook the most ravaging series of attacks on the Venetian dependencies in the Ionian and Aegean seas, Paxos being the first to suffer with the enslavement of most of her inhabitants.

In the following year, Andrea Doria was given the opportunity of

meeting Barbarossa face to face. Placed in command of the combined
fleets of Genoa, the Papacy and Venice by the Emperor Charles the
Fifth, he marshalled his vast resources in Corfu harbour and then set
forth down the Ionian Sea. Barbarossa had already been warned that
Doria was cruising in the Adriatic and hastened northwards from
Crete to give battle. He was glad, however, to slip through the
Preveza Channel into the Ambracian Gulf when he discovered that
the Christian fleet was considerably larger than his own. Doria
refused to follow because of the shallows, nor did he seize the Preveza
Fort and bottle up the Turkish fleet with his guns. Instead, anxious
for the safety of his fifty large sailing galleons, the most up-to-date
naval craft in the Mediterranean, he sailed away south.

Barbarossa went after him in pursuit. The north wind had little
strength and the long oars of his galleys soon caught up with the
largest of the Venetian galleons, which fought back strenuously, its
well-aimed guns causing great destruction among its attackers. A
wind then arose from the south which should have given Doria the
opportunity of returning to meet Barbarossa. In spite of the pleas of
his senior commanders, however, he refused to engage the enemy and
in the evening, after much fruitless manoeuvring, sailed with his
massive armada back towards Corfu, leaving Barbarossa with his
inferior numbers in command of the sea.

About three miles south of Lakke, we turned round an outcrop of
grey-white rock into the little bay of Longos. The port is even smaller
than Lakke, consisting of some twenty solid, well-proportioned,
whitewashed houses, their roofs constructed of red or ochre tiles and
their window frames and shutters painted green. Set around the
neatly paved quay and with steeply wooded slopes rising behind,
Longos looks like a stage set for an eighteenth-century comedy about
Venice. Most of the houses were unoccupied. The only sign of industry was the olive oil factory in the northern corner of the tiny bay—
black and slightly antediluvian. So heavy is the olive crop that labour
has to be imported from the mainland to harvest the fallen fruit.

From Longos to Gaios by sea takes little over twenty minutes. The
entrance to Gaios is marked by an islet which stands out towards the
distant misty heights of Epirus. This is the Panayia or Madonna
Island on which is a whitewashed monastery of the same name, now
usually empty, and an automatic lighthouse. The Feast of the Assump-
tion is celebrated here in mid-August with a gathering of Paxiots
from all over Greece and beyond—a wonderful explosion of life amid

otherwise deserted walls. Here, the boat turns inland down a well-marked channel between steep green banks, the southerly one belonging to a larger islet on which stand the ruins of a fort. It is this island which protects Gaios from the outside world. Like Lakke and Longos, the little capital is invisible to boats sailing between the Ionian Islands and the mainland except when they are opposite its entrance.

At first there is no sign that a port is close by. Then suddenly as you turn sharply round a bend in the channel to the south, you see the little town of Gaios almost on top of you. Its appearance has the same elegance as Longos but on a much bigger scale. The boat anchors where the quay opens out into a well-proportioned white-paved square, in the centre of which stands a little whitewashed chapel with a Greek-style belfry at its west end. On three sides round the square are one- or two-storey houses, washed white or pink and with green shutters; most of these are cafés but there are several shops as well. The sparkling atmosphere is enhanced by the pink and white oleanders which are planted round the square.

We arrived at about five in the afternoon when it was already beginning to cool after the intense heat of the day. We asked a gendarme in the square about accommodation as we knew that the Paxos Beach Hotel was full.

'Ah, you want a hotel? We have several here.' We followed him down the quayside to a little house no different from the rest. Gaios has in fact no hotels but rooms as elsewhere can be hired by the night.

The great problem in Paxos is shortage of water. It is collected in tanks and in Gaios there are a number of wells, often inside the house. In such cases, the lavatory is usually on the ground floor, sometimes forming part of the kitchen from which it is separated only by the thinnest partition. Water is raised by a bucket and it takes practice to drop it at such an angle that it fills at once. Visits to the lavatory often lack privacy and sometimes light as well. On occasion the uncertain traveller finds himself stranded in complete darkness, fortified only by the knowledge that there is a hole very close to his feet.

Apart from the gay little central square, there are only two or three streets interlinked by alleys, which seem to lose themselves almost at once in the olive groves which surround the town. The most imposing structure, a great four-storeyed stone house on the quay a few steps away from the square, was originally built for the

British Resident during the British Protectorate. This connection started in 1814 when the island was captured from the French by the 2nd Battalion of the Greek Light Infantry, under Church. It was from here that the Corfiot dependency of Parga was seized in the same year from the French garrison to save its inhabitants from Ali Pasha. In addition to the former Residency, the road which connects Gaios with Lakke and Longos was also built by the British.

Mr Gladstone visited the island in December 1858 during his fact-finding tour of the Ionian Islands and, as any other sensible enquirer would have done, called upon, among others, the senior cleric in the area, in this case the Bishop of Paxos. Kirkwall described the meeting thus:

'At Paxos, as everywhere else, he showed the most unbounded veneration for the dignitaries of the Greek Church. In Corfu, he had excited the perhaps illiberal disgust of the English by publicly kissing the hand of the Archbishop and dutifully receiving his blessing. . . . The simple Bishop of Paxo appears to have been ignorant of the etiquette which the High Commissioner Extraordinary practised with ecclesiastical dignitaries. Mr Gladstone, having taken and respectfully kissed the Bishop's hand, leaned forward to receive the orthodox blessing. The Bishop hesitated, not knowing what was expected of him and not imagining perhaps, that a member of the Anglican Church could require his benediction. At last, he perceived the truth, and, bending forward, he hastened to comply with the flattering desire of the representative of the British Crown. But at this moment, unfortunately, Mr. Gladstone, imaging that the deferred blessing was not forthcoming, suddenly raised his head, and struck the episcopal chin. The Resident and other spectators of the scene had considerable difficulty in maintaining the gravity befitting so solemn an occasion.'

In this gleaming, contented little summer port, with its streets spotless and untroubled by motor vehicles, with its flowering trees and its little cages of singing birds hanging under the awnings outside its shops, one forgets the long wet winter evenings, the general lack of amenities. During one visit, the island's only doctor decided to take a holiday in July. Our host's nine-year-old daughter was suddenly and inexplicably taken ill. After an anguished day and night in which all courses of action were considered, it was decided to rush the child to a clinic in Athens—although excellent medical arrangements exist in Corfu. The weekly coastal steamer was calling that night *en route* for Corfu. At ten o'clock, a rowing-boat with our friends and others pulled away from the quay to meet the steamer which was too big to enter the little harbour. The local agent, a thin elderly man, sat in the stern holding a lantern which showed up the hollows on his fine-drawn, resigned features. The boat was due to reach Corfu in the early hours but the Athens plane did not leave until ten in the morning. It must have been an exhausting and expensive journey and one which might have been too long for someone critically ill.

The meeting place for all Gaios is the square. The townspeople congregate mainly at the café in the north-east corner close to where the coastal vessels are moored. Visitors are more likely to sit at tables in the shade of the whitewashed chapel, looking across to the ruined fort, partly hidden by trees, on the island opposite. How old the fortifications are nobody really knows although they are usually said to be Venetian. There must have been fortifications here from time immemorial. The Venetians may have built on defences raised by the powerful medieval baronies of Sant' Ippolito or Altavilla, the famous Neapolitan clans of the fourteenth and fifteenth centuries, the latter of which continued to reign in Paxos long after the Venetians became masters. Eventually these fortifications became British, only to be demolished at the end of the Protectorate.

According to legend, Antony and Cleopatra dined here with their chiefs of staff the night before the battle of Acteion. An earlier sea-battle, the result of which led to the expansion of Roman influence in Greece, was fought somewhere in these waters in 228 B.C. In that year, the Illyrians who had for some years been expanding their influence southwards from what is now Central Albania, laid siege to the ancient city of Corcyra. They were supported by several Greek states, including Acarnania, who sent seven warships according to their treaty obligations. The Corcyreans had in the meanwhile appealed successfully to the Achaean League whose fleet encountered the combined Illyrian-Acarnanian force off Paxos. It was an exciting battle according to Polybius. The Acarnanian and Achaean ships engaged each other but with little result. In the meanwhile, the Illyrians seized upon the idea of lashing their ships together in groups of four and, by facing the enemy broadside, encouraged the Achaeans to charge them. This they did with disastrous results. Having got their bows fixed into the nearest Illyrian ship, from which they could not extricate themselves, they found themselves boarded and over-

powered by the combined Illyrian crews. In this way, the Achaeans
lost four quadriremes and one quinquereme. What remained of their
fleet fled, leaving the victory to the Illyrians and their allies. As a
result Corcyra was forced to surrender and to accept an Illyrian
garrison.

The tables were, however, turned by the rapid arrival of a strong
Roman force off Corcyra with over two hundred ships, intent on
inflicting real punishment on the Illyrians because of their arrogant
attacks on Roman shipping in the Adriatic. The Illyrian commander,
deeming discretion the better part of valour, allowed the Romans to
occupy the island without resistance. The Corcyreans gratefully
accepted their protection, the first Greek state to do so. From Corcyra, Roman influence spread steadily throughout Greece. Whether
Paxos was occupied by the Romans at the same time or was considered
too unimportant or remote to warrant a garrison, history does not
record.

The name of the island was known to Edmund Spenser and to
Milton through Plutarch. One of the conversation pieces in Plutarch's
Moralia is entitled 'The Decline of Oracles'. The argument pro-
pounded was that with the decline of the world's population during
the Roman Empire, fewer oracles were needed; moreover, some of the
demi-gods, though not the gods themselves, might not be immortal.
One of the speakers told of a ship returning to Italy carrying freight
and many passengers. 'It was already evening when, near the Echinades, the wind dropped and the ship drifted near the Paxi. Almost
everyone was awake and a good many had not finished their after-
dinner wine. Suddenly from the island of Paxi was heard the voice of
someone loudly calling Thamus, so that all were amazed. Thamus
was an Egyptian pilot, not known by name even to many on board.
Twice he was called and made no reply, but the third time he
answered; and the caller, raising his voice, said, "When you come
opposite Palodes announce that the Great Pan is dead." Thamus made
up his mind that if there should be a breeze he would sail past and
keep quiet, but with no wind and a smooth sea about the place he
would announce what he had heard. So, when he came opposite
Palodes and there was neither wind nor wave, Thamus from the
stern, looking towards the land, said the words as he had heard them
"Great Pan is dead". Even before he was finished there was a great
cry of lamentation, not of one person but of many, mingled with
exclamations of amazement.' Both Spenser and Milton connected this

story with the crucifixion of Christ, which would have been at about this time.

The only inland village of importance is Magasia, half-way between Gaios and Porto Lakke. It is on a pleasant road, shaded by enormous olive trees. Under these, grey stones in vast quantities are scattered everywhere—here gathered into piles to denote private grazing, there used to build little grey walls for separating one property from another, but for the most part lying haphazardly. The pale green of the olive trees, mingling with the deeper grey of the limestone, gives an impression of refreshing coolness even at noon. By the side of the road, shaded by plane trees and cypresses, stand comfortable old houses built from the same material. Around them are little beds of precious earth in which grow geraniums, carnations and roses.

The road winds uphill, past the site where several years ago oil was unsuccessfully drilled for, to the central ridge which is over a thousand feet high. Close to the summit is a great Venetian church tower, similar to that of St Dionysios at Zakynthos. A little beyond, a road branches down to Longos. From the top of the ridge, before it drops slightly downwards into the long straggling village of Magasia, a different impression of the island is gained. To the west the ground falls rapidly away to end abruptly in great cliffs which rise straight out of the sea; these can be seen through occasional gaps in the never-ending forest of olive trees. In these cliffs are an abundance of caves; those at sea-level can be visited by boat, but the upper caves are of greater interest to the historian, as they were inhabited by hermits soon after Christianity had been brought to the island by St Gaios, a Macedonian by origin. There is also an early Byzantine church named after Saints Peter and Paul which had been neglected for centuries, but which is now being cared for by the villagers, according to Mr Mitzialis-Mitziell, the island's only journalist, who lives in Magasia.

Now an elderly man, he was still, in 1967, writing, editing and type-setting the island's only newspaper, which is published fortnightly. His house in Magasia is one of the oldest and he pointed out the loopholes for the muskets built into the walls in the eighteenth century to keep raiders at bay. In his own lifetime, he thought that there had been few changes of note. Perhaps the greatest had been the substitution of the Greek language and Greek place names for Italian. Not of course that the Paxiots had ever been anything but Greek. Nevertheless, four hundred years was a long time to have been under

Venetian domination and habits are not easily changed. There was cause for gratitude to the Venetians, at least for their development of the olive oil industry through their grant of a cash bonus for olive trees planted. How else could the island have lived?

The distance from Gaios to the southern tip of the island is about a mile and three-quarters. Beyond the quay, a rough track winds over the edge of the low cliffs where the olive groves end. Below there are wonderful little coves and promontories where the water is deep enough for diving. The bed of the sea is rocky, but beware of the black sea-urchins which lurk here in quantities.

After about fifteen minutes' walk, you pass the Paxos Beach Hotel, whose bungalows are built on the slopes of a little bay with an excellent sandy beach. The further south you go the more empty the island becomes, although in ancient days there was apparently a small harbour facing across to Anti-Paxos. We did not walk to the end but went in a motor-boat to Anti-Paxos which lies about a mile beyond Paxos. A little channel cuts off the south-eastern tip of the island; we passed through this before emerging into the Paxos channel.

On its north and west sides, Anti-Paxos has vast cliffs as high as any on Paxos. The land slopes down steeply to the east coast with its wonderful white gleaming sandy beaches, completely free of tourist debris, seaweed and sea-urchins. There are no beaches in the Ionian Islands to compare with these. We were the only people present. Here and there on the slopes rising above us to the west we could see a whitewashed cabin with red roof, occupied in the summer by those who look after the vineyards which cover the upper slopes and which produce the wine for which Anti-Paxos is locally renowned. There is no village on Anti-Paxos and the few houses are deserted in winter. Most citizens of substance in Gaios appeared to own a patch of vineyard on Anti-Paxos. The best wine is a natural slightly sparkling rosé, limited supplies of which are on occasion to be found at a price in Gaios and Corfu town.

The motor caique leaves for Corfu at about seven in the morning. It is an incomparable time to set forth on a Mediterranean sea voyage, the sun rising strongly but the cool of the night still lingering. Swinging out beyond Panayia Island the central massif of Levkas some twenty-five miles to the south was still visible. By nine o'clock it would be shrouded in heat mists and would not be seen again until the following dawn. To the north, the morning angle of the sun turned the chalky-grey folds of Cape Asprokavos into pale gold. The sea was empty except for a schooner heading further east towards the Epirot port of Igoumenitsa. The radio on the caique was silent. It was still cool on the sea three and a half hours later when we rounded the Old Fort at Corfu and moved towards the harbour.

Some Books of Reference

1. CLASSICAL PERIOD

Bérard, Victor, *Les Navigations d'Ulysee*. Paris, 1929

Bradford, Ernle, *Ulysses Found*. London, 1963

Herodotus, *The Histories* (tr. Aubrey de Selincourt). London, 1954

Homer, *The Odyssey* and *The Iliad* (tr. E. V. Rieu). London, 1946 and 1950

Pliny, *Natural History* (Loeb Edition)

Plutarch, *Moralia: The Obsolescence of Miracles* (Loeb Edition)

Polybius, *Works* (Loeb Edition)

Strabo, *Geography* (Loeb Edition)

Thucydides, *The Peloponnesian War* (tr. Rex Warner). London, 1954

Virgil, *The Aeneid* (tr. by W. F. Jackson Knight). London, 1956

Xenophon, *A History of My Times* (tr. by Rex Warner). London, 1966

2. MEDIEVAL AND VENETIAN PERIODS

Bradford, Ernle, *The Great Betrayal: Constantinople, 1204*. London, 1967

Chatzidakis, M., *Contribution a l'Etude de la Peinture Post-Byzantine. L'Hellenisme Contemporain*. Athens, 1953

Geanokoplos, Deno J., *Byzantine East and Latin West*. Oxford, 1966

Miller, William, *The Latins in the Levant*. Cambridge, 1908

— *Essays on the Latin Orient*. Cambridge, 1923

Norwich, John Julius, *The Normans in the South*. London, 1967

Procopiou, A. G., *La Peinture Religieuse dans les Isles Ioniennes Pendant le XVIII Siècle*. Paris, 1939

Runciman, Steven, *History of the Crusades*. Cambridge, 1951–54

— *The Fall of Constantinople*. Cambridge, 1965

— *The Great Church in Captivity*. Cambridge, 1968

St Sauveur, A. Grasset de, *Voyage Historique, Literaire et Pittoresque dans les Isles et Possessions ci-devant Venetiennes du Levant*. Paris, 1800

Tenenti, A., *Piracy and the Decline of Venice, 1580–1615*. London, 1967

Villehardouin, Geoffrey de, *The Conquest of Constantinople* (tr. M. R. B. Shaw). London, 1963

Wheler, Sir George, and Spon, Dr, *Journey Through Italy, Dalmatia, Greece and the Levant*. London, 1678

Wood, A. C., *History of the Levant Company*. Oxford, 1935

Lane-Poole, Stanley, *The Barbary Corsairs*. London, 1890

3. NAPOLEONIC WARS AND GREEK WAR OF INDEPENDENCE

Bagally, J. W., *Ali Pasha and Great Britain*. Oxford, 1938

Church, E. M., *Sir Richard Church in Italy & Greece*. Edinburgh, 1895

Crawley, C. W., *John Capodistrias and the Greeks before 1821*. Cambridge Historical Journal, 1957

Dakin, Douglas, *British and American Philhellenes during the Greek War of Independence, 1821–1833*. Thessaloniki, 1955

Dodwell, Edward, *A Classical and Topographical Tour Through Greece*. London, 1819

Ferriman, Z. D., *Some English Philhellenes*. London, 1917–1920

Leake, W. M., *Travels in Northern Greece*. London, 1835

Nicolson, Harold, *Byron: The Last Journey*. London, 1924

Plomer, William, *Ali the Lion*. London, 1936

Rodocanachi, E., *Bonaparte et les Isles Ioniennes*. Paris, 1899.

Trelawney, E. J., *Records of Shelley, Byron and the Author*. London, 1858–1878

Woodhouse, C. M., *The Battle of Navarino*. London, 1965

— *The Greek War of Independence*. London, 1952

4. THE BRITISH PROTECTORATE

Ansted, D. T., *The Ionian Islands in 1863*. London, 1863

Bowen, G. F., *Ionian Islands under British Protection*. London, 1851

Davidson, Angus, *Edward Lear*. London, 1933

Davy, John, *Notes and Observations in the Ionian Islands and Malta*. London, 1842

Durrell, Lawrence, *Lear's Corfu*, letters edited by. Corfu, 1965

Hart, Sir Basil Liddell, edited by, *The Letters of Private Wheeler, 1809–1828*. London, 1952

Holland, Henry, *Travels in the Ionian Isles, Albania, etc*. London, 1815

Hughes, Rev. T. S., *Travels in Sicily, Greece and Albania*. London, 1820

Jervis-White-Jervis, Henry, *The Ionian Islands during the Present Century*, London, 1863

Kirkwall, Viscount, *Four Years in the Ionian Islands*. London, 1864

Lord, W. Frewen, *Sir Thomas Maitland*. London, 1897

Morley, Lord, *Life of W. E. Gladstone*. London, 1903

Müller, C., *Journey Through Greece and the Ionian Islands*. London, 1822

Napier, Col. James, *The Colonies: Their Values Generally, of The Ionian Islands in Particular*. London, 1833

— *Memoir on the Roads of Cefalonia*. London, 1825

Napier, W. P. F., *Life and Opinions of Sir James Napier*. London, 1857

Reumont, Alfred von, *Sir Frederick Adam*. London, 1855

Smith, G. C. Moore, *Lord Seaton*. London, 1903

Vere, Aubrey de, *Picturesque Sketches of Greece and Turkey*. London, 1850

Waddington, George, *A Visit to Greece*. London, 1825

Williams, H. W., *Travels in Italy, Greece and the Ionian Islands*. Edinburgh, 1820

5. MODERN GREECE

Forster, E. S., *Short History of Modern Greece, 1821–1940*. London, 1941

Frazee, Charles A., *The Orthodox Church and Independent Greece 1821–1852*. Cambridge, 1969

Mavrogordato, John, *Modern Greece*. London, 1931

Miller, William, *The Ottoman Empire and its Successors*. Cambridge, 1936

6. MISCELLANEOUS

Bradford, Ernle, *Companion Guide to the Greek Islands*. London, 1963

Butler, Alban, *Lives of the Saints*. London, 1956

Crosland, Margaret, ed., *A Traveller's Guide to Literary Europe*. London, 1967

Denham, H. M., *The Eastern Mediterranean*. London, 1964

Gibbon, Edward, *The Decline and Fall of the Roman Empire*. London, 1776–78

Hamilton, Mary, *Greek Saints and their Festivals*. Edinburgh, 1910

Haslip, Joan, *The Lonely Empress: a biography of Elizabeth of Austria*. London, 1965

Jenkins, Romilly, *Dionysios Solomos*. Cambridge, 1940

Larrabee, Stephen A., *Hellas Observed*. New York, 1957

Luke, Sir Harry, *Of Cities and Men*. Vol. III. London, 1956

Matton, Raymond, *Corfou*. Athens, 1960

Mayes, Stanley, *An Organ for the Sultan*. London, 1956

Murray's Handbooks to Greece, 1840, 1854, 1872

Pallis, A. A., *Greek Miscellany*. Athens, 1964

Politis, Jacques N., *Corfou et les Isles Ioniennes*. Paris, 1964

Polunin, O., and Huxley, A., *Flowers of the Mediterranean*. London, 1965

Rodd, Sir Rennell, *Customs and Lore of Modern Greece*. London, 1892

Spencer, Terence, *Fair Greece, Sad Relic*. London, 1954

Ware, Timothy, *The Orthodox Church*. London, 1963

Wright, H. R., *Horae Ioniae* (poems). London, 1809

Nigel Nicolson on Corfu in 'Great Palaces of Europe', edited by Sacheverel Sitwell. London, 1964

Dictionary of National Biography

Public Record Office

Index

෴

(After place-names, C = Corfu, Ce = Cephalonia, I = Ithaka, L = Levkas, P = Paxos and Z = Zakynthos)

St Gerasimos, 100, 112
San Giorgio dei Greci, Venice, 47–8
St James & St Christopher, Church of, C, 187
St James of Collas, Z, 50
St Jason & St Sosipater, 222
St Jason & St Sosipater, Church of, C, 222–3
St John of the Cisterns, Church of, C, 186
St Kiriaki, Ce, 116
St Michael & St George, Order of, 136, 201–4
St Michael & St George, Palace of, C, 59, 168, 172, 173, 183, 185, 187, 193, 201–4, 214
St Minas, Church of, L, 159–60
St Nicolas, 102
St Nicolas, Church of, L, 159
St Nicolas, Church of, Pochali, Z, 56
St Nicolas of the Mole, Church of, Z, 26–7, 33, 43, 53
St Spiridion, 180–3, 186, 189, 191, 208, 244
St Spiridion, Church of, Argostoli, Ce, 101
St Spiridion, Church of, C, 46, 50, 160, 209
St Spiridion, Church of, L, 159–60
St Theodora Augusta, 181, 186
Salvator, Archduke Ludwig, 27, 33, 55, 60, 75
Sami, Ce, 85, 96, 104, 106, 109–10, 112–13, 115, 125, 129, 149, 238
Sanderson, Alexis, 142–4
San Stefano Cape, C, 246
Santa Mavra Fortress, L, 155, 158, 161–2
Sarakina, Z, 69–72
Sarakinato Cape, Ce, 107
Sarakiniko Bay, I, 132
Sargint family, 28, 60
Sarkali Cape, I, 149
Schliemann, Heinrich, 140

Schulenburg, Count von der, 50, 172–3 ,179, 188, 193
Scopus Mt, Z, 22, 55, 56, 65, 66–7, 105
Scorpios Island, L, 152
Scripero, C, 239, 246
Seaton, Lord, 207, 238
Septinsular Republic, 36, 39, 80, 154
Sfakera, C, 245
Sicily, 31, 40, 109, 134, 218, 220, 227
Sidari, C, 246
Sikelianos, Angelos, 162–3
Sinori, Ce, 116
Sivota Bay, L, 151
Sivota Islands, 219, 252
Skino Cape, I, 131
Solomos, Count Demetrius, 58
Solomos, Count Dionysios, 25, 38, 57–9, 205, 216, 241
Sordinas family, 191, 233
Sparta, 30, 143, 219–20
Spartilas, C, 241
Sperantzos, Spiridion, 181, 187
Stavros, I, 129–30, 138, 141, 144–5
Stavrota Mtn, L, 149, 151
Storks, Sir Henry, 174, 208
Strabo, 105, 154
Strophades Islands, 51–2
Suleyman the Magnificent, 97, 171, 243
Svoronata, Ce, 101–2, 103
Synarades, C, 238

Tekia Fort, 162
Theophrastus, 79
Theotokis family, 183–4, 191, 204, 216, 246
Theotokou Sision Monastery, Ce, 105
Thucydides, 218–20, 228
Tocchi dynasty, Dukes of Lefkadia, 31, 82–3, 100, 135
Torkington, Sir Richard, 24, 171
Trelawney, E. J., 113, 142
Tricupis, Spiridion, 58